# Your Will

## A Legacy of Hearing God's Voice

Mark & Mary,
 May my story reveal to you the heart of the Father. I am thankful for the love you have shown to me and my family. Many blessings!

*Angel Hope O'Malley*

Angel Hope O'Malley

Copyright © 2020 by Angel H. O'Malley. All rights reserved. No part of this book may be reproduced in any form without permission in writing from the publisher.

ISBN 978-1-7354965-1-1

I dedicate this book to my father and mother, Virgil and Melonie Johnson, who laid for me the foundation of the reality of who God is. Through their example of selfless love and dedication to living lives that were totally sold out for Jesus, I am who I am today. Thank you for teaching me the importance of hearing God's voice.

And to my husband Brendan for walking through this process of life with me, he is everything and more than I could have ever hoped for in a partner and he is truly my favorite fulfilled promise from God. Thank you for being my best friend.

# Table of Contents

   Dedication

1   The Beginning of a Legacy   ........................1

2   Growing Up   .......................29

3   Two Becoming One   ........................59

4   I Knew Him As Dad   ........................79

5   Blank Slate   ......................101

6   Few Are Chosen   ......................123

7   When Your Will Is His Will   ......................147

8   Not Imposing Your Will   ......................162

9   The New Has Come   ......................180

# 1
## The Beginning of a Legacy

This is the story of the legacy that has been handed down to me. The beginning of this book, like many other beginnings, was born out of an ending. A chapter in my life came to a close and a new one began. Shortly after my thirty-sixth birthday the Lord rocked my world with a revelation that would not only revitalize everything I thought I knew but also change me forever. From that revelation this book was created into a seed. This legacy of hearing God's voice is my story to tell but before I can tell you the revelation that revitalized my life, I must establish some ground work. I believe my story cannot be told without first telling the story of those who have gone before me. My story begins two generations ago. It begins with my grandmother Becky Johnson. She was a fierce little lady who was called to follow Jesus and spread the gospel of God's great love for us. She is the forerunner of this legacy.

In the 1950's she was very active in the great miracle move of God known as the Healing Revivals. The services held at her crusades predominately took place under a tent. I believe tents were the gathering places of that era because it is sometimes hard for denominations to lay aside their doctrinal differences. It's a risk to walk into a new experience of a true move of God but it's one worth taking. Perhaps tents were a way around that religious fickleness that divides the children of God and was able to bring more people together in unity. The Spirit called people out of the churches and into tents because He wanted to draw them out of the normal confines of religion and have plenty of room to move.

Hearing stories about my Grandma's faith as I was growing up impressed upon me how she always got results. She believed the word of God and that every promise was true and rightfully hers to obtain. She was not highly educated or particularly special in the flesh but she had a heart after God. Because of her love for Him and her hunger to hear His voice she was projected into a life of miracles. It is often those who are measured by the world as not worthy that become world changers because in them is a strong determination to see God's will be done. She was a simple but sincere woman who's heart longed for His kingdom ways to be declared to the people so that they might know the reality of who He is.

In 1 Corinthians 1:27 the word says, "God has chosen the foolish things of the world to confound the wise; and God has chosen the weak things of the world to confound the things which are mighty;". It is hard for the intellectual, ultra educated mind to see the simplicity of

God's word and will. That simplicity can only be revealed to us through the revelation of the Holy Spirit. That revelation blatantly goes against what our minds may perceive to be possible or logical. Imagine being a woman in the church in the 1950's. At that time it was hard enough in the world to be a woman whose voice could be heard, much less in the church world. For centuries the religious-spirited church has been the number one suppressor of women having a voice. Making it harder for women who have been called by God to minister the gospel to be accepted. My Grandma was chosen of God to preach during a time when the majority of churches frowned upon women even speaking a single word in a service! Knowing that your calling is sure takes confidence that can only come from one thing and that is hearing the voice of God. What He calls us to do, He will bring about. All we have to do is just learn to follow His lead.

~

> "You have all become true children of God by the faith of Jesus the Anointed One! It was faith that immersed you into Jesus, the Anointed One, and now you are covered and clothed with his anointing. And we no longer see each other in our former state, Jew or non-Jew, rich or poor, male or female, because we're all one through our union with Jesus Christ." Galatians 3:26-28 (TPT)

~

Rebecca Margaret Sims was born on June 1, 1912 in Rock Castle County, Kentucky to Sidney and Eliza Jane (York) Sims. My Pappaw (pāp-paw) Albert Alson Johnson was born in Brazil, Kentucky on August 7, 1907 to William M. and Sophia (Rader) Johnson. My great-grandfather Johnson was a homesteader and owned thousands of acres of land in the mountains of Kentucky. At the age of about sixteen Pappaw was forced to set out on his own to get away from his abusive alcoholic father. He secured himself a free ride by hopping on a train and traveled his way north to Richmond, Indiana. There he took room and board at the home of the Sims. From the moment my Grandma laid eyes on him she knew he was the man she was going to marry. Shortly after they met they were married on March 7, 1928.

Before long they started a family and they had a life much like anyone else. But not long after they began to build a life together Grandma began to follow Jesus. She had been raised in a dead church that did not rightly represent the true love of God. So while growing up she had been told a false message of who He was. When she grew up to make up her own mind she rejected that doctrine and soon realized her need for the real deal. What she knew about Jesus was like looking through a glass darkly and not being able to see the real thing in all its detail and true form. This hunger in her caused her to begin to seek out the Truth for herself in the word. Reading the Bible gave her a picture of Christ she had never know before. She found salvation and soon after the baptism of the Holy Ghost.

All those who are hungry for who God is will be filled. From the time Grandma was saved she began to see miracles. Her faith was activated as she believed the word and all she wanted to do was keep that faith active and allow it to grow! It all began with hearing the voice of God. The pursuit of what that might lead to began to transform her and only made her hunger increase. Through her experience she began to grow in confidence. Soon she began to pour out the love that God had given her onto everyone who would receive it. She had obtained a life changing revelation and it motivated her to let others know so that they too could be made free. It started in her own family and neighborhood.

She first reached out to her family and soon saw her family around her finding freedom through salvation. She then began to pray, "God let me win over all the ladies on my street for You." And within a year every single wife on that block was saved and filled with the Holy Spirit, but the last woman to give her heart to the Lord was very resistant. Grandma didn't preach this lady into salvation, she simply told her about Jesus while inviting her to know Him. After presenting the simplicity of the love of God all she did was pray for that woman. One day Grandma was on her knees praying for that very woman and all the sudden a banging came on her door. She got up from her knees and opened the door to see her neighbor with a scornful look on her face. The woman spoke with an irritated tone saying, "Becky, I want you to stop praying for me!" Isn't it interesting how this lady knew she was being prayed for? My Grandma just smiled and said, "Not until you know the love of Jesus." All of the sudden the scorn left that woman's face and she began to weep. In that moment the love of God broke through and demolished every defense that woman had put up in her heart. Right then and there, on that door step she gave her heart to the Lord and was baptized in the Holy Ghost.

From the time she responded to the call of Jesus to "come follow Him" she was unstoppable. She began to pour over the word of God and let the Holy Spirit write it on her heart. She knew it was the only way she could know who He was and how to walk like He did. She took every promise and every word Jesus ever said as truth and it became her foundation. Miracles were just a promise from the Word and if the Word said it, she believed it! She even joined a Pentecostal Holiness church in her search for more of the Lord, in hopes she would find a community of believers to walk with her on her journey.

I am not going to tell you all the details of my grandparents lives but I do want to tell you as many miracles as were told to me so that you can know how much apart of their everyday life miracles were. Miracles are the threads that have been woven into the tapestry of this story. They are real and they are a product of a life that is in pursuit of the glory of God. Hearing His voice produces miracles and they can become apart of everyday life, if you are willing to believe.

One day Grandma greeted a man named Tom Stature who was sitting outside a gas station. Tom did not know Jesus yet but his parents were members of the church Grandma attended and he professed to believe in God. He began to tell her about his feet being in such pain that he couldn't walk or even stand. She said, "Tom if I prayed for your feet to quit hurting, would you believe the Lord to do it?" At this point in her walk she was not yet a preacher and had only been saved a few years herself but she was willing to agree with anyone who would believe for a miracle. He agreed that he would believe and she asked him to wait where he was for ten minutes because she wanted time to get back home so she could pray for him. She was a young follower of Christ at this time and didn't yet have the confidence to lay hands on him right then and there, but never the less she believed God would heal him.

When she got home she prayed and asked God to heal Tom. Shortly after she finished praying she received a phone call from Tom and he proceeded to tell her about what happened after he got home. He said that when he sat down to his dinner table to eat he suddenly felt a tingling sensation in his feet that he had never felt before nor could hardly explain. Suddenly the pain he'd been feeling was instantly gone! Tom received a miracle that day but his testimony doesn't end there because even though he believed for the miracle He hadn't yet believed that he needed Jesus. It was about a year later Tom had a stroke that left him completely paralyzed and bed ridden. He asked his parents to request Grandma to come to the hospital and pray for him because she was the only one he had any confidence in for getting a miracle. When she arrived at the hospital she asked him, "Tom if I pray for you will you believe the Lord to heal you?" he replied, "I'd believe anything you'd say!" She laughed a little and then prayed a faith filled prayer before telling the paralyzed man to get up from his bed. Suddenly he was able to stand up! But he wasn't completely healed yet as he still felt weak and showed some signs of the stroke. She said to him, "Tom if you will kneel down on your knees and give your heart completely to the Lord you can be perfectly well." He said, "I can't get down on my knees." So she and Tom's wife helped him to do so and prayed with him as he gave his heart to the Lord. After they prayed Tom raised up off his knees without any help because he was filled with the presence of God and completely healed!

~

"The Lord has been my Savior, my Keeper and my Healer for over 46 years. And since the day I was saved to this hour I have never had to have a natural physician because I always had the Great Physician. I have raised my children by faith and that in the Son of God. We never had a natural physician in our home, we never had to go to the hospital or the doctor's office, we never had to consult anybody but Jesus. Every time we called on Him He heard us and because we knew He heard us, we knew we had petition of what we asked. That's the Word of the Lord, hallelujah!" -Rebecca Johnson

~

My Grandma's life story was full of testimonies and countless miracles that took place. Like many revivalists who have gone before her, Becky Johnson will never be famous in the eyes of man but she most certainly left a legacy and received a great reward in heaven for it. She saw blind eyes opened, the lame made to walk, deaf ears to hear, cancers healed, diabetes healed, vital organs creatively made new, addictions broken, lives saved and she even saw the dead raised back to life. Raising the dead is no more or a challenge for God than the healing of a headache. We are the ones who give a certain sickness more power than another, He sees them all the same. He is willing to answer, we are just too often not willing to ask for it and believe we will receive it. It takes a lot of trial and error as we grow in confidence to see miracles and healings. It's only the fear of it not working and pride of looking foolish that keeps most from trying. Whether a person gets healed or not when we pray is not on us, it's all up to God. He does the healing, we just have to step out in faith and believe He will!

Grandma once set up her revival tent on a plot of land next to a deaf school and every single child that came to her for prayer received a miracle and could instantly hear and speak. The people who were in charge of the school were furious and even petitioned to the town to have her tent removed. They believed that by the end of the revival they would have no students left and that would put them out of business. There was a certain teacher at the school who was risking her job by seeking and receiving approval from parents to bring the children to the revival for prayer. She was motivated by her genuine love of those little ones and she wanted to see them set free. The woman did in fact get dismissed from her job but she saw many students healed. Grandma stayed and finished the revival and nearly emptied that deaf school of its students.

~

"If there wasn't health insurance there would be more people well. A preacher told me recently that an insurance salesman came to his church to sell the church a health policy. A health insurance policy! I can't even image that! It's just something I don't understand. Because if you have Jesus you already have a Health insurance policy! This is what the Word says, 'I am the Lord God that healeth thee', now that is real Health insurance!" -Rebecca Johnson

~

By 1945 she had learned more of who God was. Every opportunity there was to attend church, she was there. She grew closer to the Lord and fervently began to believe for her husband's salvation. In Amos 3:3 it says, "How can two walk together unless they agree?" Soon the Lord spoke to her concerning my Pappaw's salvation, words that most people would have rejected as the word of the Lord. He said, "You will have a child, a baby girl. You shall name her Martha. I will give her to you, but soon receive her back unto me and this will be the key to Albert's salvation." What an amazing and terrible thing to receive! How solid her foundation must have been in her relationship with the Lord to accept such a word and not be totally devastated by it. We as humans cannot see the full picture like God can but if we trust Him through the hard things, we will come to totally trust Him. Trusting Him means a joyful walk not an easy one. He understands each and every one of us so intimately and wants only what is best for us because He is only good and His true motivation is love. With God good can be produced out of a painful experience.

My grandparents were blessed with five children. The eldest was William Alson, the second oldest child was Betty Jane, the third child was Robert Ray and four years later Virgil Claude came along, making him the youngest son. Martha Sue was the last child born into the family on October 17, 1945. Dad told me about how his baby sister would toddle around the house, raising her hands up in the air saying one of the only words she had learned, "Glory, glory, glory!" It was as if she was constantly aware of the presence of God at only fourteen months of age.

Suddenly one day Aunt Betty became sick with what they thought was just a common cold but what was later believed to have been pneumonia. They did not rush to the doctor for assistance but rather began to seek the Healer for the healing. There was never a doubt in my Grandma's mind that she was up against the devil, because the word says in Ephesians 6:12 that "we wrestle not against flesh and blood, but against principalities, against powers, against the rulers of the darkness of this world,". She fought on a spiritual plane from a place of knowing the victory belongs to the Lord. Within a few weeks of Betty falling ill Martha Sue also became sick with a very high fever. Grandma prayed fervently for both her daughters but this time the miracles she sought didn't come. God was all the while working another miracle.

Having been sick for only a couple weeks Martha Sue Johnson died on December 22, 1946. My Grandma chose not to attend the funeral services held on Christmas day. Instead she stayed with Betty who was fading fast. Grandma stayed on her knees and she would rarely leave Betty's bedside. Day by day Betty's life began to slip away, she had lost too much weight and death was fast approaching. Betty began to say things like, "I can see Martha Sue." and "Can you hear angels singing?" On her last day and despite her weakness she lifted her hands towards heaven and began to speak in tongues. Pappaw was in the room at her bedside when that gift began to flow from her. As Betty raised up her arms he gently slipped his underneath her frail body and held her close to him as tears streamed down his face. In that moment he found himself able to talk to God. In that moment he finally surrendered to Jesus. In that moment he began to believe and found salvation. With

Betty's last breath she said, "Don't worry, I'll take care of Martha Sue." She passed away on January 5, 1947 at the age of sixteen, only two weeks after Martha Sue.

Even though two lives were taken from this earth to be in eternity, one life that would live well into his eighties found Jesus that day. God worked three miracles in those few short weeks. Is God a God who vengefully kills children so parents can find salvation? No. The sickness was a product of being a human in a broken world where sickness exists because of the prince of lies. Sometimes healing looks like a victory for our earthly bodies in the form of a miracle from the sickness. Other times a miracle looks like going to sleep only to wake up in heaven. Heaven is the ultimate victory! Everyone in this life will go through hard, unpleasant and even painful situations. Not one person can escape that natural law that abides on this earth of fallen man. The difference between the faithful who overcome and those who bitterly blame God for all the wrong in the world is that we have an assurance of all things working together for our good. If your focus is on the indisputable truth that God is good and He loves you, then you will be able to walk through any circumstance that life may bring.

~

"And we know that all things work together for good to them that love God, to them who are the called according to his purpose." Romans 8:28 (KJV)

~

Victory is a promise for those who are in Christ, it is literally our heritage and our birth right as we have been born again into the family of God. No son or daughter has to fight for what is rightfully theirs, they only have to know who they are, accept the promise and walk in it. If we can understand that victory comes in more than one form, then joy is not so hard to hold on to in the middle of the pain. My Grandma was an incredibly resolute woman. Once she established confidence in being able to hear His voice she could not be shaken or made to doubt the word of the Lord. She proved who God was in her life by taking Him at His word and walking it out in faith. Once she learned to identify His voice she began to live on every word that proceeded out of His mouth. It took a life time of testing and proving and seeking after God with her whole being. Many people claim to believe the word of God but it is the fruit a life produces that proves how much we believe.

If He spoke, Grandma obeyed. Even in every day settings like driving up to the gas station one day to pump gas. There she saw a member from her church and the Lord spoke a clear word for her to give him. She got out of the car and said to him, "Brother, the Lord just told me to tell you to not get that operation you are planning on having. He told me you will not come out from under the sedation." He scoffed, "Aw, Becky! Don't worry about me, it'll be alright! The doctors assured me this is a minor thing." She answered him by speaking again exactly what God had told her but the man would not listen. Three days later he went through with the operation and he died on the operating table.

~

"I have learned that the words 'God said' are not Christian bywords. It's not just something we say to make us sound more credible. We don't say 'God said' because we had an emotion or read something in the Bible that is written that He said. You only say 'God said' when you have heard from heaven. Because when He says it, it's going to happen! This is why we must learn to hear His voice for ourselves." -Virgil Johnson

~

Grandma was destined to make an impact on this world for the kingdom of God. The enemy knew this and decided to make a play to stop her. What Satan didn't realize was that instead of ending her pursuit for more of God's glory, he was about to prove that God could use her for His glory in a big way. A few months after the deaths of her two daughters the elders of the church that Grandma faithfully attended for fifteen years suddenly asked her to leave the church. They believed she had a "different Holy Spirit" than they did because the fruit of her ministry was signs and wonders. She was out being the hands and feet of Jesus, testifying of who God is and their religiousness blinded them with fear and jealousy. It was like a slap in the face to her. This woman of faith who believed in miracles and a wonderful loving Savior was only doing what she saw her Father do and these elders whom she loved and respected rebuked her because they themselves did not walk in the same power.

One day not long after all this happened Grandma was overcome with numbness in her body. My Dad was playing inside their house as she called to him with great urgency in her voice. She told him she felt like she was dying. All the sudden her feet became numb and the numbness started creeping up her body as if death was taking over. Dad shouted, "I'll go get grandma!" but she stoped him before he could go. There wasn't time for him to go get help so she said, "You pray for me Virgil." She felt that if the numbness made it to her heart that her system would completely shut down and she would surely die. So with a child like faith my ten your old Dad began to pray with and for his mother. The numbness stopped creeping up her body and went no further than her waist. He quit praying and rushed to get his grandmother but there wasn't much she could do for her daughter except watch over her until Pappaw came home from work.

I couldn't tell you medically what was happening to her but spiritually it is plain to see that her heart had been broken which opened her up to doubt and fear. Satan saw an opening to make his play and she would have to decide if the opinion of man or the opinion of God was of greater value to her. Could the elders be right? Could God be a liar? She began to question everything she believed. She hadn't lost her faith she was only having it tested. At any time she could have called on a doctor for help but she held tightly to what she believed, that God is not a liar and His word is true, and she knew He would walk with her through it. You don't always have to know the reason why something is happening or the cause of the issue but you always need to know the Answer because He has the solution long before the problem ever exists.

For the next few months Grandma's sisters would come and help her do things around the house because she was only able to sit or lay. She was unable to function normally and needed to be cared for by her family constantly. It was believed that she had a nervous breakdown of some kind. Physically she was numb throughout the lower part of her body but her spirit had been numbed first. One day while sitting in an easy chair next to the Zenith up-right radio in her living room and listening to a local gospel station, she began to hear a man speak of faith and signs and wonders. After a short sermon about how God is able to heal the sick the preacher speaking through that radio announced that he was holding a tent revival in Cincinnati, Ohio. The preachers name was Earl Ivie and he was advertising for his tent revival on the radio station to tell about the many miracles and the wonderful things God was doing in his meetings. As Grandma heard this man speak over the radio she knew that ground was being laid for a move of God that would bring revival. This man was preaching what she already knew to be the truth, so when Pappaw came home from work that evening she asked him to take her to Cincinnati. She said, "Albert, this man is doing exactly what the church told me I was wrong for doing."

That Sunday they arrived where Brother Ivie's tent was set up and there they found that from one side of the tent to the other were piles of cots, crutches, braces, wheel chairs, canes and casts that had been cut off, all tossed aside never to be used again. Brother Ivie was a man of God who had a strong anointing for miracles and healings and he played a major role in the beginning of the Healing Revivals of that era. In that healing campaign held in Cincinnati there were over thirty-thousand people healed and over five-thousand saved and filled with the Spirit.

After Brother Ivie's sermon the power of the word was already working in Grandma as she was now able to walk on her own to go up and receive prayer. Brother Ivie laid hands on Grandma and prayed with the word of knowledge in operation. He told her that her condition was more spiritual than it was physical and that once her spirit was renewed her body would be healed. As he prayed for her the power of God caused every last bit of numbness to leave her body as her broken heart was healed and her spirit renewed. In that moment she had stepped into such a life altering experience that no devil and no man could ever again shake her confidence in who she knew Jesus to be!

"People will say you sound foolish when you talk about faith! But I don't care because the reproach that was on Christ fell on me, so I don't mind!" -Rebecca Johnson

From that day on greater things began to happen in Grandma's life. Grandma didn't miss a single meeting in the rest of that revival in Cincinnati and when Brother Ivie moved his tent to Waynesville, Ohio, she followed. During this next campaign of Brother Ivie's he managed to almost completely empty a hospital of its patients. The local hospital was forced to cut down its staff in half as people would go to his meetings for a miracle rather than settling for a man's side effect riddled cures. My grandparents became good friends with Brother Ivie and before long Grandma began to help with the morning services by praying for people with needs. Hundreds of people she prayed for received the baptism of the Holy Spirit and healings or miracles as she continued doing what those deceived elders had told her that she couldn't do.

(Photo of Rebecca and Albert Johnson in front of Earl Ivie's healing campaign truck)

Brother Ivie had six ambulances that he would send, upon request, anywhere in the United States to bring the terminally ill to his meetings for a miracle. That's how confident He was in what God was doing in that great move of God. He certainly heard the voice of God and encouraged my Grandma that she could do the same. You can imagine what kind of an impression this powerful preacher left upon my family. That is how it is in the kingdom, a ripple effect. One person believes and ignites a fire in one or two or thousands and then it just multiplies! It can even effect not only one generation but several. Even I, who never new Brother Ivie, have been impacted by his ministry. My story would be completely different if that one man hadn't heard the voice of God to tell my Grandma the truth that would make her free. The love of God rightly represented is what brings the multitudes into the liberty for which Christ died to make us free.

So began the action to the clear call of God over Grandma's life. She had loved and believed God from the moment she accepted Jesus as her Lord and Savior but it was during Brother Ivie's healing campaigns that she came to know she was chosen. Chosen to lead, to set an example, to redeem the time, to set forth on a path that would not only transform her but the rest of the world around her. On that fateful night that she was healed and set free her confidence in Christ raised to a whole new level. That night when she was chosen, she found a resolve within her to do whatever it takes to be led by God. His perfect love came in and cast out all her fear. She decided to completely trust Him with absolutely everything and everyone He entrusted to her. Her faith truly became unwavering!

~

"Verily, verily, I say unto you, He that believeth on me, the works that I do shall he do also; and greater works than these shall he do; because I go unto my Father. And whatsoever ye shall ask in my name, that will I do, that the Father may be glorified in the Son. If ye shall ask any thing in my name, I will do it." John 14:12-14 (KJV)

~

Perhaps the unsung hero of my Grandma's story is my Pappaw. Because it takes a lot of faith to trust that God is truly working through someone else. He not only agreed with what Grandma was doing but he chose to partner with her in her calling. He may have never preached one sermon or laid hands on one person to pray but he faithfully did what he could do. He sought out vehicles when she needed them, he would drive her to destinations and help to set up the tent. He worked hard to provide for his family. He stayed by Grandma's side and showed his faith in her calling by being a part of everything she did. Pappaw was just a simple, hard working man who had come from a rough background but as Grandma became committed to a life of ministering the gospel it in turn impacted his life in ways he could have never imagined. He probably didn't fully understand what he was getting himself into but he agreed to join her for the ride. From the time he accepted the Lord into his life to when he went home to be with the Lord, it could be said of him that he loved his family as best he knew how and he never forsook them. He had an incredibly generous heart and loved to give to those who had need. In his own way he left a mark of love on those whose lives he touched, including mine.

As Grandma began to understand that she was chosen, God began to put a vision for ministry in her heart. The vision gave her a purpose and with her husband's help, she began to prepare to set out on the first mission the Lord gave. They bought a tent and a suitable truck to transport it in and then set out in faith to find a town where they could hold revival. Her first revival was held in a town in Ohio, about thirty miles away from Richmond. The Lord told Grandma that she would minster to those who were sick, diseased and tormented but she wasn't a preacher and did not really care to be one. So she decided to ask another minister to take the preaching part of the services while she would do the laying on of hands. On the night of the first service that preacher never showed up. There she was, with a crowd of people and never having preached before in her life. If there had been any fear in her she would have just called the whole thing off! But being full of faith and confidence that God led her to that place, she made the decision to not back down despite the unexpected twist. Her faithful statement in the face of this challenge was, "Well I guess God wants me to preach too!"

Indeed He did! And in believing that the Holy Spirit would give her the words to speak, she gave her first sermon. It was short and sweet, the best kind of sermon! She finished the service with getting every single person who came up for prayer a miracle that night. Word of her healing campaign spread like wild fire and the attendance grew each night. After that, preaching just became another aspect of her ministry. She never "prepared" for sermons in the traditional way many preachers do, with notes and days of study before hand. She would say, "I don't really prepare for a sermon, I just get up and whatever the Holy Spirit puts on my heart, that's what I teach on. I really just let Him have His say." Money might be able to buy you a Bible college degree but it can't buy you the ability to be an oracle of God!

The Lord blessed the first meetings she held and through her obedience God was glorified in it all. It changed her life. She was so full of the joy of the Lord and confidence in Him, that she decided to visit that little Pentecostal Holiness church she had once attended. Her heart still had a burden for those people and she wanted to share with them the freedom of the Truth. She had tasted and seen that God is good and she very much wanted them to partake of it. She hoped that maybe this time they would open their hearts to what the Lord was doing. She went to them and asked if they would allow revival at their church. But hardened hearts are lost upon even the simplest faith. Religiousness is a cancer to the soul that blinds, deafens and destroys. It is an unteachable spirit. The elders rejected her yet again and told her they wanted to have nothing to do with her. In that moment those men chose to remain in that place of hardness. They declared their desire to hold onto tradition and forfeited being a part of the new move of God.

Her heart mourned for those people but she was not affected in the same way as before. This time she couldn't be shaken because she had encountered the reality of who God is. He had spoken to her and she knew that she knew, that she was in the center of His will. This was her new foundation. She believed Ephesians 3:20 that says God "is able to do exceeding abundantly above all that we ask or think, according to the power that works in us,". If you know who He is and who you are in Him, He will go above and beyond our understanding., but you must be willing to believe.

~

"For if there is first a willing mind, it is accepted according to what one has, and not according to what he does not have." 2 Corinthians 8:12 (KJV)

~

After Grandma presented the opportunity to the elders of that church she immediately drove into downtown Richmond and rented the largest auditorium, the Morten Center, which seated about twenty-five hundred people. This is where she would hold her next meetings for the next three weeks. She advertised throughout the city and the first night about fifteen hundred people showed up and every night the attendance continued to increase. The very first night a man came up for prayer who had had his arm amputated by army doctors due to cancer. The cancer had returned and had appeared on his neck and face in the form of growths. With authority, Grandma commanded that sickness to leave and the cancerous growths literally fell off! This was merely one of the thousands of miracles that took place during that awesome revival. Out of those healing campaigns held in Richmond the locals who had attended responded by asking her if she would be willing to start a church. So she began to look for a building to hold church services. She rented a local hall called Beechwood that seated about six hundred people. It was usually only rented out on Saturday nights as a dance hall, so until the money could be raised to build a church, she rented it for the other six days of the week. At the very first service held at this new gathering place, there was standing room only and so it continued every night (except Saturday) with an additional service on Sunday morning. Once again countless lives were touched, people came to salvation and were filled with the Holy Spirit and many, many more miracles occurred.

The money to buy land was soon raised and so began the construction of the Full Gospel Tabernacle located at South Ninth and Q Streets in Richmond, Indiana. While the church was being built Grandma began praying for guidance on where to evangelize next. He spoke to her saying, "Go south Rebecca and I will show you where I want you to be." The next morning they were packed up and ready to go. Before they headed out Pappaw informed Grandma that they only had $11 to their name. She responded, "Don't worry Albert, God will never forsake us. He told me to go and He will make a way!" They had traveled only a few miles when suddenly they came upon a man waving at them from the side of the road. They pulled over to see what was the matter and watched as the man rushed to their truck. He jumped up on the running boards and said, "I hoped I would find you before you left!" With a grin he handed Pappaw several hundred dollar bills and explained, "God spoke to me to give this to you, I hope it helps you on your way." Thus through the obedience of one, another's obedience was rewarded. Little did they know that God was sending them to the small town of Big Hill, Kentucky, the area where Pappaw was born and raised.

As they came into town they passed by a vacant field that was beside a small general store and gas station. Suddenly Grandma told Pappaw to stop the truck because she heard God say that they should set the tent up in that very field. They went inside the general store to inquire about using the property and were willingly given permission to set up their tent. They set a sign outside the tent that read "Healing Campaign" along with the dates and times. So many people came on the first night that every seat was filled. They even had to raise the sides of the tent so that hundreds of other people could stand and look in. One night during these services the Lord said to Grandma, "Tell those who want the baptism of the Holy Ghost to fast from food the next day. Tell them that if they do so and return the next evening, they will be filled." On that next night when she went to pray for all those who had come to be baptized she simply waved an outstretched hand over the people without ever saying a word and three hundred and forty people were immediately filled and began to speak in tongues.

~

"An encounter with the Holy Spirit isn't a passive experience. One must hunger and thirst for the activation of the Holy Spirit through the baptism of fire and He will in turn respond with filling you up to overflowing!" -Virgil Johnson

~

In those meetings in Big Hill, Kentucky my Dad became active in the ministry. He was only eleven years old at the time. God laid it on his heart one night to fast and so the next morning he went up into the mountains without any food and found a secluded hollow in a cliff. There he prayed all day, not really knowing what the Lord would do, just knowing that he hungered for what he had seen displayed in his own mother's life. The very next night Grandma asked Dad to begin helping her to pray for the people in the services due to the overwhelming amount of those who needed prayer. Not knowing how to pray for people Dad asked, "How do you get miracles Mom?" She smiled and replied, "Lay hands on the person and ask God to heal them. Believe what you say and then stand back and watch God do it." Such simplicity in describing something as profound as faith for miracles and healings! Even though she was speaking to him as a child who could easily grasp simple faith, her words were filled with wisdom. Everyone, young and old, should come to understand faith in this way.

~

"Just believe that what you are praying for, God is willing and able to do! From there your faith will grow. Activating the gift of faith requires action on our part, to begin to trust and obey as we believe for what we ask for." -Virgil Johnson

~

The first three people he prayed for received miracles. The first person was a young man who suffered so badly from asthma that he was painfully laboring for every breath. Dad took the man's hands in his and simply asked God to touch him, then he stepped back and watched for a miracle. He was fully expecting to see what his mother had told him would happen and he believed he would. Suddenly the young man who had been gasping for air began to inhale deeply without a bit of laboring! He received a miracle and his lungs were made perfectly well! Hallelujah!

The second person Dad prayed for was a little lady who was one hundred and three years old and had become blind in her old age. She wanted her sight to be recovered so that she might be able to read her Bible until the Lord saw fit to take her home. Dad's heart was so moved with compassion that he just knew God would honor her request. Dad took her hands in his and asked the Lord to restore her sight and instantly her eyes were made to see with perfect clarity! Several years later the little old lady's granddaughter told Dad that her grandmother lived to the ripe old age of one hundred and six and she read her Bible daily until she went to be with the Lord! Praise God!

The third person that Dad prayed for was an eighteen year old girl who had polio in both legs. Her legs were clad in steel braces which locked her legs into position so she could walk with the assistance of crutches. He prayed for her and then said, "Now let us see what God has done!" The girl immediately sat down on a nearby chair so that the braces that were attached to her shoes could be removed. Next she stood up on her own and began to walk back and forth on the platform! Glory to God! After service Dad watched her climb over the rack on the back of a cattle truck which was her ride home and he believed it was her way of proving to herself that she was completely healed.

~

"At this same revival we were asked to go outside of the tent to pray for a man who was paralyzed from the chest down. Two joints of his backbone had been removed by Army doctors because of an accident he had suffered while serving. Where they had operated on his spine there was an open running sore that would not heal. Mother said to him, 'If God puts feeling back into your legs, will you believe that He will give you two new joints of backbone?' The man said he would. While we prayed, I pinched his legs. He cried, 'Ouch!' God had put feeling back into his legs! Two months later we received a call to drive two hundred miles to this man's home to see the progressive miracle. There where the open running sore had once been were two new joints of backbone that I felt with my own fingers and new skin had completely covered the opening." -Virgil Johnson

~

That revival in the tiny town of Big Hill went on for four months. People came from all over the state of Kentucky and bordering states. The testimonies of God's goodness were innumerable and the impact on the Kingdom immeasurable! Shortly after that revival the construction of the church in Richmond was completed on November 25, 1950. It had wood shaving floors, dual purpose chairs that were also used in the tent meetings and a furnace to give it heat. It was a humble building where those of like heart and spirit could meet and worship. Service was held every night of the week and twice on Sundays. It would continue to thrive for the next thirty years.

~

"How can one describe such a thing as this? Surrounded by the reality of God, saturated in his power, understanding the fullness of God's promises, walking in heavenly places! Being in His presence and feeling such awesomeness can only be experienced for ones self. One can not simply read about it, or hear about, or take someone's word. When you feel the power, witness the miracles with your own eyes, sense the anointing then you will know for yourself that God is who He says He is and every promise is true." -Virgil Johnson

~

At the next tent revival in Kentucky there were over a thousand attendees and the majority were from Baptist churches in the region, none of which believed in the baptism of the Holy Ghost and speaking in tongues. The first night many people were hesitant to believe that God moved in miracles because of the teaching that they had been given. So on that first night very few people came up for prayer. The few who did come all received miracles and this caused the people's hearts to begin to soften. The next night even more people came out to the meeting, including a man whom everyone knew to be a trouble maker. He would visit the various Baptist churches from county to county and make his presence known as if he were the final authority on God. When Grandma finished preaching that night she called people up for prayer and that man was one of the first to get in line.

"What's wrong with you?" she asked. He replied "I've got arthritis." she quickly replied "You are lying to the Holy Ghost." She knew this because the Lord told her that the man was in fact lying. "Oh no," he insisted "I've got arthritis!" She shook her head and again said, "No sir, you are lying, go sit down." All the sudden that hesitancy that had been caused by unbelief within the people was broken. Everyone there knew that man to be a trouble maker and that he didn't have any arthritis in his body. When Grandma called him out and identified that lying spirit, they knew she was a woman of God. Once their unbelief was broken the Holy Spirit was free to move. Every single Baptist that came to that meeting was filled with the Holy Spirit and hundreds received physical healings and miracles of all kinds. Six months later she heard a report of the man who had lied to the Holy Spirit having been suddenly struck with arthritis. It took hold of his body so badly that he became crippled and was made to remain in a wheel chair for the rest of his life.

In this same revival a woman who had the hiccups for seven years came to Grandma for prayer. This woman had been given so many different shots of medicine by doctors who were trying to cure her hiccups, that it damaged the muscles in her arms. So much so, that she could no longer straighten her arms and they were drawn up to her chest in an inward bent position. Grandma laid hands on the woman and commanded her hiccups to be gone and her arms to straighten. She received both miracles instantaneously and simultaneously! She was able to straighten her arms and stretch them in all different ways, proving her muscles to have been regenerated. The hiccups stopped immediately and never reoccurred! Glory to God!

There was another woman who came to Grandma's meetings for prayer who had three large goiters. A goiter is an enlargement of the thyroid gland that is evident in the form of nodules or lumps on the neck. Severe goiters create pressure on the windpipe or esophagus, causing shortness of breath or difficulty swallowing. This woman had not only one but three goiters causing her neck to be severely swollen. Grandma prayed saying, "Let these goiters pass like a wind!" and they did! She watched as the swelling instantly went away before her eyes and the healed woman shouted the victory! Hallelujah!

~

"Ah, Lord God! Behold, You have made the heavens and the earth by Your great power and outstretched arm. There is nothing too hard for You. You show lovingkindness to thousands." Jeremiah 32:17-18 (NKJV)

~

It is not because of miracles that we love God but we love Him because He first loved us. Fully comprehending that love causes us to believe that He will do miracles for us and through us. It is that loving kindness that draws out of us a desire to be obedient to the One who loves us. And that is what allows us to enter into the promises of God. Every day that we walk with the Lord we will be presented with opportunities to obey His voice and His leadings through unctions given by the Holy Spirit, but it's a choice. We can agree with His word or dismiss it, it truly is completely up to us. He speaks not for the purpose of us being able to do signs and wonders but so that we will stay focused on Him and His love for us. Being focused on Him will in turn let us see His will be done on earth as it is in heaven. Signs and wonders are simply the result of a life lived in obedience to God's voice.

This obedience born of confidence in His love for us must translate into every area of our lives. One day my Grandma was on the phone with a preacher who had invited her to come and hold meetings at his church. As soon as she set the date with him and hung up the phone the Lord spoke to her. He said, "If you go, I won't go." In that moment she had a choice. She could have reasoned away the voice of the Lord, she could have even come up with a dozen scriptures that argued that God couldn't have possibly said those words. But she knew, through testing, through trusting, that it was His voice. Without a moment's hesitation she called the preacher back and said, "Pastor, the Lord just spoke to me and I'm going to have to cancel the meeting. He said if I go that He won't and if He won't go I can't come." Many a religious minister would have argued with God. Argued that they needed the meeting. That they needed the money or that it was their job. But she had learned that God always worked everything out for her good, so her choice was an easy one. She didn't even stop to consider what the preacher would say in response because it didn't matter. The only thing that ever matters is hearing the voice of God and responding in obedience. Grandma knew no amount of carnal or religious reasoning trumps the word of God. His words had never failed her and she wasn't about to start trusting in her own reasoning.

Three weeks later she found out that pastor had been arrested and put in jail on charges of sodomy. He was caught in a homosexual relationship and it utterly destroyed his church. Obedience is better than sacrifice and God will only ever ask us to do what He is working for our good. That is why faith is blind and that is why submitting to His will is worth letting go of control. Believing without seeing is knowing He is working all things to our good. He is in the center of everything for the life of the one who loves Him. Obedience is always required of us so that we will be protected under the shadow of His wings from that which we cannot see. She didn't know exactly why God said don't go, but she wasn't about to go where He wouldn't! She didn't know what was going on with that preacher, or that he was lost in sin. But the Lord wanted to keep her from going there for a reason, and that she trusted.

Once the Lord gave her a vision of the church. In this vision she was walking down a hallway full of doors that were closed. When she opened the first door that she came to she saw a room full of infants that were mentally retarded and physically deformed. They were crying and wailing from hunger and there was no one to tend to them. The Lord said, "This is the church, held back and helpless because they refuse to grow up." The door closed by itself and she moved on to the next one. As she opened it she surveyed a room full of rocking chairs with preachers sitting in each one just rocking away. The Lord said, "They have knowledge without experience and can only stay in one place." She marveled at how close in proximity the leaders were to the children in the next room and how they did nothing but sit, unmoved by the cries coming from the next room. The vision showed her how many were not being taught or fed so that they could know who God is in maturity for themselves. The leaders were creating church members without power or effectiveness for the Kingdom of God. This vision fueled her resolve to be led of the Spirit to reach the broken within the churches.

My Grandma's confidence in the love of God towards her caused countless lives to be touched by God. Her greatest desire was that others would know the love of God for themselves. From that heart of compassion she made an incredible impact. Her's was not only an active faith but an interactive faith. She was willing and determined to share what had changed her life. Miracles may be what a lot of people remember her for but for those who were close to her, the greatest mark she left was love. She believed what she preached with every fiber of her being because God had proven Himself to her time and time again and He never once failed. Did trials come? Yes. Did hurt threaten to shake her foundation? Yes. Did the devil try to undermine and attack? Yes. This is the life of a follower of Christ. We are promised victory not a lack of battles. We are promised strength only when we fully understand our own weakness. We are given a great hope and assurance in the face of despair because God's goodness towards us never ceases! He knows exactly what will bring about that good in our lives if we are willing to trust the path He has set us on.

My Grandma lived a Christ-like life. Even before she was called to evangelize, people from miles around would bring the sick to her house believing for miracles. They took the sick and dying to a farmer's wife. Not to a pastor, not a great theologian, not a high ranking official of some wide spread denominational organization. They looked for faith in a woman chosen by God for her willingness to be a vessel for Him. She was just an ordinary woman who made the choice to believe and then act on that faith until she was made extraordinary through Him. She was known as a woman who completely trusted God. That is the kind of person we can partner with to push through to breakthrough.

~

"If I could get the word of God in your heart like you've got that doctor, I could really get you well!" -Rebecca Johnson

~

I can hear the fervency in her heart when I read that statement! She had a deep, deep revelation of how obeying the voice God can usher you into divine health. It is a cry for people to come and know God in His goodness! He wants to be your Healer, if you will only believe! You put your trust in man and then curse God for not bringing you an answer when you cry out on Him. If you believe the word of man over the word of God you cannot comprehend the resurrection power living inside of you. We all want to be well but not everyone is willing to do what it takes to live in that reality.

The word Christian means one who is Christ-like. In the book of Acts after the day of Pentecost when the Holy Spirit came to indwell inside of the believers, the disciples went out to all parts of the world doing the works of Christ with many signs and wonders and preaching the gospel. Only after they began to do what Christ did, did they become known as Christians. Have you seen the dead raised? Jesus did and so did my Grandma.

While holding revival for almost a year in Tampa, Florida she witnessed God's resurrection power. One night a woman came into the tent screaming, "My baby is dead! My baby is dead! My baby is dead!" She was holding the baby's body tightly to her's and her husband and a doctor were in tow. The child had been pronounced dead three hours prior to their arrival and the woman absolutely refused to let go of her child. She was unwilling to let the doctors give the baby's body to the undertaker. This woman heard of the miracle services being held in town and she refused to give up her baby until she had her baby prayed for by my Grandma. This woman was not a Christian and had never even attended church, but she believed God would honor her request.

To the right of the platform in the tent was an area set up for people to go and pray in private during services. When Grandma's preaching was interrupted she asked someone to start a song before she went over to meet the woman and her baby. She took the baby from the mother and walked to the private praying area while right behind her followed my Dad. He watched as she prayed, "Father, it seems to be that this mother misses this baby. Could you find it in Your heart to give it back to her?" Just as the prayer left her lips the breath of life came back into the baby who had been dead for three hours! Her compassion for the mother mixed together with her knowledge of how much God loved this mother caused her to ask for His love and kindness to pour out by way of a miracle. This is praying in the perfect will of God. It's not what you pray but the Spirit in which you pray.

Grandma thanked the Lord and handed the baby back to the mother. "God has favored you this night", was all she said to her. She didn't stop to ask if this woman was saved or if she was without sin in her life. She didn't tell her to stay for the service or demand a single thing. God answered the cry of that woman's heart and if that was not enough to draw her to Him, what amount of preaching could? The woman responded by coming back the following night with her family. Both she and her husband gave their hearts to the Lord that night and they returned the following evening and were baptized in the Holy Ghost.

Miracles are wonderful, aren't they?! I am so overwhelmed at the goodness of God when I think of everything He has done for my family and through my family. This has been my reality for as long as I have lived. I was exposed to all nine gifts and I believe that anyone who has them can use them. It's as simple as choosing to be an outlet for the Holy Spirit to flow out of. I am encouraged by my Grandma's life because of her unassuming relationship with the Lord. She didn't attempt to figure out how He would move, she just believed He would and He did. When I remember her story I see someone who lived and moved and had her being in God. She is proof of loving Him with all your heart, soul and mind.

    I want to share with you one last miracle that happened sometime in 1959 or perhaps 1960. This miracle is actually a series of miracles that my Grandma received for herself during the time she held revival in London, Kentucky. Dick and Gladis Carter were goods friends and ministry partners with Grandma who were the ministers of music that led song service at the revival. The Carter's had volunteered to drive Grandma to the tent meeting that day because my Grandma didn't drive. Pappaw was usually the one to drive her to the meetings but he had gone back home to take care of some business and hadn't returned to London yet. As they were riding down the road a truck turned in front of their car and hit them on the right front side of their 1954 Plymouth Belvedere. They collided so hard that the truck was knocked completely off the road and into a field.

    The car was completely totaled. The Carter's were not hurt but Grandma was badly injured. She was sitting in the front passenger side of the car which took the brunt of the hit causing the door to be crushed inward onto her. Back then there were no seat belts and her head slammed into the metal dashboard, denting it in about half an inch. The impact knocked her out and when she came to, Brother Carter told her that her nose was broken and laying sideways and her scalp was peeled back from the impact to the dash. Someone who witnessed the wreck called for an ambulance and when Brother Carter found out the first responders were on their way he told Grandma. Now this is the part of the testimony that makes people's hearts grip with fear or soar with faith! If you didn't believe what has been written thus far about this woman's faith, you are about to. She knew that the EMT would try to force her to go to the hospital as soon as they saw her nose and scalp. So the first thing she did was to put her hand over her nose and say, "Lord heal my face before the ambulance gets here!" She removed her hand and Brother Carter stood in awe as he watched the broken bone of her nose go from visibly being broken to being set right on her face again. The only evidence of it having been broken was the bruising on the bridge of her nose. "Becky! That was the most amazing miracle I have ever seen!" he declared. "You mean out of all the miracles you've seen in our meetings?!" she replied rather surprised. He answered, "Oh Becky, you don't know how bad your face looked!" Quickly she took her scalp and laid it back down against her head. She prayed that there would be no more bleeding and the bleeding ceased. When she tried to move out of the car she knew that her hip was broken as severe pain shot through her whole body. The wreck happened near a gas station so she asked Brother Carter to carry her out of the car and set her on a bench.

When the ambulance came they surveyed the wreck and began asking questions. They began insisting that she go to the hospital as quickly as possible, just like she knew they would. She refused them by saying, "I am not going to the hospital." They were stunned at her response because they assumed no one in her condition could possibly not want to go to the hospital for help. They tried again to convince her how bad her injuries were, that her hip was likely broken and then there was the possibility of internal injuries as well. One EMT stated "Oh woman! You don't realize how badly you are hurt and you must go to the hospital!" With faith and confidence she spoke, this time with greater authority. "I preach that Jesus is the Healer of all diseases, not just of the flesh but also of the bone. Whatever is wrong, Jesus heals it! I'm not going to the hospital. I am over 21. I know what I am talking about and I am in my right mind. So you just take that ambulance and go on back!" Without further argument they packed up their gear and left.

After the ambulance left the scene of the accident she had her photograph taken while standing in front of the totaled car as proof of her testimony. Brother Carter then asked Grandma if she wanted to be taken back to her travel trailer to rest and she replied, "No! The people are expecting a service tonight so we have to go and give them one." They got a ride to where the tent was set up and arrived before the crowd began to gather. Brother Carter carried her to the front and placed her in a chair on the platform. Hundreds of people attended that night. The Carter's led song service and people testified of miracles they had received the night before. Just before she was about to give the word to the people she announced, "I was in a car wreck before service and I'm just a little shaken up. So tonight I'm going to preach sitting down." And Grandma preached and prayed for the sick all while sitting in that chair.

(Photo of Rebecca Johnson after accident)

22

Once the service ended she waited for everyone to leave and then asked Brother Carter to carry her to the car. When he picked her up out of the chair the pain was so excruciating that she almost fainted. She was able to stay alert and was then carried to a car and driven back to her trailer. When they arrived they found Pappaw had returned from his quick trip to Richmond. He came and carried her from the car into the trailer and placed her on the couch. He inspected her injuries and saw the gash in her head from where she had laid her scalp back into place. He also saw small pieces of glass from the broken windshield imbedded in her scalp and said, "You know you are going to have to have that glass removed from your head." She replied, "Don't say another word, just be real quiet. Just give me time to get myself calmed down and we will see what God can do." Although she was a strong woman of faith she, like all of us, was human and going through what she had just experienced was traumatic in more ways than one. She calmed herself down by staying her mind of the Lord and focusing on His presence there with her as she gingerly felt around her head and one by one picked out all the shards of glass from her scalp. The facts of what were true in the natural did not shake her from the Truth that He is the Lord our Healer. She had to fight through the pain and the physical evidence of what was wrong to get her focus on the Answer but once she did her faith steadied.

It was a rough night with little sleep but she made it through to the next day when her sister Elizabeth Smith, co-pastor of Grandma's church in Richmond, came to pray for her. After spending just a bit of time together she said, "Becky, the Lord just showed me you that you were hurt very badly on the inside and you are bleeding internally." Grandma replied, "I knew it but I didn't want to tell anyone else about it. The Lord will take care of it, the same as He will take care of everything else." She was a wise enough woman to know that when you are trusting God you don't have to tell everyone else what He already knows. Sometimes revealing more details only causes others to respond in fear instead of faith. On that same day the two sisters prayed together and the Lord spoke to both of them confirming that He had healed the internal bleeding.

For three days she laid in bed. Every once in a while she would ask Pappaw to move her leg to see if there was any improvement and every time he did she would shout out in pain. After doing it a few times he finally said he wasn't going to do it anymore because hearing her in pain was not helping his nerves. She would later testify that for those three days not one time did anything go through her mind but that the Lord God heals. Not one time did she have a thought of calling on a doctor or going to a hospital. She continued to stand on and declared the word of God and she believed nothing could keep it from working. No matter how long it would take, she was going to trust Him.

"He may not come in a hurry but He always gets there just in time." -Rebecca Johnson

On the morning of the third day five different preachers came to pray for her, including my Dad who was at his own series of meetings and came as soon as he could. She needed a boost in her faith to help her through the fight, so she called on people of faith. Dad asked her, "Mom, why didn't you at least come home, being in this condition?" She replied, "Virgil, there's a time to lay down and there's a time to fight! I had to make my stand. Once I had made my stand then I laid down and let Him show His glory." So many of us just lay down without making a stand for what we believe in. We let circumstances dictate our reaction instead of letting faith be our declaration. My Grandma knew, that she knew, that she knew, she was the beloved of God. That love could not break the foundation of trust she had established with Jesus. She believed the word and the word says He cannot lie and if He cannot lie then how could she not put all her trust in Him?

The group of believers prayed together over Grandma until one of the preachers said, "In the name of Jesus, get up and walk!" If she had asked someone to do something they couldn't do before she would want them to do it, so when the preacher said get up, she stood up out of the bed and began to walk toward the preacher. He motioned for her to follow him with an outstretched hand, leading her in this way as he began walking backwards. She walked on a broken hip just as if there had never been anything wrong. As she walked she didn't see that preacher before her but she saw Jesus standing between them! As long as she saw Jesus she could walk, but suddenly He faded out of her sight and she couldn't take another step. As she was about to fall over someone caught her and helped her to sit down.

She looked up at the preacher who had commanded her out of bed and said, "You don't know me, and I'm not bragging about what I know or what I have. I am not meaning to do that, but I do want to tell you what to do right now. You see my leg has been hurting me for three days and it may have created a little fear in me. Maybe just the fear to move my legs but if I have even a little bit of fear in me, I can't get well. That will stop my faith from working. So I want you to anoint me and lay your hand on my head and say, 'Lord if there is any fear in her, take it away'." The preacher agreed to do it and everyone present prayed in agreement. Then suddenly Grandma heard the voice of the Lord speak to her loud and clear. He said, "Rise up quickly, I have delivered you!" All the sudden she jumped up from that couch and when she did so she felt two unseen hands take a hold of her leg and set her hip back into place. As the hip was set it hurt quite a bit and caused her to almost faint from it. But instead of fainting she started shouting, "Glory to God I've been healed!" Not only was the hip set back into socket but the breaks had also been completely mended as she was made able to stand and walk without any pain! God is so amazing!

~

"There is no other way to get well but to believe what the word says. Don't believe what Sister Johnson says, but what thus says the Lord! You don't say, 'Well, He healed Sister Johnson and because He healed her He'll heal me'. You don't base your faith that way. It won't work. You have to base your faith on what the word of God says! If the word of God says that you are healed, then you're healed! You can't believe this word and stay sick. Abide in Him and let the Word abide in you and you will have anything you ask for." -Rebecca Johnson

~

To abide in Him does not mean we know absolutely every detail about how God will work but we do know that no matter what, He cannot lie and He is working it all to our good. What it means to abide in Him is that daily we choose to actively work with the Holy Spirit to conform our minds to the word of God, thereby transforming our minds to the mind of Christ. This comes only from hearing the voice of God for ourselves and believing that the word of God is true. For the purpose of establishing a relationship between us and the Father, the Son and the Holy Ghost.

If we don't believe that He is who He says He is, all of the promises become just out of reach. Will He answer the way we expect? He will give us what we ask for if we ask for it in His will, that's the word of God, but many times the answer comes in an unexpected way. That is where we humans tend to be shaken. It is hard to see how going through something as awful as a car wreck that broke a hip in two places, broke a nose, peeled a scalp and caused internal bleeding could possibly work for good. Did He send the car wreck? No! The devil intended that accident to be just the thing to keep this mighty woman of God from having revival. But she made her stand and preached, even if sitting down, being obedient to what God had called her there to do. The proof of the Word abiding in us is that we believe it without question. This is how we walk through the test and obtain our testimony.

Three days after the miracle of her hip, six days after the wreck, Grandma was standing at her sink in her home in Richmond doing the dishes. She heard the Lord say, "I want you to go have an x-ray made. I want you to go and show it to the people because I want them to know what I have done for you." She really didn't know herself exactly what had been wrong with her hip but she knew for sure God had healed it. So she went to the Medical Arts building to a man named Doctor Wisener. There she told him that she had been in a car wreck and that she would like to be x-rayed in the hip area. He took the x-ray and examined it. A few short moments later he called her to join him in the room where they could both view the x-ray. He showed her the image and pointed out the proof of her hip having been broken in two places and also being out of socket and reset. He said, "You did walk in here, didn't you?" She replied, "Yes sir, I walked in here." He responded, "Well I've never seen anyone walk on a broken hip before!" He paused before continuing, "But I will tell you what to do! You go home and get in the bed. Because if your hip comes out of place again you'll be a cripple for life!"

She knew he was only speaking out of his limited carnal knowledge, so she did not rebuke him. He looked her straight in the eyes and said, "I'll tell you one thing, this is the most perfect setting I have ever seen!" Up until now she had not told him any details of the car crash or the miracle. She smiled and said, "Do you know why it's so perfect?" He shook his head and replied, "No." With pleasure she testified to the glory of God, "It's perfect because Jesus did it and when He does anything He does it right!" He didn't know what to say to that but recommended eight weeks of bed rest and sent her on her way with the x-ray of the healing that he couldn't explain. The doctor, being very smart in the knowledge of medicine, knew that if she had had the operation done by a doctor there would have been a pin in her hip and there was nothing of the kind. He examined the two places where the hip had been broken and how there was evidence of it being mended back together. If that man didn't believe in miracles after that I don't know what could have convinced him!

~

"Jesus doesn't half way do things. When Jesus touches you, you will be well. And if He says that He has touched you will see it, if you will be patient enough to wait on Him. If you can believe that word enough to wait on Him." -Rebecca Johnson

~

The very next day after she had the x-ray done a few friends of hers asked her to join them on a trip to Washington D.C. for the Voice of Healing convention. This meant riding in a car for about five hundred miles and long periods of sitting can be hard on the hips. She decided to join the group and so did my Dad. When they arrived in D.C. they rented rooms on the top floor of a three story hotel and never once did she use the elevators. She made it a point to walk up and down the stairs and with every step she told the devil, "You are a liar and my hip will never come out of place."

Seeds of doubt may be placed in our hearts by others after we receive our miracle. Sometimes it will require us to do something radical to counter act and eradicate the seed. Whatever it takes keep your eyes on Jesus and His word will be proven in your life. If she had believed the doctor instead of the word of the Lord she could have very easily crawled into bed for eight weeks and believed the lie. But she chose to challenge that lie and sit in the back seat of a car for over eight hours and book a room on the top floor of the hotel with the determination to literally walk out what she believed.

There is nothing too difficult for God. Nothing impossible for Him. Be it a lifelong disease, a sudden illness, an injury from an accident or even death. He does not pick and choose who He will heal but rather invites everyone to believe that they might obtain their healing. Sometimes it takes days of pain in bed to eradicate some fear that we did not know was there. Or perhaps there is a lie we were told and it has to be worked out of our thinking so that we can begin to see like He does. As we continue in His love and learn to trust in His faithfulness our faith will grow.

My Grandma was faithful! She evangelized up and down the east coast of the United States and to the island of Jamaica spreading the gospel that was followed by signs and wonders and many miracles. She ministered on the radio, created a monthly circular entitled "The Voice of Deliverance", to inform others of the miracles being produced out of the move of God she was a part of. She pastored her church, The Full Gospel Tabernacle, for about ten years before resigning to let Dad take over. Grandma ministered to anyone whose heart was open to hear the love of God up until the day she went home to be with the Lord on June 29, 1979.

(Photo of Rebecca Johnson)

Her doors were always open to anyone who needed prayer or encouragement and she loved others like Jesus loved them. She was faithful until the day the Lord called her home to heaven. Although I never personally knew my Grandma her story was told to me by many who witnessed it. I was blessed with having audio recordings of her preaching, photo's of ministry and documentation of miracles that helped me to tell her story. Her story is so much a part of my story because without it I would not be who I am today. I have been told by many that I have her tenacity, determination and boldness. Those who knew her kept her memory alive by telling me who she was. Writing her story has made me feel like I did know her and she was the best Grandma a girl could have ever hoped for. May we all live our lives so that for generations without end our story will be told of the goodness of God. Becky Johnson fought the good fight, finished her course, kept the faith and left behind a legacy.

~

"He that loveth Me shall be loved of my Father, and I will love him, and will manifest Myself to him." John 14:21 (KJV)

~

# 2
# Growing Up

Virgil Claude Johnson was one of a kind! People either loved him or hated him, there was really no in-between. He was fearless and determined! He knew exactly who he was and what he wanted and not much could stand in the way of that hunger for life that he possessed. That is describing him in the natural but it also describes him well in the spiritual. Only God could have taken someone like him and transformed him into who I knew him to be. Mature Virgil still had that passion for living life but the man I knew had come to posses deep wisdom with great knowledge and experience. He was remade from a strong willed, stubborn fighter who was resolute to get things done in his own flesh into a man who's measureless faith and unshakable confidence in God caused Him to see the will of Father done on earth.

The man he was before I came along was someone I have only recently become better acquainted with in the writing of his story. I could only know certain aspects of my Dad through my relationship with him as his child. In my immaturity I could not have fully understood him even if he had tried to tell me every single thing he went through to get to where he was when I knew him. I grew up watching him partner with the Holy Spirit to work on his flesh so that he would no longer be Virgil Johnson but a reflection of Christ Himself. From this I learned that I too could work on my flesh and live in victory over the Adam mind. He taught me how to embrace the good traits of my inherited nature and how to let the Holy Spirit do away with that which was not of Christ. The Virgil I knew never made life about him but always about Jesus.

Everyone who knew and loved him will first recall his smile and laugh. That is just a testimony of the true joy he carried with him. Oh, that infectious laugh of his! You couldn't help but laugh with him for the bubbling over of his happiness. When he laughed you could see in his eyes genuine love, honesty, and a truth that spoke of how he really just wanted to be your friend. And at times you could see just a wee bit of mischievousness. Then there was that look he often had when you just knew he had your number and you couldn't hide because that love he held for you shed such a brilliant light on whatever was in your heart. That presence of joy would either make you realize you were bitter and joyless or that you could partake in that joy with him and there was freedom for you in the partaking. It would make you get mad or get glad real quick!

He was a powerhouse and as solid as they come. If you ever needed help, he was one you could turn to. He never told you how to live your life and he would never make decisions for you, but rather offer you what He knew about God from his own experience and let you choose to receive it or not. He poured out wisdom and knowledge that held the key to your breakthrough, if you had ears to hear it. His way of teaching was so incredibly simplistic that it allowed the word to be readily applied to everyday life and he made you believe you could obtain it! He knew, through experience, that you cannot work out anyone else's salvation for them. You can however love them and lead them towards their own revelations of who God is.

Countless lives were touched by his life and ministry because he lived it. Ministry was not a job or a position he held. Ministry was an all out, die for you, never turning back, radical kind of love that was displayed to bring glory to God! And it showed up in every aspect of his life that was lived unapologetically. Take it or leave it, love it or hate it, he was the real deal! It took him many years of learning how to lay down his own life for the purpose of taking on Christ's nature so that he could share his testimony with all of us. But he chose to walk that path knowing the prize was worth it.

As I have said before, miracles are the threads with which this story is woven. This is the word of our testimony. My Dad's story builds upon my Grandma's story. Both of who's stories are the very fabric upon which my story is built. It would take a lifetime to relay a lifetime of miracles. So I will outline his life in a way that will show you what I know to be true of who my Dad was. I want to start at the very beginning so you can see how he was affected by his mother and her ministry. The simplicity of his way of life testifies of a heart that longed for one thing, to hear the voice of God. His life is the next chapter in this legacy.

On the 25th of February in 1938 my Dad was born in the family home on Water Works Road in Richmond, Indiana and he was born dead. The umbilical cord had wrapped around his throat in the birth canal and he was stillborn. Satan was actively trying to end his life before it could even really begin. The doctor told my Grandma the grim report and she told him that she was praying. Dad was purple and non-responsive but she told the doctor to keep trying. The doctor massaged his limp body as she asked God to spare my Dad. Ten minutes later he began to cry! The doctor placed Dad in Grandma's arms and said, "Well, Becky, it seems your prayers have worked!" That was the first attempt the devil made upon Dad's life and many would follow it. Satan knew my Dad was destined to give him hell.

When Dad was about three years old the family moved to a house on Fourth Street in Richmond. One day while he and my Uncle Robert were playing in the back yard on a pile of discarded boards, Dad's bare foot stepped on a board that had a nail sticking up through it. His brother rushed him into the house where he was quickly placed on my

Grandma's lap. She didn't panic she just calmly began to pray. She laid her hand on the wound and thanked the Lord for touching it and when she removed her hand the bleeding had stopped. More to Dad's delight his foot had also stopped hurting. "God healed you Virgil." she said, "Now I need to finish dinner, so go on back outside and play." He went back outside to continue his playing in those bare feet with no evidence of there ever having been a nail through his foot.

~

"You have to believe God. It's a simple kind of faith. You can not believe the Word and stay sick. You can not believe the Word and stay in a financial need. You can not believe this Word and have trouble and stay in trouble. This Bible is right and the promises of God are yea and amen!" -Rebecca Johnson

~

When Dad was about five years old the family moved again. Pappaw was always looking for an opportunity to get a good deal on a property that he could fix up and sell. As the family grew in size the need to move to a larger house was necessary. They bought a property on which the house had burned down and only the foundation was left standing. The other structures on the property were a very large hay barn, a smoke house, an outhouse and a one car garage. They turned the garage into make-shift home while Pappaw began to build the new house. They moved into the garage in the fall after insulating it as best they could, just before the cold set in, and by the following autumn Pappaw had built a one floor two bedroom house for his family. The eldest son lived in the newly remodeled garage and the rest of the family lived in the newly constructed house.

Living on a farm was exactly what an energetic little boy like my Dad needed. There were places to run, places to explore, places to swim and climb and let the imagination grow. The hay barn was a particularly fun place for a rambunctious child like Dad. To give you a glimpse into how fearless he was I will tell you about the day he decided he was superman. He tied a kitchen towel around his neck, climbed to the top of the roof of the barn and shouted to everyone about his new found superpowers. Grandma looked up at where he was perched and told him to immediately get down from there! He obeyed but she couldn't watch him climb back down, so she just turned her back until he was down and then proceeded to give him a swift swat to the bottom so he would learn to never do it again.

Another time Dad decided he was going to look inside a gas can to see how much fuel was in it. He did so by lighting a match. This was not fearless, just foolish, but he was too little to know better. As you can probably guess, the struck match caused fire to shoot up all over his face that was so close to the gas can. He received third degree burns from this accident and Grandma hurried to his side at the sound of him crying. She laid hands on him and prayed and immediately the burns on his face were healed. All the redness and pain left and even his eyes were not hurt. The only evidence of the accident was that the tips of his eye brows were missing and they never grew back. A reminder of the miracle.

At the age of seven he began to attend school. For an active boy such as himself it was like torture and being made to be still was like cruel and unusually punishment. The class had very little hands on learning, which would have suited a child such as himself much better. It couldn't have been easy to go from a life of freedom on the farm to being constrained to a class room. The teachers really didn't know how to handle him. It's not that he didn't love to learn, he actually had quite a passion for learning, just not in the way the school system was going about educating. It is no surprise that Dad only made it to the eighth grade before he chose to drop out of school. His reading skills were quite limited because of being passed from grade to grade without actually having learned much of what was being taught. The only book he could ever read with some amount of ease was the Bible.

As my Dad grew physically, his mother was growing spiritually. Her prayer life had been increasing with her spiritual growth and now he was beginning to notice how often she prayed. People began to come out to the house to receive prayer and everyone who came needing a miracle left with that need met. He was raised up in an atmosphere of faith. One where he was being taught the reality of who God is and what He is willing to do for a life that it fully submitted to Him. He was always attentive when his mother would say the words "God said".

~

> "I remember waking up many nights as a child at three in the morning hearing Mom praying. She would cry out, 'Lord save my brothers, save my sisters, God touch my church, anoint my pastor!' She asked God for the desires of His heart to come forth over those she loved." -Virgil Johnson

~

During the Second World War Grandma's two brothers were in the armed services, one in the Army and one in the Navy. It was exciting for a young boy of Dad's age to receive letters in the mail from overseas. Letters that would let the family know where the uncles were and the battles that they had fought. Grandma's brother Thomas was actually a part of General Patton's outfit and was in the Battle of the Bulge. She prayed for her brothers the entire time they were at war. When you cry out on God, it pleases Him. When you please Him, He will speak to you more often. When He spoke to Grandma she openly shared it with her family and it impacted my Dad greatly.

One night Grandma woke up and the Lord said, "Pray for Thomas, I want to spare his life." She obeyed and prayed for hours through the night until morning. Just before morning light the Lord spoke again and told her that her brother had been part of a direct hit but he was spared and he was the only one who survived. She told my Dad what the Lord had said and two weeks later they received a letter from her brother confirming that everything the Lord had spoken to her had happened. His letter described how his entire outfit was in a two story building that was hit with a bomb and he was the only one that walked out of that building alive. The only injury he suffered was a cut on his cheek from a piece of flying glass.

The very next night after receiving the letter about her brother Thomas, the Lord woke her up to pray for her brother Sidney Monroe, who was a trigger man on a destroy in the Navy. After she had prayed for him the Lord told her that her brothers ship was positioned in the South Pacific and that He had just spared Monroe's life. She told my Dad and the rest of the family that the Lord specifically said, "Monroe's life was spared by just moments and his ship was damaged. He will be coming home soon." Once again a letter came. The first thing Monroe said in the letter was that he was coming home! He also wrote of the night he was standing watch on deck in a really heavy fog (the same night she was awakened to pray for him). When it came time for him to be relieved of his duty, another sailor took his place. Monroe further wrote that he made it from the watch point to the top of the stairs and just as he was about to go down inside the ship to his quarters the destroyer collided with another destroyer. He was thrust down the stairs by the impact but not badly hurt. The only evidence left of the man whom he had switched watch with was the man's bloody glove. I'm so glad we serve a God who answers prayers! Through my Grandma's obedience and the grace of God both of my great-uncles returned home safe from war.

~

"I'd rather have the voice of God than ten thousand gifts! Because the communication only comes through a relationship with Him." -Virgil Johnson

~

One day a lady driving by in her car got a flat tire in front of their house. Dad watched as the lady got out of the car and asked my Pappaw for help with changing her tire and he gladly obliged. While the tire was being changed the woman and Grandma visited with one another. Grandma noticed how the woman seemed weak and even acted faint a time or two. As the woman was leaving the house Grandma told her that if she ever needed anything to not hesitate to call on her. About a week later the husband of the lady called. He told Grandma that for the brief time his wife spent at her house she had never felt such peace. He also told her of how his wife, a mother of three children, had experienced a nervous breakdown and spent time in a mental institution. He implored her to let his wife come and stay with them at their house for a while, believing that she could really help his wife. Grandma was notorious for laying aside her own life, comfort and convenience and sacrificing of her time and self to help anyone who truly wanted it. Grandma gave her consent for the woman to come and stay and her husband brought her to the house the next day. At the end of a three week period the woman was set free from demon possession. She also accepted Jesus into her heart and was baptized in the Holy Ghost. The woman returned to her own home with a sound mind and was a wonderful mother to her children and wife to her husband. She and Grandma remained friends for many years.

Dad began to see God move in such a great way in his mother's life and all around him. Miracles were increasing and his interest in the kingdom ways increased as well. He would say, "Some people get their children hooked on football or baseball, my mother got me hooked on miracles!" Seeing God work in her life caused him to become acutely aware of the goodness of God and that God does speak to His own. It was at the age of seven that Dad first heard the voice of God. God simply called his name, "Virgil". It was so real and so audible, that he turned around to see who had called his name but it was no one on earth speaking to him. Then he heard the clear voice speak again and it said, "Some day you will preach My gospel." He told his mother what he had heard and in her wisdom she spoke to him in a way a child could understand. "That is good Virgil, keep what you heard in your heart." Grandma did not present him with religiosity or confusion or rebuke. She didn't tell him that he was too young to hear God. She neither confirmed nor denied his calling but she knew he needed to learn how to identify God's voice for himself. The calling itself was not as important as the identifying of His voice. If the Lord spoke once she knew He would speak again to him. She also knew that teaching Dad to listen for God's voice was vital so that he could learn that when God speaks, His words are good, they edify and they are true. It was about a year later when the exact same thing happened to Dad again. It was the same voice and the very same words. He told his mother again about hearing the voice and she replied very similarly telling him to keep it in his heart, but this time she confirmed that it was indeed the voice of God.

The year my Dad experienced the loss of his two sisters, many things changed. From that year forward Christmas was never the same for their family because it brought memories of the loss of Betty and Martha Sue. They also sold their home, packed their belongings in their car and headed out west. The year he turned eight Dad had his first taste of the west and the beginning of what would be a lifetime of travels. It was a big change but a good experience. From this very first adventure of traversing the states westward a passion for seeing the sights would grow in him. He would come to love frequenting many of the nations national parks and historical landmarks and enjoy sharing this love of the outdoors with others.

The family of four hit the road, not even knowing exactly where they were going, but they ended up deciding to head towards Missouri. It was the first time the family had ever left the eastern side of the country and a wonderful time for a little boy who loved adventures. Traveling created a passion inside of Dad for geography and history. Seeing it first hand was a better education than any book could have offered. On their way to Missouri they passed the Mississippi river, which at the time was flooding the worst it had ever flooded and he witnessed history in the making. They traveled through Missouri and down through the pan handle of Texas and onto Albuquerque, New Mexico. Upon arriving in this state known for its dry and hot weather they ran dead into a blizzard. They headed on into the snow storm to Flagstaff, Arizona towards Phoenix where they knew it would be warmer. From Phoenix they traveled onto El Paso, Texas in a more southern direction soon finding themselves in Pecos, which is where they made up their minds to stay for a while. They rented an efficiency room in a small hotel and that is where they made their home for the next several months. Pappaw found work as an auto body repair man at the first shop he enquired at. The man who owned the shop liked him so well that within a few weeks he turned the entire business over to Pappaw to manage. Pappaw was an excellent auto-body repair man as he had learned the skill from working with family who were in the automotive trade. With this skill he was able to make a decent living on restoring wrecked cars.

While living in Texas the family would go sightseeing whenever they had free time. They may have lived in Pecos but when work was done and school was out they traveled much of the western part of Texas. They visited the Davis Mountains near Ft. Davis where the McDonald Observatory is. They visited the Rattlesnake Bomber Base in Pyote that was established in 1942 to train replacement crews for bombers during World War 2 and served as a storage facility for aircrafts. Almost every weekend they traveled together as a family to see the sights, so it was at a young age my Dad came to love traveling and sightseeing and history and geography. He fell in love with creation and learned of how easily it is to connect with the Creator in this setting designed for us to enjoy. Later in life some people dubbed him the "vacationing preacher" because of this desire to enjoy where he was while he was there. It wasn't that he was vacationing when he went to minister to different lands, but that he had learned to live life to the fullest and that God wanted him to enjoy it.

~

"Texas was a time of healing for my parents. They needed a change of scenery after the loss of my sisters. Time to seek God as to what was next in their lives. It was a great time of just being together as a family and letting him prepare us for the next chapter."
-Virgil Johnson

~

After a little over a years worth of traveling and living out west, it was time to return to Indiana. Upon arriving home they bought a house on 10th Street in Richmond and once again my do-it-yourself Pappaw began to remodel it. Not long after all of this my Dad witnessed his mother having a nervous breakdown. The story of which I have already shared. He was just a child but he remembered every detail of what happened. How she called him for help, how he prayed for her and how the numbness stopped creeping up her body. He remembered his grandmother and aunts helping his mother keep house because she was unable. He was ever observant and always learning. This is how he remembered the day his Dad took his mother, his brother and himself to Earl Ivie's healing crusade.

He described it like this, "The tent was set up on Route 4 right near the stock yards. To this day I can picture the tent and remember the exact location. When we arrived we found from one side of the tent to the other were crutches, wheel chairs, canes and casts that had been cut off all which were laying about, tossed aside. We sat down and the service began with an anointed song service followed by the entrance of Brother Ivie. He began to preach a word that stirred the hearts and spirits of the crowd, building up each and everyone's faith. When the prayer line was formed my mother and I went up for prayer. Brother Ivie laid hands on my mother and prayed and then and there she was fully restored, inside and out. She began praising God and then Brother Ivie looked to me. I had been having a lot of bad stomach pains and needed a touch. He prayed for me and then gave me a very small bottle of anointing oil and told me to drink a teaspoon of it when I got home. On the way home my mother continued to praise the Lord, she felt as if she had been made new. Her body was healed and her faith was renewed. Perhaps I was inspired by my mother's rejoicing in her miracle, or perhaps I was too impatient to wait until I got home to take a sip of the oil that Brother Ivie had given me, but whatever the cause I decided to open the bottle and take a swig. Not a moment later I hollered to my father to stop the car and as soon as he did I jumped out and threw up. Whatever it was that had given me pain came up right then, cleaning my system out. Then and there I was given a miracle, never suffering from another stomach pain ever again."

Brother Ivie's ministry continued to have an impact on the entire Johnson family for three years from 1947 to 1949. And it was in the last year of their time with Brother Ivie that Dad was brought to a place of decision at the age of ten. On December 12, 1949 Dad broke his usual routine of playing outside with the other children during services. This night he decided to sit in on the service and participate. He seated himself in the middle of the large audience covered in a canopy of white, the sound of voices being raised to Jesus in song filled the air as the offering plate was being passed. Suddenly he heard a familiar voice amidst all the singing. A voice he had already learned to identify as the Lord's. God spoke, "Virgil, give me all the money you have in your pocket and I will give you something that money cannot buy."

At first this nearly eleven year old boy was devastated at the gentle request. He said to himself, "Give Him all I have?" He immediately thought of the money he had been saving up to buy himself a toy for Christmas. Buying it for himself seemed like a sure fire way to get exactly what he wanted that year. He had spent countless hours collecting bottles and turning them in for two cents apiece raising a sum of $6.80. This seemingly small amount was a great treasure to a ten year old boy who thought of himself as real live cowboy. His greatest desire in life at that time was to obtain a set of shiny cap pistols with black leather holsters to certify that he was indeed a real life cowboy. Although there was a bit of sadness from the thought of giving all he had away, he knew that as the offering plate was being passed in front of him, he must obey. He put every last penny in the plate without hesitation, although he didn't fully understand God's request. But more than wanting a set of toy guns, he wanted to be obedient to that Voice. This was what his mother had been preparing him for. This was the time of deciding to lay down all that he had, even his own life, in exchange for a covenant with the Lord. Everything he witnessed up to now in his own mother's life had prepared him to be obedient to God's voice, and what he felt next was conviction and awe in the realization of what the Lord was offering him in return for his obedience. Tears began streaming down his face as he submitted to the call of Jesus.

He put that experience into these words, "After I put my savings in the offering plate, I felt Him drawing me to the altar. There I would give to Him the only thing left I had to give. I fell to my knees weeping and asked for His forgiveness of my sin. As I knelt before the altar I could hear the voice of my mother and my aunt Elizabeth encouraging and praying for me as I asked the Lord to come in my heart. The two women of faith came to my side and helped me walk into His arms. Before I got up from my knees I was saved and speaking in tongues, having received the baptism of the Holy Spirit. I had never felt such peace and joy as I did in that moment. That night I gave Him my all and what He gave me was more than I could have ever hoped for! Praise the Lord for His mercy and grace! Glory to God! Hallelujah!"

It was through giving that God brought Dad to salvation by getting his attention when He spoke. And it was also through giving that he taught him to better hear His voice. For the next several years of his life as he began to better learn and identify the voice of the Lord, he would be told specific amounts of money to put in the offerings at church. Once when he was around the age of fifteen, Dad received a bonus in his pay check and wanted to give $50 in the offering. Before he could put it in the plate the Lord said to put in $1. It grieved him because he wanted to give more but he was obedient because he had come to know the voice of the Lord. Why would God be so specific in this way? Years later he realized that God had used this way of speaking to him to train him to be comfortable with not only hearing but responding to His voice. He said, "I learned the voice of God through giving and I received something better than anything money could buy." It's not about how much you give it's about being obedient to the voice of God in how much He would have you to give. Obedience is better than sacrifice.

Dad experienced salvation and the baptism of the Holy Spirit at the age of ten and began laying hands on the sick at eleven. And after his decision to give all he had he became actively apart of every single meeting that his mother held. One of his jobs was to gather up prayer cards from people attending service. Another thing he did was play a mandolin for the worship part of the service. And at every service he joined his mother at the prayer lines to lay hands on the sick. The more victory ground we gain as warriors for Christ the more we will begin to see push back from the opposing side. The devil came to counter act these amazing breakthroughs. Not only in Grandma's life but Dad's life as well.

One night Dad was awakened by excruciating pain. He immediately went into his parents room crying and screaming. He told his mother he was hurting so bad in his stomach that he could hardly bear it. She prayed and the pain ceased for a little while so that he was able to fall asleep again. But it wasn't long before he woke up again with that same severe pain. This time Grandma heard the Lord say, "Pray for his appendix, it's ruptured." So she prayed for him again and he stopped hurting. Though the pain subsided his legs began to draw up to his stomach and his belly became largely swollen. Grandma felt she needed some reinforcement for this battle so the next day she put Dad in the back seat of the car and took him to an auditorium where she knew Brother Ivie was holding services. He came out to the car to pray for Dad and took one look at him as he laid in the back seat and said, "Do you know what's wrong with this child?" She didn't want to tell Brother Ivie just yet what that the Lord had told her, because she wanted to see what God told him first. This strategy is helpful when learning to hear God's voice because it can confirm for you that God did indeed speak to you. Remember, at this time she was just beginning to gain confidence in her ability to hear the voice of God. Brother Ivie quickly confirmed what God had spoken to her by saying, "His appendix has ruptured." After Brother Ivie prayed Dad felt better and was able to eat some food, but he wasn't completely healed yet.

Grandma had a tent revival scheduled in Somerset, Kentucky and she wasn't going to let the devil win by keeping her from what the Lord called her to do. She continued in faith and laid my Dad in the back seat of the car as they drove to Somerset. My Dad was a small framed child with not too much meat on his bones and at this point he had lost eleven pounds from not eating for three days straight.

~

"Now most people who had a sick child who had lost eleven pounds, whose legs were drawn up to their stomach with a swollen belly, would have had their child to every doctor in the world! They'd have had him to the hospital and they would've fretted themselves to death. Fretting won't do a bit of good but faith will move mountains!"
-Rebecca Johnson

~

Taking your children to the doctor or the hospital in time of emergency is not a matter of right or wrong. Everyone can only stand on the faith they have. This is not a testimony given to condemn but to bring the light of the truth. To tell what faith in God verses faith in man can do. Man's knowledge can help you, it is true, but his knowledge and ability are limited while God is unlimited. If we are ever to grow in faith it is vital we have testimonies of how others trusted Him at His word and operated in their faith. Everyone walks at their own pace with the Lord, at their own level of experience and knowledge of Him. There is therefore now no condemnation for those of us who are in Christ Jesus and we should all walk in freedom because of it. This is a true recalling of an amazing miracle and proof that God is not a liar. It is given to encourage you and to bring glory to God. Becky Johnson's faith was her faith, but I hope that this testimony will cause your faith to grow in the knowledge of who God is in you. He will save us out of the snares of the devil, if we can only believe.

They arrived in Kentucky and set up the tent. That very night the intense pain returned and Dad cried out to his mother, "Oh, mom! If the Lord doesn't heal me I am going to die!" This was his fourth day of being sick, and though the pain did subside after Brother Ivie prayed, this night it returned with a vengeance. I want you to be very clear on this one thing, this was an outright attack of the devil and an attempt on my Dad's life. Our enemy seeks not only to destroy us but to get us to believe that the circumstance is the truth and God's word is a lie. If he can deceive God's children in this way, he wins. May we all walk in faith like my Grandma who was not willing to back down.

Filled with the fire of unwavering trust in the word of God, Grandma kneeled next to Dad's bed and prayed, "Lord, I'm going out to preach in that tent tomorrow night but unless Virgil is able to go out and play his mandolin I will not preach divine healing! Because if it doesn't work for me, it doesn't work for anybody else! I will go out and preach salvation but I won't preach divine healing!" God showed up when she cried out in faith! She was believing with everything she had in her and willing to trust the word, even to the extent of being faced with the death of her son. But defeat was never an option. That very moment she cried out to God Dad was given a miracle! The ruptured appendix was either miraculously put back together or replaced all together with a new one. The pain left, his legs straightened, the swelling in his belly went away and his appetite returned. The tent was set up on a plot of land that belonged to a strawberry farmer and the next day Dad ate as many strawberries as he could fit in him, plus three full meals! That same day he played like any other healthy eleven year old boy and on that first night of revival, he played his mandolin!

~

> "Truth is, if you cry unto the Lord He will deliver you out of all your troubles! This is the Word of God. Anything that the Word of God says you can believe it, if you want to believe it. Of course if you don't want to believe it, that's another thing. But if you want to, you can believe it. Don't you believe that that mind works? And you can put it to believing anything as easy as you can put it to doubting everything?"
> -Rebecca Johnson

~

Just over a year later, at the age of twelve Dad fell ill with a common childhood disease of that era known as polio. This devil attacked his right leg. He soon became bedridden with fatigue, fever, muscle weakness and pain. His leg muscles would spasm and were very stiff until he began to lose the use of his leg as it became paralyzed. Grandma knew right away that something was seriously wrong and as she prayed the Lord told her it was polio. She prayed and fasted for three days and nights until she began to see the symptoms subside. The fever broke, the pain left, the leg began to straighten and work again. Soon there was no sign of permanent damage or even of side effects that often came with polio. He was made perfectly whole! Praise God!

During their time of ministry in Tampa, Florida when Dad was around the age of fourteen yet another notable miracle took place. One day he was outside wrestling with a friend. Dad was short, light and wiry, whereas his friend was taller, heavier and had a more solid frame. The odds were more in his friends favor but Dad would give it his best. As they wrestled on a grassy field Dad was suddenly flipped up into the air and landed directly on his head. The last thing he remembered before becoming unconscious was hearing a loud pop noise. His friend hurried to get help as Dad lay convulsing on the ground. Someone carried him to his bed and Grandma began to pray. The Lord spoke to her that Dad had broken his neck and she knew this was life or death. She refused to believe that the circumstance was greater than the ability of her Deliverer. Again she stood in faith as she was on her knees, clinging to the promises held in God's word for her and her son. After six hours of prayer he stopped convulsing and slept through the night. He awoke the next day completely recovered and well enough to attend school.

I can see how my Dad and Grandma were growing spiritually as I tell these stories. They were growing separately and yet together. She never pushed him into ministry but how could he have made any other choice but to serve God when being witness to so many miracles? She would never back down on what she believed and what she believed caused Dad to believe too. God spoke and she responded and all the while he was watching and learning. That very fact that she never quit pursuing the Lord, whatever the cost, was raising up a great man of God.

When Dad turned fourteen he began competing in speed roller skating races. He started pursuing the sport as soon as a skating rink had been built in Richmond in 1950. As he learned to skate he also began to realize he was good at it and quickly became a member of a team that raced in championships. He put in countless hours of training at the rink and would train all day, sometimes until two in the morning. It is hard work to train for any sport and it takes discipline, effort and time. As in every area in life, Dad wanted to be the best he could be. Soon he was winning all his races and made it to the state championship. Next he made it to the regional championship which included racers from five states. This championship held in Dayton, Ohio consisted of three days of races. In this series of races participants were eliminated out of each race until the six best skaters were left. This would determine who would compete in the final race. Dad made it to the final race in which he was up against the reigning national speed skating champion. This race was to be won for the opportunity to represent the United States at the summer Olympics in 1952.

He said in these words just what he was going through on that day, "Perhaps at the time I didn't realize how pivotal that moment was in my life but the Lord knew what would be brought about. On the last day of the championship I woke up with a purpose to win. But reason would tell me I wasn't fast enough to beat this national champion that I was up against. So I prayed, 'Lord, this guy is clocking faster than me, he's better and I can't beat him with my own ability. I need your help.' He answered saying, 'If you will give up your opportunity to go to the Olympics and go full time into the ministry you will win this race.' And that sounded like a good plan to me. I knew I was called into the ministry from a very young age and I knew one day I would have to answer the call. In that moment when He called, I willingly laid down my earthly pursuits and obeyed Him. Before we left for the race mom gave me two cloths that she had prayed over and I stuffed one in each toe of my skates. How could I lose?!"

Grandma and my Uncle Robert were there for the race to cheer Dad on. They watched as Dad lined up with the other five skaters. All the racers were now in position, just waiting for the sound of the starter gun and wouldn't you know it, the national champion was a little bit anxious and before the gun went off he did a false start! The penalty for a false start was being set back three feet from the starting line. Once the champion took his penalized position, the racers prepared to start the race yet again and when the gun went off, they were off! Before the race Dad worked out a strategy of how he was was going to win. His plan was to let the racer in first position skate in front of him to block the wind resistance. At the opportune time Dad would pass him and take the lead. Everything was working according to Dad's plan but behind him the champion was skating so fast that he had already made it to second place position shortly after Dad took first. Though the champion was right behind him he held his position on that last lap, crossing the finish line in first place! You've probably already guessed it, but the national champion who worked his way from the very back to finish in second was only three feet behind Dad!

~

"Having been given a promise and honoring the call of my Jesus, I turned down the opportunity to compete at the Olympics and began to walk into what God had planned for my life. I have never done anything without God!" -Virgil Johnson

~

Giving up the desires of your flesh will always be the price for being transformed in the spirit. It wasn't a hard choice for my Dad to give up going to the Olympics because he had seen the glory of God displayed in his mother's life. Most people are content with living the life of their choosing, following after goals they set for themselves. There is nothing wrong with that but if you want to see God move in your life in miraculous ways you must first be willing to lay it all on the line for Him. Our will submitted to His will creates in us a new heart, a new mind and a determination to see His will done on earth as it is in Heaven.

Shortly after Dad's championship victory and resolution to go full time in the ministry he began to seek God for direction. One night he went to church with a desire to pray and ended up praying all night. In the wee hours of the morning while down on his knees the Lord spoke to him saying, "Get up and go down to Montgomery Wards to meet your cousin. Both of you will go to Florida and have a revival." As soon as he could he went down to the department store where his cousin was a manager. As Dad pushed on the revolving glass door he saw his cousin on the other side coming out. One told the other that he was looking for him. It turned out that the Lord had spoken to his cousin as well and had told him to resign his position at the department store and go with Dad to Florida for revival. He also told Dad that he had just quit his job and was bringing a sewing machine to his wife to give her as a peace offering and help soften the blow of the news of him resigning. Dad was also working a job and went directly from there to tell them he was quitting.

The very next day after God spoke to them they headed for Tampa, Florida. They knew a man who was a friend of Grandma's and he offered to let them both stay at his house while they were visiting. They arrived in Tampa and told their host that God had sent them down to have revival. The man said that there was a vacant church in Plant City that was owned by three old maid sisters. Their host suggested that they ask the ladies if they might let them use the church for revival. So Dad contacted the ladies and found that they were glad to let them have use of the church building. Dad and his cousin went to the vacant church and dusted and swept to make it ready for service. For the next two days straight, they prayed for revival.

On the first night of service they turned the lights on and just waited. Not a single advertisement was made for the services and they were totally relying on God to bring the people. Suddenly one by one the sanctuary that held about seventy people began to fill until it was a packed house. Dad asked the people what had caused them to come to the service that night and each person said the same thing, "We were driving by and saw the lights on so we came to see if church was being held." The revival went on for four weeks! This was the first meeting in which Dad operated in the gift of the word of knowledge. He heard the Holy Spirit so clearly it almost scared him to death. As a woman was coming up for prayer the Holy Spirit told Dad exactly the name of the sickness she had. It was a really long and complicated medical term that he could have never known out of his own knowledge. When the woman came up to him and asked for prayer, she told Dad what was wrong. It almost blew Dad away because it was exactly what the Holy Spirit had told him. From then on he began to develop the gift of the word of knowledge through prayer and fasting and within about three years he became very comfortable with hearing from the Holy Spirit in this way.

~

"Mother always taught me that I should develop a gift before I am comfortable enough to walk in boldness in that gift. It's like having a product. It must first be developed and tested before it is put on the market. I began to separate my thoughts, which ones were from God and which ones were my own thoughts. The first time I was confident enough to speak out what God was giving me through the word of knowledge, was in a Sunday afternoon healing service. I said, 'There is someone here who has cancer that the doctors have diagnosed as terminal and they have sent you home to die.' A man stood up and said, 'It is I; the doctors sewed me up yesterday and told me there was no hope and sent me home to die. I heard about these healing services and came.' In obedience I released the word of knowledge and God gave him a complete miracle that day. When God reveals something to you it is always for His purpose." -Virgil Johnson

~

Dad said there were many, many miracles in that first revival he and his cousin held. There was an outstanding miracle of a child that had bone tuberculosis, a sickness that effects the spine and the joints. The boy wore a pair of braces on his legs and could not walk on his own. Dad's attention was drawn to the boys knees that were swollen up twice their normal size. He prayed for the child three times in the prayer line but nothing happened. After the service Dad spoke with the father of the boy on the front porch of the church. The father told Dad how they were driving to an Oral Roberts tent revival in Saint Petersburg as they just happened to drive by this little church and something made them decided to stop there for the morning service. When Dad heard the story of the family he asked if he could pray for the little boy once more and they agreed. Suddenly he felt an overwhelming compassion for this child as he was reminded of when God had given him a miracle from polio. This boy must have been about the same age as Dad was when it happened to him. He made his request known to the Lord for a fourth time and this time the boy not only felt the healing but they all saw the swelling in his knees disappear. They quickly took off the little boy's leg braces and as soon as he was free that little boy took off running! Hallelujah!

~

"You see, it is never for our glory that signs and wonders come. Miracles and healings and deliverances are just different facets of the nature of God and when these things come about we can give glory to none one but Him!" -Virgil Johnson

~

You may be in awe as you read these testimonies with one glaring question in your mind. How? How do I work the works of God? How do I walk in a place of seeing signs and wonders? How do I get miracles for myself and others? You may not like how simple the answer to the question is. How do you do all these things and greater things than Jesus did? (John 14:1-21) Believe! Only believe! It is a common theme in the Bible that is repeated over and over and over in hopes that we will understand what it means to believe. "I do believe!", you may say as you are reading this. I believe you do believe to a certain degree. Then how do you believe the way Jesus says to believe? Believing is the key but being able to think like Jesus is the door that the key opens to bring you into doing the works and great works than He. How do you believe? You may be asking that question next. I'm glad you asked. Believing can only come by the cultivating of an intimate relationship with Jesus and taking on His mind. The evidence of that relationship being strong enough for you to believe in the impossible comes only from being able to hear His voice. If the spiritual mind overrules the carnal mind, you will be able to hear Him clearly and with ease and then do the works that He did.

When I was young I would have believed my Dad if he had told me the sky was green and not blue. Even though I could clearly see with my own eyes that the sky is obviously blue. I would believe his word over my eyes because my Dad never lied to me. He never lied to me or hurt me and he always lived before me a life that was in complete submission to God. That was my example and that is why I can say so plainly that I could believe him in this way. Both my parents were great examples, they taught me it is easy to take the Father at His word. If I could trust them, I could trust Him. It is a foreign concept to the Adam mind to understand this idea of complete and unquestioning trust. The heart of man is full of rebellion and wanting to have its own way, that is why most people look at their parents and decidedly want to do the complete opposite. Many even become resolute in their flesh to do life differently than their parents because they reject the way that was lived before them. My experience is rare, I know, but because my parents were submitted to the will of the Father, when it was my turn to learn to take God at His word, it was not so hard of a reality for me to grasp. Dad said, "My children do not give me any trouble because I don't give God any trouble. I am submitted to His will."

I know how much my parents loved me, it was the one thing I was always sure of. I grew up in that love to understand they only did what they did for me because they knew, out of their love for me and by the Spirit, what was for my good. How much more is the love of my Heavenly Father towards me than that of my earthly father? If you become resolute to know God, as He longs to be know, then you will grow up in the knowledge that His word is true and it cannot fail and He works all things to your good. Perhaps this is being repeated throughout this book but repetition is often the best way to bring someone else into an understanding. You have to have a foundation in knowing His voice before believing becomes second nature to you. A relationship with Him, not a church, not a man or a woman but God Himself. Cultivating the relationship is what casts out all fear and doubt from your heart and mind. If you can believe He loves you without restriction, then you can believe all things are possible. That love He has for us frees us to do His will, or keep His commandments, with ease because we are His and He is ours. Then we know it is not a severe restriction that He places on us, but rather one that says that if we take Him at His word, we will overcome the world by our faith!

~

"Whosoever believeth that Jesus is the Christ is born of God: and every one that loveth him that begat loveth him also that is begotten of him. By this we know that we love the children of God, when we love God, and keep his commandments. For this is the love of God, that we keep his commandments: and his commandments are not grievous. For whatsoever is born of God overcometh the world: and this is the victory that overcometh the world, even our faith." 1 John 5:1-4 (KJV)

~

1953 was the year my Dad began to preach under the guidance of his mother and other great Godly influences around him. The nearly sixteen year old young man was set out on a path of righteousness. If he had not fallen in love with Jesus at such a young age no doubt his life would have been very different. He was set apart by God when he chose to obey His voice. He became very different from the rest of the Johnson clan. So much so, that in later years they would tell him he was no longer a Johnson and that was music to his ears! He loved his family but he didn't want to be like them, he wanted to be like Jesus. No higher compliment can be paid to a follower of Christ than to be told you are not like who you once were.

My Dad became aware of the stark contrast between carnal pursuits and the pursuits of the kingdom of God. Pride, anger, lust, pleasing of the flesh, all these are not only carnal traits but part of what he was exposed to as a young man predominately from his father's side of the family. His grandfather Johnson was an Irish bare knuckle boxer and it was a family trait to fight just to prove you could beat the other fellow. This was fueled by a quick temper and rooted in pride. His grandfather Johnson was a gambler, a drinker and a womanizer who was shot five times and stabbed seven. He died with a bottle of whisky in one hand and the other raised up to heaven in a fist as he cursed God with his last breath. You can only pass down to your children who it is that you are and what it is that you know. So this nature was the mark of Dad's family and when God revealed Himself to Dad he began to see how vital it was to change.

That "fighting spirit", as Dad used to call it, was in Dad and it had to be dealt with. He was a scrapper in his school boy years and one day while fighting in the school yard at the age of fourteen his opponent pulled out a knife. He said to himself, "If this is where fighting leads, I don't want any more to do with it." He backed out of that fight and never fought again. Once he realized what the consequences of that carnal fighting spirit would lead to, he began working with the Holy Spirit to deal with his temper and pride. The need to prove himself was strong inside of him, just like so many other young men. He was, after all, of the "fighting Irish" stock. The Lord began to show him that what was in his nature could be eradicated, and he began to pay attention when it would rise up and then ask the Lord to take it from him. He knew that if it hadn't been for his closeness to his righteous mother and the example she led before him, that he never would have been able to break the cycle. God would give him a choice to give in to it or to let the Holy Spirit take it away. Even in his old age God saw fit to test him again on this very subject.

He was tested as we were on a plane traveling home from Australia after a seven week evangelistic trip. The plane was full of boisterous Australians having too much to drink while watching a rugby game. It was a replay of a game that their national team had just won and sports fans tend to be easily over excited when it comes to their favorite team. A man sitting behind us was getting louder and louder as he cheered and shouted at the little screen in front of him. All of the sudden he got so excited he jumped up out of his seat and spilled beer on my Dad. I watched as my Dad quickly rose up from his seat and turned around to face the man. I saw a glimpse of anger being brought forth from my travel weary, jet lagged, worn out Daddy. It was a fleeting moment, less than half a second and it was gone. His reaction was not only out of frustration at the man being loud and drunk and spilling beer on him, but for protection over me as I was laying on the seats beside where Dad was sitting. Commenting later on that experience Dad said that God just wanted to see if any of that Johnson nature was left inside of him. Here he was a fifty-seven years old with a great track record of being an overcomer and he was being tested yet again. I was witness to a man who, though he was flesh, had conquered that flesh. The drunken man apologized and Dad sat back down and I laid my head back down on his lap and fell asleep.

Many of Dad's extended family members were into racing cars, some even made careers out of it, including his eldest brother and a few older cousins and uncles. Having that example set before you as a young man would make street racing and alluding the police with hot-rods and exciting and fun pass time. You can imagine how a young man just learning to drive would thrill at the adrenaline rush of speed. For a short while Dad would drag race on a main street down town at night and he was pretty good at it. He had learned the timing of the stop light so perfectly that he would usually get a good jump on his competition and win. But breaking the law is, breaking the law and he found himself in more than one dangerous situation. Grandma stayed up all night praying many a times when Dad was out with his friends on those nights, and he knew her prayers kept him alive and out of jail on more than one occasion. It wasn't long before the Lord showed him the wisdom of turning away from that pursuit for the purpose of fully focusing on what God had for his life.

Once he got a good scare from a fast car. He and his brothers had just added a super charger to this souped up car giving it a lot more horse power and thus speed. Dad was elected as the one to give the car its first run and when he started it and put the pedal to the metal, he quickly learned that the linkage on the throttle was stuck! He pumped the gas pedal frantically but it just wouldn't come unstuck, so he tried the break and that was unresponsive. Before he knew it that super powerful car had gotten away from him and shot him into a corn field. Once he had his wits about him he realized that cutting the engine off was the only way to get the car to stop. The car did stop but his heart almost stopped with it!

There were also a few miracles surrounding cars that Dad witnessed. One very unique miracle that he told of happened to someone who attended his mother's church when Dad was still a teen. This man had an old Plymouth that was in bad need of a paint job. It just so happened that he was in church the night after he scheduled to have the car painted, having finally saved up enough money to get it done. At the beginning of service it was made known that the church had a financial need. Suddenly the Lord spoke to the man and he knew he had to give that money he had been saving. Obediently he gave the

$250 to meet the churches need. He joyfully did so and went home that night full of that good feeling you can only get when you are obedient to the voice of God. The next day was Sunday and that morning when he walked out to his car parked in his driveway he found that it had a brand new paint job and it was even the color he wanted! He arrived to church that morning and excitedly asked everyone to come and look at the car and marvel at God's glory. He was jumping and shouting praise to God as he testified of this truly miraculous work. He told them all about how he had saved the money and how the Lord spoke to him to give the savings. What a testimony it was to glorify God and His goodness! Dad knew a good paint job when he saw one so he carefully inspected every inch of the car as he was in total awe of this supernatural thing God had done. After his inspection he said it was the most perfect paint job he had ever seen!

~

"God doesn't need your flesh to get things done, He just needs your obedience and trust!" -Virgil Johnson

~

Another automobile testimony that will blow your mind is what I like to call the miracle of the gas tank. Money was scarce back during those early years of Dad's ministry and he was just a young man learning to trust God in a big way. The Lord decided to get Dad's attention by showing him what He was willing to do. One day he had driven his car quite a few miles and happened to notice that the fuel gage was not going down. He thought that there may be something wrong with the gage, so he pulled into a gas station and tried to put gas in the tank. As soon as he did, the fuel over flowed. So he put the cap back on and went on his way. He went on driving it for a few more days and the fuel gage needle never once moved from that full mark. A week went by and he tried to put gas in it a second time with the same result as before. After the second attempt at filling the tank, and a thorough inspection of the gage itself, he began to believe it was a miracle. Two months went by and he never ran out of gas, even though he put a lot of traveling miles on the car. Then one day his brother Robert asked to borrow the car to run an errand. Dad didn't think anything of it and he gave him the keys. The minute Robert started the car and tried to go, the fuel gage dropped from full to empty and the miracle of the gas tank had passed. Dad used to laugh and say, "If only I had never let him borrow the car!"

He stayed close to his mother's ministry as he was growing in maturity spiritually but as he grew he also began to evangelize on his own. During those teenage years of his ministry he would describe himself as being a firebrand. After all, the style of preaching he had seen as an example was that Pentecostal way of being loud and excited and getting your point across with a lot of passion. He would say, "I was an excellent preacher but I wasn't someone you could follow back then." The first place he traveled to evangelize on his own was Dayton, Ohio when he was eighteen years old. He was scheduled for four nights of services. On the first night the preachers wife received an instant miracle from a life long condition which resulted in the preacher getting very upset. Imagine that! He had so much pride that he couldn't even rejoice in God giving his wife a miracle because he felt threatened by a teenager being able to do so when he could not. So Dad's first night of meetings was his last.

His next scheduled meeting out on his own was in Hot Springs, Arkansas where he was invited to minister for six nights. He ended up only preaching two nights before this pastor also became threatened by the ease in which Dad could get miracles. Out of the first six series of meetings he had scheduled, four got canceled. That alone would be enough to discourage anyone just starting out. When the last one was called off the Lord spoke to him and actually told him a specific address to go to in the state of Texas. Dad didn't recognize the address nor did he know anyone who lived in the town God had spoken. He didn't even exactly know where he was going, except to look it up on a map. But knowing he had heard the voice of God, he packed up his truck, assembled his crew, and headed to Texas.

Dad traveled down through Texarkana and into the logging country of Piney Woods. The address God had given sent him to a barber shop in that little town. Dad walked inside and said to the barber, "God sent me here for a revival." The barber was so shocked by it he almost cut the man's throat that he was shaving! Turns out that barber was an Assembly of God pastor. He asked Dad to meet him at his house where they could talk a little later. Once he heard Dad's story he believed it was God and invited Dad to set up his tent on the church grounds. On the first night of service hundreds were saved. The next night hundreds received the baptism of the Holy Spirit, and the night after that hundreds of people received healings and miracles. This meeting didn't get canceled and revival broke out! Transforming not only that pastor and his church but the entire town.

Around the age of eighteen Dad married a woman named Juanita Roberts. I don't know a lot of details about this part of his life. I do know he married a woman who loved the Lord and she sang and played the accordion and piano in their ministry. My Mom used to talk about Juanita fondly and said that she had the sweetest spirit. Juanita came from a family who wanted nothing to do with God and didn't like my Dad because he was a preacher. That tension must have hurt Jaunita's heart. Dad and Juanita truly loved one another but they did face a lot of challenges during their marriage. Dad had a job when they were first married working at a relative's casket factory. He didn't stay long at this job because God spoke to him to go full-time in the ministry. To Dad this meant trusting God completely for every need he had and not having a steady income to rely on. He made the decision to obey the voice of God, although it was not an easy one. I'm sure they had their own struggles and many things to overcome due to that fact alone as offerings back then were an average of just a couple dollars a meeting. These offerings were the only means by which they had to live off of. Dad used to say he thought preachers were supposed to sleep in the back of cars or church pews back then because there was never enough money for a hotel. They lived without many luxuries but they never went hungry and every need was always met.

One time he and Jaunita traveled all the way to South Carolina from Indiana to minister and the offering at the service was not enough to get them back home. So they got a day job picking cotton, which earned them just enough money to travel home. Another time they were so low on money they didn't have enough for a meal and would have to wait until the next day after service to eat. Dad had just enough change in his pocket for Juanita to buy a soda. That night they were using the church's sanctuary as a place to sleep and they happened to meet another couple who was using this sanctuary for the same purpose. A man from South Africa named Drummond Thom who had a ministry based out of Louisville, Kentucky. He was a second generation evangelist like Dad. The son of an evangelist and author named Robert Thom. Drummond and his wife Charlotte became very good lifelong friends of my Dad's. They were even named my godfather and godmother at my dedication. Good things often come out of hard times.

Not long after they were first married, Dad and Jaunita decided to move to Miami, Florida. They headed south in their used '55 Chevy pickup truck pulling a thirty-seven foot house trailer that they recently purchased. On their way to Miami they were planning to visit Birmingham, Alabama where they were invited to minister. When they arrived the meeting was canceled and so they headed on down the road a day earlier than planned. Just outside of the pan-handle of Florida the oil pump on the truck gave out and then the engine stopped working. As providence would have it, this unfortunate event happened just near a trailer park where Dad was able to use a telephone to call for a tow truck. The mechanic informed him it wouldn't be a cheap fix and Dad didn't have enough money to pay for the work. He made another phone call to his mom and dad to help him out by lending him $300. Grandma told him she would send the money via a money wire which would take a few days and all Dad could do next was wait for the repair to be completed and the money to arrive. The trailer park manager who had let Dad use the phone felt sorry for the stranded couple and offered to let them park the trailer on a vacant lot for free while his truck was being worked on.

On their first night at the trailer park Dad was suddenly awakened by a woman screaming bloody murder. He jumped out of bed and ran toward the screaming to see what was the matter. In the trailer parked next to his he found the screaming woman and her husband who was trying his best to calm her down. Dad saw an infant in the mother's arms and when the man saw Dad he suddenly took the child from the mother and without explanation handed it to him, perhaps to see if separating her from the baby would help her to calm down. The mother had accidentally smothered the child as she slept with it near her in bed. Dad holding that lifeless little body walked outside the trailer. A great compassion swelled up inside his heart as he spoke to God simple words very much like what he had heard his mother pray when she was faced with a similar situation. "Lord, these parents seem to really miss this baby, could You find it in Your heart to give it back to them?" As this request to an infinitely good God was spoken, the breath of life came back into the baby! Dad wept for joy as he hurried back to give the child to the parents. The wife's tears of panic and sorrow instantly turned to relief and gratefulness.

Dad had witnessed a resurrection once before and never forgot what he heard his mother pray, nor how God had responded to the need in that moment. It affected him. He didn't know he would one day be faced with the same circumstance, but he did know God would do the same thing again, if only he believed. This resurrection wasn't in a church setting or even an ideal situation for him. He was waylaid on his journey by a blown engine. And if that engine hadn't given out at exactly where it did, he would not have been where God wanted him. But God knew that night would come and those parents would need help. The Lord let Dad suffer an inconvenience to ultimately work the situation for his good. God even had a hand in the Birmingham meetings being canceled. Because if the meetings had not been canceled he never would have been in that trailer park on that night! You can't make this stuff up!!! And we could certainly never fully understand how and why God does what He does, but we can know through reading these experiences that He is God and He is a rewarder of those who diligently seek Him! For Dad it must have been the best $300 he ever spent in his whole life!

Dad and Juanita were in Miami for three months during the winter season for what Dad called a resting period. Both he and Juanita worked jobs and enjoyed the warm Florida weather while taking a break from preaching. Dad had not received many invitations to speak at churches for the past year and so many times when he did get invited the meetings were then canceled. That time spent in Florida was to pause and let God take the lead. At the end of three months of living down south, preachers began to reach out to Dad asking him to come and have meetings. They were seeking him out instead of him seeking them. This was when things began to turn a different direction for his ministry. They left Florida and moved back to Richmond and more and more meetings began to open up in Indiana, Illinois, Kentucky, Ohio, New York, and the Washington D.C. area.

~

"I preach my testimony. It's my life. One time I was destitute in Washington D.C. after traveling there to preach and I had no money to get back home. So instead of being depressed and worried I decided to take a walk to enjoy some of the national monuments because they are free. As I was walking I looked down and the wind was blowing something toward me along the sidewalk. I looked and saw it was a hundred dollar bill! I knew it was a gift from God. I didn't even bat an eye, I just picked it up! I didn't care if God sent it by raven or whatever, it was for me! I didn't even look around to see if there was anyone who looked like they were missing it. David didn't feel bad when he broke in to the store house and ate all the offering. I like to think that a window in the mint was open and God caused a wind to blow a brand new hundred dollar bill out onto the side walk just for me." -Virgil Johnson

~

By the age of twenty-two Dad had been preaching for seven years. By this time his mother knew it was time for her to step down as pastor of the church and time for the next generation to lead. Dad succeeded his mother as pastor and changed the name of the church to Congregational Tabernacle. Most transfers of pastors within a church are not easy and this one was no different. Many people didn't want new leadership and rejected the idea. Many members of the church would not acknowledge him as pastor but called him "Becky's boy". They would say that he received the pastorship only because he was her son. They refused to consider that the reason she chose him was because he had been preparing for it since he was fifteen. They didn't want to admit that he had worked many years as an evangelist or that his heart was to help people. This was another struggle he and his wife had to face.

Even though Dad became a pastor he never stopped evangelizing. In 1962 he set up his tent in Flint, Michigan for revival services. Four local pastors were backing the meetings and invited Dad to come and minister. On the third night of the service the four preachers came to Dad and proposed a way to get the service attendees to give big offerings. They wanted to plant a hundred dollar bill on someone in the crowd and ask that person to stand up and shout that they were going to give that hundred dollar bill in the offering. These men wanted to cause the crowd to get excited and give more. Dad was appalled that they would even propose such a thing. He said, "If you do this thing I will back out of these meetings. I will not take part in it, it's wrong!"

That night the Holy Spirit had Dad pick out three people from the crowd to pray for. One needed a miracle from cancer, one from diabetes, and the other was a Nazarene lady whose body was so swollen that she was nearly twice the size she should be. He prayed for the person with cancer and the pain and symptoms left instantly. The diabetic was healed next. Last he prayed for the woman who was swollen and she went down several dress sizes, so much so that she had to grab her skirt and fold it over at the waist so it would not fall off! She also got baptized in the Holy Ghost in the same moment and began speaking in tongues. After the service God told him to speak these words to the pastors, "This is what you could have had but God has said 'no'." God gave those men just a glimpse of the many miracles that would have come about during the next five nights had they not schemed to deceive the people out of their money. In response those pastors said they wouldn't give Dad a dime of the offerings that had already been taken for him. Dad knew if he didn't receive an offering he couldn't pay for his expenses but he also knew that God could not fail and in the confidence of that truth he ended his dealings with those men. As he was about to walk out of the tent, a woman came running up to him and said, "Here Brother Johnson, God told me to give this to you." He looked down in his hand and she passed to him several thousand dollars! The Holy Spirit told him it was more than what was received in the offering the preachers had refused to give him.

~

"Never comprise. And be willing to make the hard decisions, whatever the cost. God is a rewarder of those who diligently seek Him!" -Virgil Johnson

~

December 1963 was Dad's first trip overseas. He and Juanita joined his mother and a group of people to minister to a few churches in Kingston, Jamaica. Dad established a relationship with a pastor there named Jeremiah T. Bryson and became good friends with him. He loved and greatly respected Brother Bryson so much that he even named my brother after him. He traveled back to Jamaica several times in his ministry and even sowed the money into Brother Bryson's ministry to completely fund the building of an orphanage. That building has Dad's name engraved on its cornerstone. It was also in 1963 that Dad met Gordon Lindsay who after hearing Dad preach, asked him if he would be interested in helping him start his college. A college that would one day be called Christ For The Nations Institute. Although Dad was humbled by the offer he knew that the work Brother Lindsay was doing was not part of what God had planned for him. So he turned Brother Lindsay down but thanked him for considering him to be a part of it. Dad's ministry continued to grow and his opportunities to share the word of revelations that God gave him increased. Ministering the gospel was what Dad loved to do more than anything else.

During these years of change in his ministry came an unforeseen change of great importance that was beyond anything Dad could have ever known he would have to experience. In the summer of 1964 Juanita believed she was pregnant. More than anything in the world Juanita wanted children. She and Dad were both excited as her stomach began to grow larger and the signs of pregnancy more obvious. They never saw the need to go to a doctor right away to confirm her pregnancy but instead waited until a few months had passed. She finally went to a doctor and found out that instead of being pregnant she had a cancerous tumor growing inside of her. Juanita did not want to go the route of the doctors trying to prolong her life but decided to trust God for a miracle. They battled together for eight months. Dad didn't even go out and preach during this time because he had to be home to take care of her around the clock.

This long fight without a victory was beginning to wear Dad out and he knew it. The stress of all the months of fighting for her was almost killing him. One day he began to see in the Spirit that the devil's strategy was to wear him out. Dad believed the devil was trying to get him to stay focused on the fight instead of what God had called him to do. Being made aware of this plan of the enemy he decided to draw a line in the sand. He cried out to God saying, "I either want a miracle or for you to take her home by February 13th." This date was specified because it was a week before the time he was expected to be in Jamaica for revival. In having made this declaration he also decided that he was going to go out in faith and preach, even through the midst of the battle. I believe that you do not need to understand why he was led this way but you do need to understand it happened the way it did so that he could learn what only he needed to learn from this experience. Dad rebuked the snare of Satan by saying, "Devil, you are not going to discourage me and you are not going to defeat me!"

The day after this declaration he set up some meetings for the next few days and asked his mother to stay with Juanita while he went out of town to preach. He had contended for a miracle for all those months and had not yet received an answer and at that moment he had to make a decision to stay and be defeated or to go and declare the good news of the Gospel in the midst of his pain and trial. Broken, hurt, confused, and desperate, but always, always trusting God. Perhaps that last move to step out in faith and go and preach was a way of proving to himself that he did believe God would move on his behalf, one way or another.

~

"Do we have fight in us to where we can stand fast in the midst of the battle? Brother and sister we need to identify when Satan is trying to wear us out and make the decision to push back." -Virgil Johnson

~

He went to preach at those meetings and had amazing services full of miracles. On the third morning of his meetings he got a phone call asking him to come home because his mother knew Juanita wouldn't be alive much longer. He came back home to be by Juanita's side and began to fast and pray for seven days. He was in the battle of his life time and he was crying out to God, "Is this required of me God? Is there any other door? Is this what You expect of me? Is there another way I could move Your hand?" Five days into his fast Juanita spit up the cancer that was inside her body. Dad began to rejoice as God had given them a miracle, but Juanita had already purposed in her heart that she wanted to go to heaven. She said to him, "Honey, just let me go on home, I'm so close to heaven, please let me go." She spoke to him of how her heart could no longer sustain the atmosphere of the church world and all the persecution and hypocrisy within it. The life they lived in the ministry was an uncertain one and most days were full of struggling for her. Her experience, though shared with him, was different from his. It is very true that the life of ministry is not for the faint of heart. "Won't you live for me?", he pleaded as her decision broke his heart. She could not. She had lost her will to live on this earth and her desire for heaven was too strong.

It was in the midst of this battle that Jesus Himself appeared to Dad. The evening after Jaunita told him of her desire to go on home Dad was sitting in the kitchen in his undershirt and shorts, listening to a sad country song that he was playing over and over on his record player. He got up to go into his bedroom and as he went to flip the light switch on his bedroom lit up with a brilliant light. He was taken back a bit and even flipped the light switch off to see where that light was coming from. It filled up the entire room and he knew it wasn't the light fixture but heavenly light. He described the light as looking like "florescent rays of sparkling diamonds." Suddenly he saw Jesus coming into the room through that light that was streaming out of the wall. Jesus came and stood between the bed and the dresser near Dad and then Jesus spoke, "I have come. What would you ask of me?"

In that moment Dad knew whatsoever he would ask for, God would give it. Selfishness would have had him ask for his wife to live and the flesh could have justified it in a million different ways. But what was God's will? Having Jesus appear to him was not just a blessing but a test. Tears started rolling down his cheeks as he trembled from the Presence. He looked Jesus in the eyes and answered, "I want a ministry like Yours. One that is sovereign so that I can reach the dying of this world. Make me a preacher amongst preachers and send me around the world." Jesus replied, "You have asked wisely and not according to the flesh. That that you have asked, I will do." Jesus left as suddenly as He had appeared and the room went dark again. Quickly Dad called out, "Jesus! How do I know it was you?" And amazingly the room filled up with that same light and Jesus showed Himself once more, even if only to satisfy Dad's doubt of what had just happened. It was a time span of less than ten minutes, but that conversation with the Lord forever changed his life. When he laid down to sleep that night he wept. He wept all night until his pillow was completely soaked with his tears. As he wept he finally yielded to his wife's will by saying, "She's yours God, take her."

For the weeks that came after that encounter with Jesus, Dad began to read through the bible to find what ministry he truly wanted. He took into consideration with great care the question the Lord had posed to him. He had asked Jesus to make him a preacher amongst preachers and he mediated on this. He poured over the list of the different administrations of ministry given in the Bible only to come to the revelation that he didn't want to be an apostle, a prophet, an evangelist, a pastor or a teacher. After weeks of studying in the Bible he went to his knees and said to God, "Lord there is only one thing in the Bible that I have found that I want you to make out of me and that is an ass. Lord I'm tired of serving the flesh and the Spirit, I'm tired of being tied at the fork of the road like that foal of an ass that was waiting on you to ride him so he could carry the word into the city. I just need to be loosed! And Lord you know if you loose me I can carry your gospel into all the world." As he prayed this the gentle voice of God spoke confirming again, "I will do that that you have asked."

The day after the night Jesus appeared Dad cleaned himself up and got dressed. He told those who were at the house with him that morning that he was going out for a little walk and he knew in his heart that as soon as he walked out of the house, Juanita would go on to be with the Lord. Not even fifteen minutes after he went for his walk Juanita died on February 13, 1965. Victory was won for Juanita and she was in the arms of Jesus in the glory of eternity! For that Dad was truly thankful even in the midst of his grief and loss.

Dad had walked through persecution from others during the battle for Juanita's miracle but now that the battle was over the persecution increased. It came from those who claimed to be his brothers and sisters in the Lord, those who professed with their mouths to love him. The most frequently thrown dart was, "What did you do to make God mad at you?" Oh what a petty, religious-spirited response to death! They reasoned, "Well, if you didn't get the answer you really wanted to see from God, then your faith must not work!" But faith is believing without seeing. It is knowing that God is who He says He is. It is fully trusting Him while giving Him complete control by submitting to Him the outcome of your circumstance.

~

"I had a great healing ministry by the age of twenty-seven and many ministers believed I would be the man that would take the healing message around the world in this move of God. Here I was at the prominent place within the church world and then the devil told me I couldn't even get my wife healed. I hope that you are never put in a position like that, in a battle like that, with a decision like I had to make. But it changed my life, it renovated my life and made a new creature out of me." -Virgil Johnson

~

Do we really believe? So much so that we are willing to be made into a new creature? Something that is totally opposite of the carnal and mans understanding? We can't know until we are tested and many come to the test and don't want to walk through what it may take to get to the other side. We are free to walk at our own pace and God will work His good either way but there is a reality in which we can live trusting Him for absolutely everything. He has already won the victory on the cross. He has already given us the weapons to walk through this life. He has already given us the power and authority through the Holy Spirit. It is up to us to decide to overrule the flesh and let our spirit live in unity with the Spirit of the Living God dwelling inside of us! Are you willing to walk it out, even if you can't see how it will play out?

It is good that we talk about our tests and trials for it is by testing that we obtain our testimony. Talking about our struggles, questions, doubts and shortcomings is not a lack of faith but an attitude of transparency by which our faith can grow. This way of sharing with one another our experiences causes us to be real with one another and encourage one another. Having questions means we will be willing to do whatever it takes to seek out answers and he who seeks will find, that is the word of God. Even Jesus struggled in the Garden of Gethsemane with the path that God had for Him. So much so, that it caused Him to sweat blood. He knew the road that was set before Him and yet He had to talk it out with the disciples and then talk with His Father. Jesus didn't cry out from unbelief but from the need to have confirmation of who He knew God to be.

~

"(Jesus) went a little farther and fell on His face, and prayed, saying, 'O My Father, if it is possible, let this cup pass from Me; nevertheless, not as I will, but as You will.' "
Matthew 26:39 (KJV)

~

Did Jesus want to walk through everything the cross required? It seemed to break His heart that this was the path chosen for Him but He willingly laid down His life because of the good it would produce. Jesus walked with His Father and knew His Father's heart so well that He was willing to say, "Not my will, but Yours be done." He knew that God's purpose was greater. He knew that being falsely accused, beaten, spit on, mocked, ridiculed, hung on cross and dying was all part of the most gloriously beautiful plan. The plan that would bring the children of God back to the heart of the Father. Jesus had never experienced those things until He walked through them, but He had been prepared His entire life for coming to that place and He was willing to lay down His will to become the sacrifice that would defeat Satan once and for all. Pray and listen. Just listen. Don't get caught up in your flesh. Cry out to God for your answer but do it yielding to His good purpose for you, even if you don't fully understand what it is. It will change you and make you like Jesus. It will bring you into a place of victory and freedom and a place of knowing God in a more intimate way. Then you will be sure of His presence in the midst of the storm.

(Photo of Virgil Johnson)

My Dad never stopped believing for a miracle even though Juanita had made her decision. His faith never wavered because He knew God was Truth. He had seen God provide for Him over and over and over. Nothing could change his mind about who God was in him. Not even death, though it tried. This had to be proven in Dad so that he would know and have a confidence that only God could establish in him by walking through the test. That battle built up in Dad such a disregard for the opinion of man that he came to a place of victory that he never retreated from. One of the hardest things for a follower of Christ is to stop caring about what other people think of you. God must come first no matter how crazy it might make you look. David danced his clothes off, Job lost everything, Mary told people her son was God's and not Joseph's. Crazy? Yeah. But that is the very definition of God's ways being higher than ours. The Lord wants us to lay down our will for His perfect will out of a great desire to have His good work in our life. My Dad told me that the year his first wife died was the year he could say without a doubt that he had grown up.

~

"As I grew up in the natural I was growing up in the spiritual and I had the two to compare. I tasted of the world and the carnal and all it had to offer and I tasted of His goodness and saw that the one who trusts in Him is blessed. He let me make the choice and I chose to live by the Spirit." -Virgil Johnson

~

# 3

## Two Becoming One

After the death of his first wife my Dad did not give up or give in. He was working through overcoming the outside voices that ignorantly wanted to bring him under condemnation through religiousness. Christian soldiers make it through the battle by wearing the full armor of God. So called friends and associates would ask, "What have you done to get out of the will of God?" Or they would say, "God is punishing you for something!" and "You've missed it Virg'!", and on and on. He said the only thing during those months of persecution that he could reply was, "I am saved." It was his answer to every question posed that was a lie and no one could talk him out of it. Even if he was searching for answers himself he knew for sure that nothing could separate him from the love of God. If no other explanation could be offered up, that was indisputable!

A week after Juanita died Dad traveled to Jamaica and held a great revival. He was ridiculed for his determination to carry on with life after death. Tradition of man demanded he mourn in a particular way and they wanted him to conform, but going on with living life is the best way to heal your heart from a loss. For an entire year he struggled. He even prayed to God, "Let me die, let me die!" He literally asked God to take Him from this earth. If walking in the ministry meant living in an atmosphere of religious games and the farce and fantasy that it was within the church world, he wanted no part of it. He begged God to kill him with the sacrificial knife or to just let his heart stop beating. That entire year he prayed and fasted more than he ever had before.

Through the struggle the Lord was about to send him another great change. Many months after his first wife died Dad sat down with his mother and asked her advice on a matter of great importance. "I would like to marry again Mom, but this time I want to marry within the church. I want to choose a woman who will be a good preacher's wife." Grandma suggested a young woman who attended their church that was near to Dad in age. He considered her suggestion for a moment and then brought up another name. The name of a girl who attended church but was eleven years younger than he. "What do you think of Melonie Burdette?" he asked and she thought about it for a moment before decidedly replying, "Yes, I believe Melonie would make an excellent preachers wife!" This is not some archaic way of choosing a mate but rather a Godly way of choosing one. To consider not only who she is but where she has come from is choosing in wisdom and it is always a plus if your Godly mother approves.

God himself said in Genesis 2:28 "It is not good that man should be alone." He loved his first wife dearly but now he realized that what he wanted was to choose a woman from, as he used to put it, "the right camp". His first wife had come from a family in the world, a family who rejected faith. And although he thought no less of Juanita because of it, he had come to realize that choosing a woman who came from a family of faith would be better for his life and for the path he had chosen. Melonie had literally been raised in his mother's church. Her parents were active members since she was little and their seven children always attended church with them. They believed in the word of God and miracles. They loved God and one another. They were faithful members of the church and her father was even a deacon.

Melonie Ann Burdette was born on June 11, 1949. Her parents Ralph Benjamin Burdette, born January 30, 1907 and Hazel Cordelia Ketron born November 6, 1910 were married on September 30, 1932 and both received salvation shortly after they were wed. They began to dedicate their entire lives to Lord and their closeness to Him grew and grew. They had three boys and four girls. David, Nancy, Janice, Daniel, Melonie, Debra, and Steven. The entire family was musical and loved to sing in church. The family never missed a service and genuinely cherished being a part of their congregation. Much like my Dad she was raised up on a farm in freedom and simplicity while surrounded by the love of family. Her father worked with his hands his whole life farming and doing production work at a metal working company while her mother took care of the household.

Melonie had quite an exceptional voice but even more than that she had such a heart for worship. There was a purity to her heart and she was earnest in her desire to be used of the Lord for His kingdom. She and her siblings would sing in church together and they shared a closeness because of their common love of worshipping the Lord. She actually never wanted to marry a preacher because she had observed how uncertain the life of an evangelists wife was and it didn't much appeal to her. But she did know she wanted to serve God and follow Jesus, however He desired and wherever He lead.

Melonie had quite a legacy of faith that was handed down to her and the testimonies of God's miracle working power were part of the firm foundation of her parents. It was at a William Branham miracle service in Indianapolis, Indiana that her dad received an instant miracle in his body. The doctors had diagnosed him with arthritis of the spine and told him within a few short years he would be totally crippled by the disease. At the end of the service Brother Branham called him out to stand up in the large crowd. Brother Branham proceeded to tell him that the Lord had revealed to him that he had arthritis of the spine and that God was going to heal him of it that night. The pain and stiffness he felt in his back suddenly left and he began to shout the victory as he twisted and bent over to test the miracle. On his next doctors check up they found that there was not a trace of arthritis in his body! He never had a bit of arthritis reappear anywhere in him for the rest of his life on the earth.

Melonie's mother had a stroke and traveled to a miracle campaign in Ohio being held by Earl Ivie. When she went up for prayer Brother Ivie laid hands on her and every sign of stroke left her face and body instantly! Later in her life she had another stroke and her dear friend Becky Johnson prayed for her and the effects of the stroke left her body as she received a full miracle, never again did a stroke come upon her after that! Both of my grandmothers loved each other dearly and were good friends. They even did ministry together in a ladies group that Grandma Johnson started out of her church. The ladies would go from house to house or to the hospital and pray for the sick and oppressed. Long before they were family by marriage they were family in the Lord.

Dad decided to begin to date this sixteen year old young lady who's heart was after following Jesus and it wasn't long before they both were in love. Growing up I would ask Mom to tell me the story of Dad proposing because I thought it was the sweetest story and it really painted an accurate picture of Dad's way of doing things. He proposed while he was away on an evangelistic trip in Boston, Massachusetts and he had been seriously considering wether or not he should propose to Mom. They had only been dating a couple months but when you know, you know. He made his decision and then made a long distance phone call from his hotel room that night.

This is what she journaled in her wedding scrap book about that proposal, "The phone rang and it was Virgil. When I heard his voice my heart skipped a beat! 'How are you?' he asked, 'Good, but I miss you.' I replied, 'I miss you too.' He told me how lonely he was without me. He also told me about how some of his preacher friends were telling him he should just stay single, now that he had a second chance to be free from marriage. All of these advice giving friends were married and had children. He couldn't understand why they wouldn't want him to be happy and despite the advice, he knew in his heart what he wanted. And Virgil made a decision. 'Will you marry me?', he asked so sweetly, 'Yes.' I replied, 'But first you will have to ask my father'. I handed the telephone to my father and he asked Virgil, 'Will You be good to her and take good care of her?' Virgil replied, 'Yes'. My father already knowing that Virgil was a good man added, 'Then you have my blessing.' We planned a small wedding in my parent's home and two weeks after the day that he proposed, we were married!"

My Dad understood the meaning of God giving beauty for ashes when Melonie Burdette became Mrs. Johnson on her seventeenth birthday June 11, 1966. Before they wed, Dad told Mom that it was likely they would never have children because he and his first wife had not been able to conceive. She smiled and said, "I'm not marrying you because you can give me children. I'm marrying you because I love you." Although there was a bit of an age gap between them they shared a common love of the Lord and love for one another. They had a small, intimate wedding held in her parent's home with only family and close friends attending. They honeymooned in a little cabin on a lake on the Canadian side of Niagara Falls for one week and then it was straight into evangelizing at meetings in the New York area. Only twenty-eight years old and Dad had buried a wife and married another. He had a message to carry and now once more he had a help mate to carry it with him. He would know in the years to come that he could not have made a better choice than she.

(Photo of Virgil and Melonie Johnson on their wedding day)

My Mom was that woman of virtue that the Bible speaks of and her worth was far above rubies. She loved her husband and walked beside him, not behind him, as they lived life together. In their early years together she did a lot of growing up but even through the difficult times she proved her resolution to be committed to my Dad. She had a kind and tender heart and anyone who knew her called her a precious friend. She worked side by side with Dad in the ministry and she was never the lesser of the two. Perhaps more attention was drawn by the man with the word, but he always viewed her as his equal and she was a source of joy that made life so much more worth living. They had an amazing trust built between them and they learned to draw from each others strengths as the two became one. Their backgrounds were not so different but when they were first married they were very different. One element was the age gap, another was him being a man and her a woman. Two people who thought differently and had different ways of doing things eventually became one flesh, as the word of God puts it. Not by osmosis from having lived together for so long, but by the Spirit. As she yielded herself to the Holy Spirit and he yielded himself to the Holy Spirit that third and essential element in their marriage caused the two to become one by the Spirit. When people observed their marriage they would see a freedom like very few other couples had. They would note an equality that testified of not law but liberty that allowed them to love one another so fully. No marriage on this earth is perfect every moment of the day and the two may not always agree but in the lives of those who have purposed to let God do the work in their spouse instead of they themselves trying to change the other, there is evidence of true oneness. The Holy Spirit bridges the gap between two flesh and so only by the Spirit can they become one and enjoy the benefits of a truly happy marriage.

During this time of transitioning in their lives God was revealing within Dad that he had some changing to do before he could be ushered into the new move God would be doing. One thing the Lord revealed to him was concerning the style in which Dad was accustomed to preaching. All of the sudden he lost his voice for three months. He cried out to God in his heart, "Who's side are you on?" He wanted to preach so badly that He said he wished he had known sign language! But God was using this time of quiet to reach Dad, to transition him from the strong Pentecostal way of preaching loud and fiery and very emotionally to a more laid back approach of presenting the gospel. It was a key situation he had to walk through to step into the next level of maturity. One of the revelations he received from that time of being made mute was that you don't have to scream and yell when you have God's authority to speak.

Even after marrying Mom my Dad struggled to understand what God was doing in and through him. He realized that he needed to just get away for a while and be with the Lord. He asked Mom if it was alright with her if he took a little time by himself to travel out west on his motorcycle. She was happy for him to be able to go and take that time. He decided he would ride his motorcycle to California and back and just before he was about to set out he received a phone call from the Wayne Works Corporation. This Wayne Works was the leading school bus producer in North America at the time and they had two buses they needed desperately to get to California within a week. Dad had a relative who worked at the bus company in the distribution department who suggested that they contact Dad since he was planning a trip to California. They asked if he would be willing to take the buses and they offered him $800 to do the job. Who would pass up a chance to get a paid vacation? He found another driver for the second bus by inviting one of his elders, who was also a motorcyclist, to come along and then agreed to do the job. He secured his motorcycle in the back of the bus and headed west.

He made a quick trip to California to meet Wayne Works deadline and then journeyed north up the California coastline into Oregon and into Washington. From there he went to Montana and visited the Glacier National Park and went south to Yellowstone National Park in Wyoming. He had taken with him one change of clothes and a sleeping bag so he could sleep out under the stars when he didn't want to be in a hotel. The mountains had always been a place he felt close to the Lord. He parked his bike and took a hike to the top of a mountain by himself and sat in the quiet while taking in the great beauty of the Rocky Mountains. There he felt the presence of the Lord and knew that his spirit was being renewed.

On the last day of his trip, in a hotel in Toledo, Ohio, Jesus appeared to him once again. This time Jesus walked into the room while Dad was on his knees in prayer at the bed side. Suddenly that same glorious light he had seen once before filled the place. Jesus said, "You have been asking to die and you have died but not in the way you have comprehended. You have died to the flesh that you may live in the Spirit. That which I have told you, I will do. I am going to show you a new way, because I have reserved your ministry for the last days. Now, go and do what I have called you to do." The Lord spoke to confirm what had already been spoken before. This encounter gave him a second wind and brought an understanding of what would be produced from all he had recently walked through. It reassured him that he was on the right path and to keep going. He had walked through the hurt and the hardships and the persecution. He passed the test of being able to stand on the Rock during the storm. He had to learn so that he could teach.

Sermons began to come fresh to him and revelations of a new way of seeing scripture were imparted. This new revival was just breaking out and now was the time for forward action into what God had set before him to do. He was being released into a greater knowledge of who God is, in ways he had never known. He would say these new revelations were not only for the church but first and foremost to edify him. So that he could prepare and really focus on working out any religious traditions or wrong mindsets inside of him that would get in the way of moving into the new. Mom was his sound board for all of the revelations God gave to him. He would first let her partake of the word with him and then give it to others who would receive it. She would even offer interpretation by the Spirit when it was given to her and her knowledge of the scripture was of great help to him as they would meditate on the word together.

Soon the Lord began to open up the western side of the country to Dad and Mom for evangelizing. Mainly in Kansas, Nebraska and Iowa. It was in Iowa that my parents met their future brother-in-law Gary Batchelder. He not only married my Mom's sister Debbie but also became a part of my parents ministry. He is an excellent singer and song writer and played the guitar while accompanying Mom and her sister in the music ministry. They became known as the Living Word Singers of the Living Word Team. A name Dad had chosen for their evangelistic ministry.

During a revival in Nebraska there was a young man brought to the service who was dying from overdosing on drugs. This young man grew up in the Mennonite church and after falling away from the faith became addicted to drugs. That day one of his friends found him overdosed and having violent seizures. This friend knew about services being held in a tent where they advertised miracles so he carried his friend to his car and put him in the backseat. Instead of taking him to the hospital he took him to the tent. When they arrived he carried the young man into the tent and brought him to the front interrupting the service. Dad immediately stopped preaching and went to lay hands on the young man at deaths door. The friend explained that the seizures were caused by an overdose of drugs and Dad quickly commanded that devil of addiction to come out. Instantly the seizures stopped. His body relaxed and his eyes opened. He was completely made well! The young man gave his life to Jesus that night and was delivered from his drug addiction from that day on. Many years later the friend of the overdosed young man met up with Dad and testified of how he vividly remembered that experience and how it changed his life forever. From seeing that miracle he began to see God in a new light and it really helped him break away from the religious path he himself was on. Being of a religious mind set is as dangerous as being addicted to drugs. Seeing his addicted friend completely set free, set him free to know God in a way that the church had never taught him. That young man who was willing to help his drug addicted friend ended up with an even greater miracle.

After years of use on Dad's first tent he realized he needed a new one. So he researched to find which one he wanted and then waited on God to provide it. One day while preaching in Tennessee the Lord woke him up in the early morning. The Lord instructed him to call the Chattanooga Tent & Awning Company, which was located in the same town he was ministering in and to ask them to set aside the tent he wanted. Dad called up the company and did as the Lord directed him. He also told the man that he didn't have the money to pay for it but he believed the Lord was sending it in. The man replied, "You're the only preacher I've ever met that I believe when you say the Lord said it, so I know it's going to happen. I'll lay aside that tent for you and make sure it is available when you come to buy it." After that Dad left the room where he was staying to go out to his truck and as he went to open the door a lady came up to him. She said, "Did you get a phone call this morning Brother Virgil?" He looked puzzled because he hadn't received a phone call. He replied, "Is the pastor trying to reach me?" She shook her head no and then changed her question, "Did you make a phone call this morning?" He smiled as he suddenly realized what was going on, God had set up this appointment. He grinned and said, "I did make a phone call this morning." She replied, "God told me about a phone call and that you had a need. He also told me to write you a check for whatever your need is." Not fifteen minutes after God had awakened him to tell him to call the tent shop this lady came along in obedience to be the one to meet the need for the purchase of the tent and confirm the word Dad was given.

Not long after the new tent was purchased Dad had need of a new truck to haul the tent in. He began to seek God and then one day the Lord gave him a vision of the truck. He saw in the vision that on the side of the truck it read, "The Word Saves, The Word Heals, The Word Sets Free". He began to thank the Lord for the truck and for the next six months he was in and out of every truck dealership he was near. He would get in a truck and say, "Is this the one Lord?", and there would be no reply. Until Dad was ministering out in corn country Iowa. A man there said he knew where a truck was and that Dad might be interested in it. So they drove about forty miles outside of Des Moines to take a look at it. It wasn't at a dealership but someone's personal property and as soon as Dad got up inside of the truck he heard God say, "This is it."

(Photo of the truck with the lettering added to mirror what Dad saw in the vision that he was given)

Dad didn't have two pennies to rub together but God had spoken to him and that's all he needed to believe. It was on a Friday that he found the truck, so he told the owner he would come back the following Monday when the banks were open so he could get the money for the purchase. They drove back to where he was staying and he shut himself in his room and began to pray. He had barely begun to pray when a knock came to the door and his host said he had a phone call on the line, so he picked up the phone and said hello. The voice on the line said, "Brother Johnson, you're a hard man to find! I've been trying to find you for three days! God told me to write out a check for whatever your need is." This man was from the area but he didn't know that Dad was in Iowa at the time. Even before Dad found the truck the Lord had spoken to someone to give the money to provide for it! Dad told him the price of the truck and the man gave him the money the very next day.

During this time changes were happening at the church that Dad and Mom pastored. In the midst of their evangelistic outreaches, including another trip to Jamaica, Dad had a vision of adding onto the church. This addition would be an area dedicated to the youth and their education. Dad had such a heart for the youth and that addition would do so much to expand how he could reach the youth. Being young and surrounded by deceptions in the world can make life harder than it should be and Dad wanted to build a place where youth could have an option to come and be free, safe and loved while surrounded by faith. The church did not have a lot of money coming in at the time but Dad had that vision in his heart for the addition. Almost every week he took half of his salary and put it into the addition for the church. Dad and Mom sacrificed a lot during those years but hard work always requires sacrifice.

The addition to the building was an L shape that extended seventy feet by seventy feet out from the main body of the church. It had five Sunday school rooms, a new office, a kitchen and restrooms. Dad and Mom did a lot of the work themselves but they also had a lot of friends and family who pitched in. Mom's brother-in-law, Paul Azbill, who was married to her sister Janice and also happened to be a preacher, helped to show them how to lay a block foundation. From the foundation laying, to framing the building, and finishing sheet rock as well as putting on the roof, they did it as a community. The youth even did some fund raising to help with the cost. It took a total of four years to complete the addition. Many people are not fond of change and some members of the church stopped attending because of their disapproval of this change.

The ministry continued to have finical needs, as all things do, but Dad refused to give up believing the Lord was working all things to his good. He began to pray for the Lord to send three people to give $10,000 a piece to help pay for all the needs the ministry had. He prayed this way for seven months solid and after the building was completed they went to have meetings in Vinton, Iowa. Funds were almost nonexistent but they were invited to have revival and Dad never turned down the opportunity to bring the gospel. Offerings were never guaranteed but that wasn't his motivation. He was focused on making his calling and election sure and being faithful to that commission God gave him. Preaching was not a means by which he thought he could make a good living, but an opportunity for him to give freely from his heart what God had given him.

A woman came to him at the end of service one night and said, "Brother Johnson, I wrote out this check for Oral Roberts today and I was going to send it to him in the mail tomorrow. But the Lord spoke to me and said, rewrite this check and give it to Virgil Johnson." She smiled and handed him a check for $45,000. He smiled and thanked her and thanked God. He brought the check to Mom and said, "This is the pay check for every block we laid." With that money he bought a new organ for the church and one thousand wooden folding chairs, the stackable kind. He paid for Mom to record an album entitled Sounds of Heaven and had albums made so they could begin to distribute her singing. The rest of the money went right back into the ministry. With the exception of $20 that he used to buy himself a new pair of pants. He said, "God gave this money to me so He gets it back. I knew I was being tested. I knew if I didn't spend it right, if Daddy couldn't trust me with this money, I wouldn't get anymore." He knew that check was to be the first big financial blessing of his ministry and that it was really a test. Faith pleases God, in fact according to Hebrews 6:11 it is impossible to please God without faith. Ask and believe God hears you when you ask and that He is willing to give you what you ask, and you will have it.

After the woman gave him a check for more than what he had been praying for he asked the Lord to forgive him for trying to figure out how God would do it. As he was praying the Lord said, "I don't need three, all I need is one." It wasn't a rebuke it was just a reminder to trust God within the realm of His ways being higher than ours. It doesn't matter whether we know how God will do it, it only matters that we believe He is a God of His word and He will do it. God is limitless and He loves when we step out in faith so that He can show up in an even bigger way than we could ever imagine! Dad asked for $30,000 and God gave him $45,000. Just believe that He is a rewarder of those who diligently seek Him and He will do what only He can do!

While ministering in Sydney, Nebraska Dad received a phone call from a grandfather who's eighteen month old grand baby was dying of spinal meningitis. Which is an inflammation of the lining that covers the brain and spinal cord. The doctors would have transferred the baby to the children's hospital in Denver but it was about an hour helicopter ride away and they believed the baby wouldn't have survived the trip. Dad was asked to come as quickly as he could and pray for the baby, so he jumped in his car and put the pedal to the metal. His speeding resulted in a police officer pulling him over and when the officer asked why Dad was going so fast he explained what was going on. In response the police officer said, "Just follow me, I'll get you there." So Dad followed the police car with his flashing lights and made a quick trip of that eighty mile drive to the hospital. When he arrived the grandfather was waiting at the entrance for Dad to show him to the room where the child was. The baby was being kept in isolation with his head packed on ice to try to bring down the deathly high fever.

Every once in a while you find a devil that tries to stop you from getting a miracle for someone. This devil came in the form of the head nurse who refused to let Dad into where the child was. "It is contagious and I will not let you in the room," she said. Dad confronted that devil by telling the nurse forcefully but with great love, "Ma'am I'm going in that room, get out of my way." She protested and he restated. Three times he said it and on the fourth time he said, "I'm going to say it one last time. Whatever it takes, I'm going in there to pray for the child and you won't stop me." Finally she relented and told him he could go in the room but he would have to wear all the proper attire. He said, "I can live with that, go and get those things here now." He spoke with authority because he knew time was of the essence. That nurse may not have believed in the power of prayer, but he did.

He covered his head, face, hands, clothes and shoes and walked into the room where the mother and father were sitting on a couch. Dad asked the mother how she was holding up and she replied, "God gave me the baby and today I decided it's His so whatever He wants to do, I am willing." Then he asked the father how he was and he told him, "Brother Virgil, the Lord called me to preach during one of your meetings about a month ago. He called me and I haven't answered him and today I told Him I would do what He called me to do." With that, Dad went over to the baby whose body was jerking with convulsions. A nurse was standing right next to the child as Dad laid his hands on the little body. The baby's head was enlarged from the inflammation attacking it's body. The Holy Spirit rose up inside him to declare boldly, "God, we'll wait five minutes, five hours, five days, five weeks but right now we want a miracle. Give us a miracle for this baby." All of the sudden the baby's rigid body began to relax. His little hands had been tightened into fists and Dad watched as those tiny fingers uncurled. He looked over at the nurse and said, "Would you do me a favor and take the baby's temperature?" She quickly responded and took the baby's temperature and as she viewed the results she began to cry. As soon as Dad saw her reaction he started crying too because he knew the baby had gotten a miracle. She retook the baby's temperature to double check it and said, "Reverend, the temperature is normal."

That woman was the first to witness an amazing miracle that God did and about three hours later the doctor came to check on the child expecting he would find the baby dead. Instead he discovered that the child's temperature and breathing were normal, the swelling in the head had completely gone and there was no trace of the infection that had threatened to kill this little one. That child received a miracle and the doctor could not explain it! About twenty years later Dad got to see that little baby boy grown up and healthy. He was working with his father in the ministry who had become a pastor of a church in Washington state.

~

"You have been given the power. Years ago I came to the conclusion that through Jesus I have been given the power. They call that power dynamite, Holy Ghost power. You have the power to choose life or death. You have the power to fill that head with world knowledge or the knowledge of God. You have the power to harden your heart or to let it conform to God's. You have power to take the land wherever you set your feet. You have power! Christians seem to go around endlessly searching and asking, 'What does God want?' He wants what you want! How can I be so brazen to say such a thing? How can I be so bold? Because I want to see people blessed and He's in the blessing business. Hallelujah! I want to see people saved, He's in the saving business. I want to see people healed, He's in the healing business. I want to put the word in their heart and He wants His word in their hearts. The problem most people have is that they don't know what they want. So they never learn to move in the things of God. They don't know which end is up. Let this mind be in you that was also in Christ Jesus! I don't use this power to glorify self, I use it to glorify God." -Virgil Johnson

~

Our whole relationship with Jesus should be that we live with the purpose of keeping our focus always on Him. I want my focus to be on Jesus. I want go where He goes, speak what He speaks, see how He sees, think how He thinks and love like He loves. So in reality blind faith is full of vision, heavenly vision! Vision to see His goodness, to see beyond the circumstance. It's knowing you are walking in victory because He is in you, He goes before you, He walks beside you and He has got your back. I share with you all these testimonies because I know if you could see just a small fraction of the miracles I have witnessed then you would know why I trust Him. Just like the generations before me, I choose to stay focused on the goodness of God. In that dwelling place of hope I live. It is this reality that has given me this confidence of knowing life is only good with God. God is good and if we make Him the center of our life then life can only be good.

~

"When Peter saw Jesus on the water he asked the Lord to 'bid me come unto thee on the water.' (Matthew 14:28) Only one out of twelve disciples got out of the boat and walked on the water. The others thought that it was an illusion and could not comprehend the purpose of walking on the water. Peter wanted to be with Jesus, no matter where He was. Even if it was on water, which in all reality should not have held them. Many times in my life I stood by faith when no one had ever done it before. Jesus had spoken to my heart and given me the vision. That is why I have won so many battles over the years. I saw Jesus. I was willing to stand or walk with him where He bid me to come. Like the time the Lord told me to pour a bottle of oil over a man's head. I didn't know that this man was a Nazarene preacher who did not have the Holy Spirit. I also didn't know that one of his legs was over an inch shorter than the other. I didn't want to cheat him out of a blessing because I didn't know his circumstances, so I obeyed the Lord! In pouring out the oil, the man began to speak in tongues. He didn't even know what was happening to him. Suddenly he became very excited because he felt his leg lengthen! He had to take off his shoe to stand level! I was so glad I obeyed the Lord!" -Virgil Johnson

~

Not being able to see or hear is considered a handicap in the natural and so it is in the spiritual. Nothing handicaps a Christian more than traditions of man. According to Matthew 15:6 it is tradition which makes the commandments of God of no effect. If you can't hear His voice how could you ever be expected to comprehend the things of the kingdom? So many within the church world are impaired with religion and religious ideals that have been ingrained in them since childhood. That which is based in flesh yet peddled off as Spiritual. Thoughts that were placed in your mind and heart and developed by carnal thinking. Things that were maybe even meant for your good but they are none the less wrong. Put in you by preachers, denominations, parents, relatives, friends and sometimes ideas you've conjured up yourself. You read every book to better understand these carnal opinions of what is Spiritual until you almost don't know who Jesus is and become nothing but confused. You know what He stands for but you don't understand His heart. God knows this and it can be undone but sometimes it is a lifelong battle for Jesus to just get someone's attention long enough for Him to break through all the lies. If instead, once you find Jesus you become determined to set your eyes on Him and nothing else then your walk will not be so hard but full of the liberty He always intended you to live in.

~

"Let us fix our eyes on Jesus, the pioneer and perfecter of our faith, who for the joy set before Him endured the cross, scorning its shame and sat down at the right hand of the throne of God." Hebrews 12:2 (Strongs)

~

I see my Dad as someone who fully comprehended the connection He had with Jesus. The Lord is even now sitting on the throne of grace so that we may boldly come to the Father through Him and obtain help in the time of need. Living this life in complete trust of the Father takes faith. It takes hearing the voice of God and mixing it with faith so we can believe it and enter into the rest He offers us. When we work out of our own ability we labor and become heavy ladened or burdened with trying to make things happen on our own. But this walk with the Lord is not about how good we are in our ability but how well we believe the word that He has spoken into our lives. It's about believing the promises and our faith being perfected as it is daily proven in us through our obedience to the word. Dad comprehended the intimacy of this relationship we have with the Most High God and the oneness we can obtain with Him. Dad was tested time and again to see if he really believed what he heard the Father say, and if he would keep his eyes on Jesus.

Once Dad set up the tent in Topeka, Kansas during the middle of tornado season. As the service was underway that evening the tent began to shake from the violent force of wind and rain that suddenly occurred. The locals must have known when a storm like that comes it most likely means a tornado is about to hit because they all got out of their seats and ran for other shelter. Dad and his crew did their best to hold down the poles that held the tent to the ground as they prayed. One of the women who attended service didn't leave the tent but came to stand near Dad with her daughter by her side. He looked at her and asked, "What are you doing?" She replied, "I know that the safest place to be right now is where you are. If this tent goes, we are standing right beside you because God will protect us!" Dad laughed and said, "Honey, you are wise!" She knew, and Dad knew, that the devil could not destroy that tent if he was standing inside of it. He let go of the pole he had been holding onto and while standing near the entrance of the tent he saw the tornado in the distance touching down. He outstretched his arm and commanded the tornado that it should not come any nearer and he watched as it took what appeared to be a sharp left turn. Within minutes the rain and wind ceased and the tent and everyone in it was safe. The next day it was reported in the news that the tornado did something that was extremely uncharacteristic, by suddenly turning from its path. Little did they know that a man of faith had believed that night for something supernatural and God caused it to come about.

 Only a few years after Dad's first wife died he received a phone call from a husband who asked Dad to come to his home and pray for his wife who was hemorrhaging to death. She had lost so much blood that she couldn't move from bed and she knew she was dying. When Dad arrived at their home the devil spoke to him and said, "You had better not pray for this one because if she doesn't get a miracle people are going to talk about you and blame you for her death." Satan wanted to see if he could get a reaction out of Dad and cause him to waiver on this new solid ground he had gained over the past few years. For a split second the urge to grab his coat and go came over him but suddenly he overcame that thought with this response, "Whoa! Wait a minute! You just made this personal devil. You tried to come against me and the call of God on my life. You tried to get me to run and now it's personal!" If the devil was desperate enough to try to stop him from praying for this woman, he knew she was definitely going to receive a touch from God. So he walked into the room where the woman was and spoke with authority, "I don't care how sick or how weak you are, you will get out of that bed! If your husband has to drag you out, you will get your miracle!" Dad spoke and then left the room to instruct her husband to help her out of the bed but before he could do so they both began to hear the woman crying and shouting for joy. She suddenly came up from out of her sick bed, walked out into the hallway, arms raised praising God and declaring the the bleeding had ceased and her strength had completely returned. She did indeed get her miracle!

Once there was a young lady who came to Dad's church and found salvation. She had been living with a violent man and when she had her personal encounter with Jesus she knew she had to leave that destructive relationship. But the young lady was estranged from her family due to her decision to go and live with this man, so she had no where to go and no means to support herself. She came to Dad with her issue and Dad invited her to come and stay with him and Mom until the young lady could get back on her feet again. He not only gave her room and board but also found a job for her to work at. A few weeks later the woman's ex-boyfriend interrupted a church service by walking in with a hand gun pointed at Dad. Dad was standing on the pulpit as his sermon was cut off by this man announcing that he was going to kill Dad. Dad's reaction was calm and collected and he went right to discerning the spirit in the man. Discernment will let you know if a persons words are empty or if they fully intended to do what they say. Dad responded to the man's threat by saying, "No you won't." The man answered, "Yes I will!" Dad shook his head no and replied, "If you pull that trigger the gun will either not work or back fire and blow your hand off." The man paused to consider Dad's words before responding, "Then I will go for my knife!" This made Dad smile because now he knew he had the devil going for his backup plan. "You reach for that knife in your pocket and your hand will become paralyzed for the rest of your life." The devil in that man decided to believe the Holy Spirit in Dad and he lowered the gun and then turned and walked out of the church. The man never bothered his ex-girlfriend or Dad ever again.

There is another testimony that I would like to share about the victory of going home to be with Jesus. My Mom's youngest brother Steve was a young man on fire for God who wanted nothing more than to be in the presence of God. His heart was after the ministry and he had a great desire to be active with what God would have him to do. He loved my Dad so much and wanted to learn from him about how to follow the Lord. Steve decided to became a part of the Living Word Team. He contributed by helping set up the tent and sound system and also played bass guitar with the Living Word Singers. He also managed the selling of Dad's literature and Mom's music at each evangelistic service. While they were all ministering in the state of New York my Uncle Steve got a nose bleed that wouldn't stop. Dad would pray and they would stop for a while and then come back. Steve decided to go back home upon the counsel of his parents and when he got back they took him to the hospital. The doctors diagnosed him with acute leukemia and gave him two weeks to live. He was nineteen years old.

When faced with the question of what he was going to do Uncle Steve told the doctor, "Well, I see it this way doc, if God heals me or takes me home I'm a winner either way." He chose to decline treatment and went home to be with his family. Being surrounded by people of love and faith he was constantly lifted up in prayer. They were believing for a miracle.

For six days they believed for a miracle. The first three days Dad was at the Burdette house praying for Steve and would not leave his side, he didn't take a break to even shower for those three days. The bleeding Steve was experiencing would stop while Dad was at Steve's bedside and then come back when he did finally leave to go home and sleep and shower. During the last three days Dad would feel death coming on Steve and tell everyone to pray with him to rebuke it and then the presence of death would leave. Steve would sit up and talk and even eat. On the last day however, Steve began to bleed so profusely that a dishpan had to be used to catch all the blood. Aunt Debbie was tending to Steve during those final hours and on this last day the blood was not ceasing. While sitting next to Steves bed, Dad looked out the window to see the angel of death outside waiting for Steve. After that Dad got up and went to ask his mother-in-law what she would have him do. "Do you want me to let him go or keep fighting?" She did not want to be faced with that question but knew it was time to give Steve over to heaven. With the decision made and knowing Steve was already ready to go, Dad went back in the room and asked Debbie to step out of the room for a moment. Once she had gone he looked up and said, "God, I'm not standing between you and Steve any more." And immediately the breath of life went out of Steve's body and his spirit was ushered into heaven by that angel. Steven Michael Burdette passed into eternal life on January 23, 1974 thirteen days before his 20th birthday. If ever there was a fighter who learned the utmost importance of submitting that fight to God, it was my Dad.

Victory is winning. Winning is exactly what my Uncle Steve did. He boldly declared the love of God towards him by telling the doctors that he knew he was winner no matter the outcome of the battle. There is no force on the earth or in hell that can come between you and God. He wants to establish in all of us absolute trusting in Him so that we can reap the benefit of knowing what it is like to have Him work all things for our good. He doesn't want you to be afraid, ever. He understands that sometimes we will be afraid but He wants the knowledge of His perfect love for us to overrule that fear and completely cast it out! If your heart is already in heaven and there is nothing on earth to hold you here then letting go of this life is much, much easier.

In the spring of 1973 Dad and Mom took a family vacation to Yellowstone National Park with Papaw and Grandma Johnson. While there my Mom told Grandma she thought she might be pregnant. So Grandma took her down to the park clinic to see what the results would be. I think Grandma was even more excited about it than Mom! Sure enough, the test result was positive and Mom went back to tell Dad that they were going to have a baby. They praised the Lord together for this amazing and unexpected blessing! Eight months later the time came for the baby to be born and Mom went into labor. During the final stages of the birthing the doctors found that the umbilical cord was caught up under the baby's arm. It was cutting off the flow of oxygen and there was nothing they could do to change it. My sister, Jennifer Joy Johnson, was born dead on November 30, 1973. This was a great sorrow for my Mom and Dad.

The news of Jennifer's death was given to Dad by the doctor and shortly after he was given a vision by the devil. In this vision he saw Satan in the delivery room standing over the bed where Mom was laying. Satan said, "This is what your God does for you. Builds your hopes up, gives you a child and then takes it away from you. Come and serve me." Then the devil pointed to a corner in the room and spoke again, "Look in the corner." Dad's eyes followed that pointing finger and saw himself rocking back and forth and moaning in the corner. He saw himself as having lost his mind and completely gone mad. Again Satan spoke, "Come and serve me and you will never have to feed yourself again, you will never have to dress yourself again, you will never have to work another day in your life. Come, serve me."

It was a vivid vision but his spirit cried out, "No!" The oppression was so strong from the enemy that he told my Mom he had to get out of the room. He was sorry he couldn't be with her in that moment because he knew she needed him but he had to go. He spent the next three hours in the men's room on his knees in prayer until that evil spirit that was trying to take hold was lifted off of him. He made this declaration to put the prince of liars in his place, "Devil, I will never serve you! For my God is a just God!" He stood on the edge of insanity and prayed his way back. When he returned to Mom's side he said, "Honey, what has happened is part of our life now but God is just and I cannot bring railing accusation against Him."

Dad knew he could not speak out in protest and accuse God of being anything but just, no matter how much loosing Jennifer hurt. He had been married nine years to his first wife and seven years with Mom, only to have his first child taken back as soon as she had been given. Dad always had a desire in his heart to have children but how could he cry out to God as if he had been robbed? For he knew God had the absolute best plan for his life. How can an absolute best plan involve the death of child? Only God knows. But I believe His ways are higher than ours and the word in Jeremiah 29:11 is true, that His thoughts for us are only to prosper us and not harm us, to give us hope and a future with Him.

When I asked my Mom how she felt when she experienced loosing Jennifer she told me, "My heart was sad but I never stopped trusting God. And God was faithful because He gave me Jeremiah and you." Such a woman of faith and faithfulness! To have withstood the pain of losing a child that she carried full term. To then walk through the opinions of the religious voices that bombarded both she and Dad afterwards. People are never short of opinions and church people can especially be brutal when they believe that God is a being that goes around handing out punishments to His children for kicks. God is full of love, so full in fact, that He is the source and definition of the word. He is all things pure and holy and good and He loves His children fiercely. So much that He holds them through the pain that they experience in this broken world. So much that He gives them the promise of the oil of joy for mourning and the garment of praise for the spirit of heaviness.

This trial was yet another circumstance that reinforced their faith and caused their commitment to one another to be stronger. When there are more questions than there are answers it is hard sometimes for the mind to get away from the pain of the experience and focused on the truth of God's love. My Mom's heart was as broken as my Dad's and although she did not experience the same level of oppression that day she still had her own hurt to overcome. She drew strength from the Lord and became a source of strength for Dad. He testified of how her resolution to get back up and walk again helped him to do the same. Two becoming one is a process and we can't do this thing called life alone. God emphasizes in His word how good it is that two should become one. He said that His Spirit would cause the one to submit and love the other, and vice versa, so that it would glorify Him in the union. It creates an equality that allows the two to become one so that they can walk together in His love and strengthen each other to make life so much more full of Him. What a beautiful mystery. My parents lived that oneness and I am witness to it. Their oneness with Jesus made their oneness with each other the reality of their marriage.

We will all have our faith tested multiple times during our sojourning in this world. How else could we grow unless situations arise that we may learn? It is all to cause us to come into oneness with Him through the relationship that is established by learning to trust Him more. In the beginning we are all ignorant of the knowledge of who God truly is. The life of a follower of Jesus is just the stage on which we have our story of the learning of who He is unfold. My parents never stopped loving God and they never blamed God for that great sorrow they endured. Dad and Mom carried on loving Him and loving each other and loving the church. It was through this trial that

Dad said he truly learned to not question the plans that God had for him. A revelation of knowing that God had never failed before and this time would be no different. He didn't hold onto the pain of losing a child but began to activate his faith and believe that God was indeed going to give him another child. My parents held onto that expectation of good by setting their minds towards the unshakable truth that God's love for them was unfailing.

The very next year after Jennifer's death Dad and Mom found out they were pregnant again. This time they didn't tell anyone that they were expecting for the first fews months of the pregnancy. Until one day they received a letter in the mail from a dear friend who lived in Nebraska. This woman had been widowed and was left with small children to care for by herself. When she first met Dad the Lord gave him a word of prophecy that God was sending her a husband and not a month later she met the man that God had spoken about. They were married and he proved to be a husband who loved the Lord and cared for her children like they had been his very own. This woman wrote to tell my parents that the Lord had spoken to her saying that Dad and Mom would have a child and that this time everything would go perfectly with the birth. The Lord also spoke saying that this child would be a little boy who would one day follow in his father's footsteps. Since no one knew Mom was pregnant, it was easy to believe that God had indeed spoken to her. This confirmation caused their confidence to soar and on July 22, 1975 it came to pass that Jeremiah Jonathan Johnson was born. He weighed eleven pounds and six ounces and was twenty-two inches long, and there was not a single complication. This blessing of a big, healthy, perfect baby made Dad laugh and say, "If you wait on God, He gives you the biggest and the best!" Oh how their hearts were full! Such a joy Jeremiah was to the entire family. He was the second grandson born to Grandma and Pappaw Johnson and they loved him so much! Grandma had never stopped praying that Mom and Dad could come to know the love of a child and God was faithful to answer her prayer. Jeremiah grew into a fine man who's heart is a big as his daddy's.

Only a few months after my brother came into this world my Grandma Burdette passed away on September 28, 1975. Her heart had been homesick ever since the loss of her baby boy Steve and she was aching to go to heaven. It was her heart failing that ended her time here. I never got to know her but she is in my heart and I look forward to that great day of celebration when I will meet her face to face in heaven!

Four years later my Grandma Johnson joined my Grandma Burdette in heaven. Towards the end of her days she would sit and listen to Dad preach. Tears would roll down her checks as her heart reflected on how the Lord had helped her to raise up a rambunctious boy to be a great man of God. She once said to him, "Virgil, sometimes I don't understand the revelations He has given you, but because of the anointing you speak with, I know they are from God." The evening before she passed away Dad was sitting by her bedside and she said to him, "I am so proud of you Virgil. You've gone beyond me and whatever you do in the future after I'm gone, do it big. Because God is with you!" That next day after she spoke those words, as Dad was sitting at her bedside, he watched as an angel came in through the window and carried his mother's spirit away. She went to be with Jesus on June 29, 1979.

The 70's passed with more miracles than there were trials. Yet the trials were hard. Where there is life there is a shadow of death. It is part of the cycle of living. This mortal body was not made to last forever and it must be shed to step into life eternal. There is an old song that says, "Everybody wants to go to heaven but nobody wants to die." Yet dying is what must take place in order to reap eternal life! In every natural thing death is part of the process. Which makes it part of the beauty and the glory. We should look at death as the final part of the process and rejoice when the race is won! It is only fear that causes us to look upon dying in a negative way. Death for each of us who are in Christ Jesus is only a going to sleep and waking up to being glorified with Him forever. For us there is no end, only the ultimate beginning!

~

"For God hath not given us the spirit of fear; but of power, and of love, and of a sound mind. Be not thou therefore ashamed of the testimony of our Lord, Who hath saved us, and called us with an holy calling, not according to our works, but according to his own purpose and grace, which was given us in Christ Jesus before the world began, But is now made manifest by the appearing of our Saviour Jesus Christ, who hath abolished death, and hath brought life and immortality to light through the gospel:" 2 Timothy 1:7-10 (KJV)

~

# 4
## I Knew Him As Dad

(Photo of my Dad and I)

After Grandma passed away Dad new it was time to move from the old building of the Congregational Tabernacle. So he began to look for a new building to hold services and put the newly remodeled building up for sale. He would sell the building, which was now worth more money due to the addition, and find something that better fit his vision for the church. Finances began to increase out of the many revivals held out west. Frequently ministering in Nebraska for almost two years solid and about a years worth of ministering in the state of Kansas. Dad wanted a building with more capacity to expand the grade school and youth program as well as room to grow for the congregation. The old building ended up being sold to Trinity Broadcasting Network (TBN), which they turned into a television broadcasting station. Dad soon found a property that was just right for his vision, a foreclosed twenty-five acre golf course called Stone Valley Country Club. The property included a club house and an attached metal building that severed as an indoor driving range. Inside the club house was a full kitchen and dining room, several conference rooms, offices and full size his and hers locker rooms. Also included with the property was an olympic sized outdoor swimming pool complete with utility building and showers.

Working through a real-estate agent, Dad was told that the properties listing price was much less than what it was valued at and it was a great deal. So he began to consult God on the subject and soon made a decision, putting in an offer of $85,000. This was considerably lower than the already low price they were asking. The property was valued at $500,000, but the association that owned it needed to get rid of it so they agreed to Dad's offer. During this process a banker who was handling the financing became aware of Dad's purchase price and thought that it was a ridiculously good deal. He also thought it would be a great opportunity for making an offer, just slightly higher than Dad's offer, with the intent to buy and sell the property for the use of development. Since Dad's offer was not yet in writing, the owners withdrew the agreement and took the banker up on his offer.

When Dad found out what was going on he began to pray and claim the property for the church. He knew the Lord was in this deal and that God would make a way. Weeks went by and the man who made the higher offer could not come up with the financing. When the sellers found this out they were very upset, knowing they had almost blown the deal that they made with Dad. So they contacted Dad saying they would absolutely accept his original offer, if he still wanted the deal. Dad praised the Lord and put the $55,000 from the sale of the old church building down on the purchase. Taking on a mortgage of only $30,000 which he knew the Lord would provide for in a short time. Purchasing this property valued at $500,000 for only $85,000. The favor of the Lord should show up in every business dealing we have in this world and my Dad really lived by that truth.

(Photo of Dad in the newly remodeled sanctuary)

Once the purchase was made, they set to the task of remodeling it. First things on the list were to insulate, drywall and paint the inside of the metal building that was formerly used for an indoor driving range. They also built and installed a platform in the back of the building and carpeted the entire area. This became the sanctuary and was also utilized as a set for Dad's tv broadcast entitled The Living Word Telecast. My Uncle Gary created a logo as a back drop for the set that was an image of a dove, which represented the Holy Spirit, within a circle and from the circle four arrows pointed in all different directions coming out of it to signify taking the Holy Spirit to the four corners of the earth. A logo that would be on Dad's first book and is still being used to this day as a logo for my own ministry.

Most of the conference rooms became the grade school but one became a dwelling place for my family. That room was turned into a bedroom and this church would be the first place I called home. What better way to utilize the space than making it into a parsonage? It already had a kitchen for cooking needs and locker rooms for bathroom needs. Plus, whatever money was saved from living in a house separate from the church would be able to be put right back into the ministry. We literally lived in church!

In 1976 Dad and Mom traveled to London, England for the first time to minister and not long after that Dad traveled to Cairo, Egypt to be the featured speaker at the Charismatic Pastoral Conference. While ministering there he took the time to sightsee and got to experience riding a camel, seeing the Pyramids of Giza and also witnessing the mummy of Pharaoh Ramesses II being relocated from France to the Cairo museum. Dad watched as they unloaded the sarcophagus and spoke with one of the curators at the museum who pointed out to Dad some interesting history about Ramesess, the one believed to be the step-brother of Moses. The curator pointed out the image of what appeared to be two tablets of stone engraved into the sarcophagus, ones that he believed were depictions of the stone tablets of the ten commandments given to Moses by God. The curator said, "It would seem the God of Moses left a lasting impression on Ramesses, so much so that he would include a symbol of the God of Moses amongst the other gods he had marked on his coffin." Being a lover of history Dad truly enjoyed getting to have all those experiences in Egypt.

Dad also made his first evangelistic trip to India in 1976 with his good friend Drummond Thom and again he went in 1977. Dad would evangelize to India six more times throughout his life, holding eight separate crusades. He always took a team of preachers with him to help minister because the need was so great. One crusade he took part in drew in a crowd of over two hundred and fifty thousand people. Larger crowds than Gandhi ever had in that country. Oh, the testimonies that came out of those crusades! Twenty thousand Hindus were saved each night in that first crusade that was held. It would take a much longer book to tell of all the testimonies but there are a few that must be shared for the glory of God.

The first is the testimony of a little nine year old girl. While in India Dad befriended a French nun. She was reverend mother superior of a local Catholic school who greatly admired Dad and wanted to benefit from his teaching of the word. She invited Dad to come and teach her students every afternoon after the morning services were held at the crusade. She would meet him after service and accompany him to the school every day. The nun came to him after service this one day and told Dad that she had seen a group of six Indian men trying to cast a demon out of a little girl. She said they were doing things like holding the girl down on the ground while pulling her hair and yelling at her. She knew what they were doing wasn't right but she wanted Dad to confirm it. He said, "I don't know what book they are reading on how to cast out a demon but it isn't the Bible."

The next day after morning service the nun alerted Dad to that same group of people doing the same thing again. Together they went over to where the people were. The nun made it there before Dad and told them to leave the child alone. They obeyed and the little girl went to stand in the shelter of her mother. The nun wiped the dust off the cheeks of the child and stroked her hair out of her face before she looked at Dad and said, "Brother Johnson, they say she has a demon." He replied, "Why do they think she has a demon?" The nun was fluent in several languages and began to interpret what the Indians had said in their defense, "They say that when they put this crucifix in front of her she knocks it out of the way." The moment he saw the child he discerned that she was not demon possessed but he wanted to hear from those who thought she was so he could better communicate with them the truth. Then the Lord spoke to him saying, "She was born with a mental defect and has the mind of a two year old." He proceeded to tell the nun what the Lord said and she in turn told the others.

The Hindu mother of the child spoke up saying, "The doctors told me she has been this way since birth and that she has the mind of a two year old." She used exactly the same terminology the Lord had given Dad. He looked at the people who thought they were trying to cast out a demon and spoke while the nun interpreted for him, "When you put a toy in front of a little child that doesn't know you, they knock it out of the way every time." He said this to explain why she batted at the crucifix when they put it in her face. Truth is, a crucifix has no amount of power to discern whether or not someone has a demon. Demon's aren't afraid of relics, they are afraid of you, if you have the Holy Ghost. It is wrong thinking and bad doctrine that made them hurt this little girl who's mind had not developed properly. He laid hands on the little girl and a prayed that the Lord would touch that defect in her brain and God gave her a restorative miracle right before their eyes! The mother of that child gave her heart to the Lord that day and turned away from the Hindu religion.

In another crusade Dad became stranded after service because he had stayed late to minster one on one to some of the people. Time had gotten away from him and as he arrived to the back side of the staging to catch his ride, he found that the other preachers had already been driven back to their hotels. His transportation had left without him, but he did not get mad, instead he asked God what He was doing in the situation. Suddenly he saw a mother and father coming towards him carrying their little girl who was crippled. They presented their child who had braces on her legs and could not walk. In broken English and with a little sign language, the father got across the story of how they tried to get to the stage to be prayed for but they could not make their way through the crowds. They came to the backside of the stage in hopes they could find one of the ministers to pray for their crippled daughter.

Dad said to the Lord within himself, "This is why you had everyone leave without me." He smiled at them and said, "You made it to the right man." When he looked at the little girl he remembered the battle he went through when he was young and how God had given him a miracle from polio, saving him from ever having to wear leg braces. He said that in that moment such a powerful anointing came upon him that when he laid hands on that child, he could barely speak a word of prayer. "Thank you Jesus", was all he was able to speak as he laid hands on those crippled legs. That was it and he knew it was done. He motioned for them to remove the braces and they did so. The father stood her on her feet and she began to run!

Every child or adult Dad ever prayed for who had braces on their legs received a miracle. There were several cases throughout his ministry and he had a one hundred percent healing rate in this area. He believed it was directly tied to his own experience as a child receiving a miracle from polio. That thankfulness had anchored in him a specific compassion for those who were afflicted in this way. He knew that he knew, that God can heal crippled legs, so when he petitioned God for it the miracle always came. I can't explain it fully but I do believe it.

During one of Dad's trips to India there were protestors rioting in the streets. It happened to be the day Dad had to go to the airport to catch his flight home and as he came out of his hotel he viewed the chaotic scene. Thousands of people were crowding and pushing one another as they marched down the middle of the road angrily shouting. The atmosphere was complete turmoil and he had to find a way to get to the other side of the street to catch a cab through the massive crowd of people in front of him. There was absolutely no room to cross to the other side of the street, so he began to pray, "Thank you Lord for making a way." Suddenly some of the people in the procession stopped walking forwards as the rest of the rioters kept moving. He watched as the crowd parted before his eyes and gave him a window of opportunity with just enough time to get across the street to the cab. He often chuckled about that experience and would say that it was his Red Sea parting. Like I have said before, the miracles in India are too numerous to tell, but God did a great work through his generals that were sent on those missions to India. Dad would go back often bringing with him different groups of preachers to present the gospel to the hungry people of India. Dad described Indians as being people who were desperate for miracles. Those people who came to the crusades did not have much money or technology or doctors to depend on. When you have nothing to lose it's often easier to believe.

~

> "There were so many blind eyes and deaf ears opened and lame made to walk that we couldn't keep count. Miracle after miracle. Thousands saved and set free. It was an amazing display of the goodness of God who came and healed all our diseases. People were healed without anyone laying hands on them to pray. We had to press our way through the crowds of people who wanted prayer, praying our way out every night just to get to our cars. There was one person who was blind and could not reach us but as we were getting in the car the wind came and blew Drummond's coattails causing his coat to touch the persons face. Suddenly they began to shout, I can see! That person received a miracle in such an awesome way!" -Virgil Johnson

~

The early 80's were full of miracle testimonies, but one that is crucial to this story must now be given. This is a testimony I heard over and over again growing up. It was told at every new church we visited by my Mom for as long as I can remember. She shared this particular testimony because she was the one who fully experienced it. In 1981 Mom found out she was pregnant again. She said that when she told Dad about it you could have knocked him over with a feather! Dad's reaction was, "My Lord! I'm too old for this!" Mom laughed and replied, "Apparently not!" At the end of 1981 Dad was given an invitation to go and minister in South Africa. It would be the first of nine different evangelistic trips he would have to that country during his lifetime. The doctors predicted the birth of the baby to be around the 16th of March. So Dad scheduled his flight to South Africa to be two weeks after the due date. You guessed it! The baby decided to come on March 31'st, two weeks after the due date, the same day he was scheduled to fly out of Indiana.

They did not have an ultrasound done but God spoke to Dad and told him the baby was a little girl. So the day before he was to leave for South Africa he and Mom settled on a name. They would call me Angel Hope. My name means "a messenger of God who is confident of good". Though my parents didn't give me my name because of that meaning, they did say they called me Angel Hope because they had hope I would be their angel. Dad did not want to leave Mom but he knew he must. So that day when the contractions started, he left for the airport, while my Aunt Debbie went with Mom to the hospital.

My Mom would tell the story like this, "I checked into the hospital at 3:30 and had Angel at about 5:30. Afterwards I felt like I could have gotten up and gone shopping at the mall. I didn't feel like I had just had a baby and believe me I know what that is like, because Jeremiah was eleven pounds six ounces and twenty-two inches long! With Angel I had a completely pain free birth. When the contractions came I would feel pressure but no pain. The nurses would be in and out of the room during that time and they would say to me, 'Mrs. Johnson you have such control!' I would just chuckle to myself and think, I'm not in control, God is in control! My sister Debbie was with me the entire time and in-between contractions we would be cutting up, laughing or praising the Lord. What a wonderful atmosphere there was. Later that day Virgil called me from the airport in New York and told me he had cried the whole flight there. He had cried and prayed 'Lord, I'm going to South Africa to take care of Your bride, won't you please take care of mine.' And He did!"

Like I said, this is by far my favorite testimony! What a miracle and what a beautiful reality to be born into. Mom had a completely painless delivery and that was a miracle! Anyone who has ever given birth can testify to that. Mom was doing so well after my birth that the doctor released her that evening so she wouldn't have to stay the night and incur more cost. I can't tell you how many times I sat in the crowd of a church on the front row and listened to my Mom give the testimony of my birth. It would fill my heart with joy until I thought it would burst. My Dad would often add to her testimony of how they decided to name me Angel Hope and he would always boast in the Lord of how I did grow up to be their angel. God poured out His goodness upon my parents and I am living proof.

Dad traveled to South Africa and had amazing meetings. One particularly notable meeting took place in Port Elizabeth at a church that held close connections with Drummond Thom and where many miracles happened from Dad praying for the sick. Several ambulances came from near by hospitals transporting several terminal cancer patients to these meetings. Each and every patient who had been brought from the hospital was instantly healed of cancer! That series of meetings stirred up a lot of attention for Dad's ministry, so much so that a preacher from Australia that had been present at the services invited Dad to come to his church. This preacher said he had never seen miracles like the ones he saw at those meetings and his country was so hungry for the message Dad was carrying. Of course he wanted to go home and see his baby girl, but he knew God was making a way for the doors in Australia to be open to him, and so he agreed to go. There he had wonderful services and made a lot of connections, some of which would last a lifetime. While in Australia he received another invitation to go and minister in Puerto Rico. God was up to something good in this entire series of events and Dad was along for the ride. Four weeks went by before he got to hold me in his arms. When he arrived in Puerto Rico he bought tickets for Mom, Jeremiah and I to come and join him. The flight attendants on the plane were all amazed at how good I was on the flight. They said if they hadn't seen me with their own eyes they would have never known there was a baby on board. It's plain to see I was born to fly.

We arrived in Puerto Rico and my Dad's heart was so full of joy when he met me. He used to tell me about how he first got to know me while walking up and down the beach in Puerto Rico. When he had me alone in his arms he said to God, "Lord, I'm too old. I won't have the time to take her places and show her the world." God reassured him with this reply, "I will give her a husband who will take her around the world." That comforted his heart but little did he know that he would have many opportunities to take me around the world during the rest of his time here on earth.

I have been traveling the world since I was four weeks old. I have slept in hotels, airports, on planes and in the back of a car more times than I could count. During my childhood I probably spent more nights in hotels than in my own room at home. Besides Puerto Rico I traveled with my family in the ministry to Canada, England, South Africa, Australia and New Zealand as well as forty-eight of the United States. Dad was able to take me to many places and show me how to enjoy life while working in ministry for the Lord. I know not every preacher's kid has this kind of story but I can't imagine my life being any better than it has been living in the pursuit of fulfilling God's purpose.

My first calling was worship. Having been in the womb of one of the most anointed singers, it is seems only natural that I came into this world singing. I have ministered through song in countless churches and lead song service along with my Mom at our home church. Though I had the gift of song it was Mom who taught me how to worship and that is a gift that goes beyond a melody. I was taught that it was not my song but the anointing poured out on me and through me that would touch people's lives. That lesson translated beyond singing and into my very being. Had I not been trained up in this way I would simply be someone with a nice voice, and there are plenty of people like that in this world. It took years of growing up to fully comprehend this but because of my Mom I was taught how to worship through song in spirit and in truth.

We returned home from Puerto Rico and almost as soon as we did we were invited to go back to South Africa, this time with an open ended schedule. So many had been touched by Dad's ministry that the news spread across the country and many people wanted him to come and minister. Dad having literally traveled the circumference of the globe from Indiana to South Africa, then to Australia and back around to Puerto Rico, was featured in the local Richmond news paper. It's not often a small town man goes around the world. And many people who knew him as he was growing up had a lot of doubt he would ever be able to claim such a thing.

Dad explained his success in this way, "I had a vision. I told everyone I knew when I was about fourteen years old that I would build the biggest church in town, be on television and go around the world. By the time I was forty-four the local news paper put me in their front page headline and wrote an article about how I had built one of the largest churches in town, had a telecast from that church and had just gone on my first trip around the world. That was fourteen to forty-four. But guess what, I had a vision. A lot went on between fourteen and forty-four, but I never lost sight of my vision. My faith is knowing that as I seek Him I will be rewarded but that is not enough. I had to have that vision to keep me on that road that He had laid before me. From the time He said, 'Come follow Me.', I was determined to see His will be done."

Dad began to make arrangements for us to go to South Africa. He didn't know exactly how long we would be there, but he knew it would be for a while. He decided to go there a little bit ahead of us so he could make arrangements for us to live there. This is when turmoil began to brew at Stone Valley. Dad's lifelong friend and board member of the church began to plant lies about Dad in the hearts of some of the other members. This man, whom Dad loved very much, saw himself as the one who should be in Dad's place leading the church. The devil had spun a story in his mind and he chose to believe he was the one who should be pastor. This man thought that the church was prospering financial and that was most likely his biggest motivation in wanting to take over the church. Money and power and control are seductive agents. Truth of the matter was, that the church itself was barely bringing in any money. Dad was financially supporting the church by going out and evangelizing and pouring most of the offering money he received into the church's financial needs. I do not know exactly what made this man act the way that he did, but I do know what he did was not of God and what he did hurt my Dad's heart. But Dad never hated the man for his wrongful treatment, in fact he loved him. So much so that whenever he would visit Richmond throughout the years Dad would always invite the man out for a steak dinner, just to remind him of that love. After all, love bears no record of wrong doing.

This deceived man who wanted control of Stone Valley church threatened to take Dad to court over the matter, claiming he had enough support from the board to overthrow him as pastor. This was a pivotal moment in Dad's life and God was about to speak yet again. This time when Dad sought the Lord the Lord presented him with a question, "Where is your heart? Is it in the church or in Me?" It was a big question to ask. Most pastors would have been in total panic mode when they learned someone was attempting to usurp their power by trying to take over their church. But Dad had come to know the nature of God so well, that if he was being posed with a question such as this, there could only be one answer. Because his heart was in God he knew he had to walk away from the church that he had spent so many years working to build. He answered the Lord's question, "Surely Lord you know my heart is in You." The Lord replied, "Resign." The next day he told the man who wanted control that he could have it, and that day he signed Stone Valley church over to him.

After the transfer of the church was complete Dad realized something about himself. He said, "I was pastor and I ran my church and my ministry. But then God broke me and He runs it now." When Dad resigned and moved away from Richmond his ministry began to go in a completely new direction. A direction that Dad could have never known would be a part of the plan unless he had walked away from Stone Valley. While living in South Africa God unleashed a message through my Dad that would impact the Kingdom and countless lives through a detailed teaching of the gift of discernment. That revelation was birthed through the test of being willing to let go of the kingdom he had unknowingly built for himself. Dad was not only being tested on obedience but God wanted to know how he would react in the situation. There must have been some part of Dad that was building the church for himself in the name of God, if God saw the need to ask him where his heart was, and this situation was exactly what needed to happen to shine light on that very thing. God already knew the answer to the question but God asked this to reveal something about Dad to himself. Sometimes human nature wants to hold onto what we have known in the past, especially if what happened in the past was good. But sometimes we are required to let go of good to obtain better. That's why obedience to His word is so key to an abundant life. His ways are higher than ours and if in humility we are willing to bow to that Life giving flow He will take us to places we could have never reached on our own. God was not only leading Dad out of that church in Richmond but He was truly setting him on a new path. It was his first step in being led out of what the church world has created into a form of fleshly service to God. No more would Dad be working out his own plans for his ministry but would now fully submit to God having complete control.

~

"Man wants to be in control of God's work rather than God being in control of man's work. When God is in control, men get no glory." -Virgil Johnson

~

The church world as we know it has become a manmade instrument used to glorify the flesh and achieve its own end. Or perhaps more simply put, the carnal has tried to mix itself with what is Spiritual. God wants no flesh mixed with what is of the Spirit. It is the most seductive thing to the religious mind to think that we should have some sort of say in how the Holy Spirit does things. So people gather together in church and implement order and ritual and make everything exactly the way they think it should be and afterwards invite God to come. This is totally out of the order in which the Spirit was made to operate and yet so many are surprised when He doesn't show up in power in that pre-orchestrated service. No one can manufacture the power of the Holy Spirit, though many have tried. Maybe God is saying to you right now, "Is your heart in the church, or is it in me?" How will you answer? Can your mind even see the distinction between the two? Church is God, God is church. Wait, what? No. God is God. His children are the righteousness of God in Christ who make up a world wide church that He calls His body. His church is comprised of members of His body each having a specific function that is used to help the other members so that together it all works in perfect unity and for His purpose. The Holy Spirit is the Unifier and flesh does nothing but cause division. When the carnal has submitted to letting God lead, having been transformed by the mind of Christ to be overcomers, then there is perfect unity and liberty among the brothers and sisters in the family of God.

~

"It is time to speak the truth in the Spirit to identify who we are that we may be overcomers in Christ. How difficult it is to explain the facts of life to a child who has not matured to a level to have need of relationship? We are dealing with a church world that is immature, that has not yet seen the need spiritually to grow up and have a relationship with God. The only need that we have identified as children, is to build a building to give us security and identity. The security of children is identified by the home they live in. But mature adults realize that a house is not security. But it is love that makes a home." -Virgil Johnson

~

In the book of Acts chapter 17, Paul said that God made all things and He does not dwell in a temple made with fleshly hands. Flesh and Spirit cannot be mixed to create something Spiritual. My Dad found that out during what most would call the peak of their ministry. He finally obtained all he had labored for. It was not wrong that he did that work, in fact it was good. But God had something better and Dad had to have his eyes opened to see this reality to be able to make that separation. When his eyes were open to see the truth he realized the only way he was able to make the right decision was because he had dug his foundation deep on the Rock Christ Jesus.

~

"I have built my foundation on the rock. I've had my first wife die, my associate pastor try to destroy my church and I've had people slander and lie about me. But my foundation was dug deep in Jesus and built on that solid rock. You had better know who He is. You had better walk with God and talk with God. You had better be able to hear His voice. You had better be able to call on Jesus and He be right there! We are living in a day when you had better be able to command the devil to flee and then watch him run! You better know God and know who He is and that you are one with Him." -Virgil Johnson

~

My family lived and traveled throughout the country of South Africa for an entire year. When we first arrived, a supporter of Dad's ministry gave him a top of the line Mercedes diesel motor home so that we would always have transportation and a place to stay while in the country. This was one of many provisions the Lord made for us during our time there. While in South Africa we ministered at many, many churches. As well as the native villages of the Zulu and the Xhosa tribes. There were even adventures and milestones for us children. My brother got to ride an ostrich during our adventures and I took my first steps. We also had the opportunity to go on a safari in the Kruger Nation Park. A place where the visitors are kept safely in an enclosed area while the animals run free in the wild.

It was while we were in South Africa that God gave Dad the idea to put into book form his revelation of how to define and use the gift of discerning of spirits. Many great men and women of God moved in this gift ever since the outpouring of the Holy Spirit but there were very few who taught on the gift, what its function was and how to operate in it. If you have not read How To Discern Spirits I would highly recommend you pick up a copy after you finish this book. It is a detailed yet simple teaching that explains how the gift of discernment is ultimately meant to be used to discern yourself. To know your thoughts and the intents of your heart and to learn how God thinks and speaks so that you can compare the two and know the difference. This is how we learn to separate the flesh from the spirit. Once you know His voice it is easy to know when the enemy tries to speak his lies. If you know what is in you, then it becomes easy to identify other spirits around you. It's a beautiful gift and the key to being set free from the carnal mind.

~

"What captivates us? What motivates us? What rules us? What makes us who we are? We must examine ourselves with the gift of discernment. And it's not a one time examination but an almost daily examination." -Virgil Johnson

~

(Photo of Mom, Jeremiah and I with Zulu natives)

On our first time driving our motor home in South Africa we happened to get a flat tire while traveling through uninhabited areas on our way to the next city to preach. There were no gas stations or houses around for many miles and no traffic or hope of someone stopping to assist. We were strangers in a foreign country in a vehicle that was just given to us and it was just after dusk in a country where lions and cheetahs roam wild. Most people would have gotten a little worried or very scared being stuck in a situation like this, but when your feet are shod with the gospel of peace you can not be shaken. Thankfully there was a spare tire and a lug wrench in the motor home. Dad gathered the tools and went out to change the tire but as he was removing the lug nuts the last one would not budge and suddenly the lug wrench broke. Dad told my Mom to put us kids to bed as he got a lawn chair out of the motor home and sat outside near the tire to have a talk with his Best Friend. He said, "Lord, I know I could get aggravated, I could feel frightened but I won't. I'm going to stay my mind on you." He sat for maybe fifteen or twenty minutes praising and thanking the Lord and then the Lord spoke very specifically to him, "Get up and look under the driver's seat. There are a pair of vice grips." Obediently he opened the door and reached under the seat and there was the very tool the Lord had said would be there. The Lord spoke again, "Put the tool on, squeeze it tightly and don't yank it but lean on it." As Dad did just as the Lord said an unmistakable metal squeaking sound could be heard as the lug nut loosened and soon became free. The Lord is an ever present help in the time of need! With praise on his lips Dad changed the tire and we drove on into the next town and got a good night's sleep.

Dad spoke about what he had learned from this experience and shared it with us in these words, "I went beyond the carnal mind. There was nothing I could have done in the natural, I didn't know there were vice grips under that seat! But I went beyond the carnal mind and its limitations and reached into the realm of the Spiritual mind and the Lord began to reach me and gave me an answer. There is an answer for your family, there is an answer for your problems, there's healing for your body, there is peace for your mind, there's financial blessing for you! There is a reality that you can raise your children on! But we can't continue to go in this carnal mind of limitations and fears! We must operate in the Spirit so that we glorify the Father in the Son! Then He will say, go ahead, whatever you ask I WILL do!"

Our year of evangelizing in South Africa was so full of God's provision that it was the largest amount in offerings Dad's ministry had ever received in one year up to that time. With this money we had every need met while living in South Africa and also secured us a place to live when we got back to the states. Louisville, Kentucky would be the next place we called home. It was where my godfather Drummond's ministry was based and one of the reasons why we chose Louisville to be our temporary home state. Shortly after we got back to the U.S. Dad published the How To Discern Spirits book and it soon became in great demand. After the release of the book he was being sought after even more to hold seminars on teaching the gift of discerning spirits.

Here are some excerpts from the How To Discern Spirits book:

"Today most Bible colleges require a course in psychology, a study of the process of a person's mental nature and behavior. Discerning of spirits is not psychology, but GODchology, God's plan to deal with man. 'But Jesus needed not that any should testify of man: for he knew what was in man.' John 2:24-25"

"The only way the antichrist will be able to work is through the lust, lies, and deception of man. God is now trying to prepare us, through the gift of discerning of spirits, for the battle, so that we may not be deceived and the last great battle may be won. This is why God has laid it upon my heart to write this book... that people may know the working of the gift of discerning spirits and that we may prepare man for the battle."

"If I do not deal with myself then I become the blind leading the blind and we both fall in a ditch. How many church boards are blind? How many congregations are blinded to this truth? They may be able to organize according to the flesh or the tradition of the church but are they able to discern the needs of those around them? It seems today that the role of the church has reversed. Instead of getting a group of people together to meet the needs of the people we get a group of people together to meet the needs of church organization. It's now time for our eyes to be open according to the Spirit that we may preach deliverance to the captive and recovering of sight to the blind, to set at liberty those who are bruised (Luke 4:18). Then we shall know what the scripture means when it says 'Quick and powerful and sharper than any two-edged sword.' It's time we let God deal with man instead of man dealing with man."

"In the day in which we are living, with all the books and tapes and literature that are available, we ought to be great teachers. Man has taught from head knowledge, not remembering the first principle of God; God is a Spirit (John 4:24). Therefore, if we discern the Spirit of God which is good, then it is not difficult to discern that which is evil. That is why I feel this book is so necessary... that as long as we teach from the dead letter, how shall we find life?"

"Today it is very hard to find pastors who want to go into battle. They would rather compromise with and pacify the devil than stir him up because they do not have the weapons of warfare...the nine spiritual gifts. They know that if they go to battle they may lose the position they hold. It is time that the church be equipped with the nine spiritual gifts and ready to go to battle; that last great battle to be fought. Pastors can no longer hide behind the pulpit or find excuses any more."

"If the church will awake and hear God's voice, they will pass from darkness into life. The main hindrance today in the church is condemnation because of not knowing the voice of God (Romans 8:1). There is now no condemnation to them which are in Christ Jesus, who walk not after the flesh, but after the Spirit."

"When we know His voice it is so easy to flow in the Spirit of God. This is the reason I have been successful in using the gifts around the world. Accurately and quickly, I have been able to separate the thought which is from God, whether I am in church or in a restaurant, or sitting in someone's home. It does not matter if I am standing among a group of unbelievers or standing with the righteous of God. The reason we have seen the gifts manifested at times in church services is because we lay aside flesh and enter into the Spirit for a time. But in the day which we now live, we need to walk in the Spirit. We do not have time to wrestle weeks and months over whether God has spoken or not."

"But today hearing the voice of God seems to be absent in the ministry. We have seen many rise to success, not because of their hearing the voice of God but because they were good organizers. In this great move of God, we will find that the anointing breaks the yoke for those that can hear the voice of God and those that are truly called of God."

Almost as soon as we got back into the country we settled into our new home in Louisville and then left the state for my first trip out west. We ministered through many states on our way to Denver, Colorado. Dad was invited to be a speaker at the World Missionary Conference held in Denver in 1984. He was invited to teach classes on discerning of spirits for three days, and on his first day of teaching the room was packed and there was standing room only. They had to move the class to a larger room the next day to accommodate everyone who wanted to learn. T.L. Osborn was attending the conference as a speaker and told Dad he had read the book on discernment and that it greatly impacted his life.

God gave Dad a specific message to share with the crowd of five thousand ministers on the morning he was key note speaker at the conference. This was a service separate from the classes he was teaching. The sermon was entitled God Needs More Asses. A message born out of the word the Lord had given him when He appeared to him in his room in 1965. It was a beautiful message of how we as ministers of the gospel are not the Word but only carriers of the Word. Like the foal of an ass that carried Jesus into the city, so are we to be broken by Him that we may be able to carry the gospel. That little donkey was not the focus of the people as Jesus rode upon him but he did carry Jesus to the people. The people on palm Sunday never said hosanna to the ass only hosanna to the King! The only thing recorded in the bible as having the right to rebuke a prophet is as an ass (Balaam's donkey). And it was with the jawbone of an ass that Samson defeated the Philistines. The key part of us that the Holy Spirit wants control of is our mouth or jawbone so that we may defeat the enemy as the oracles of God with the word of our testimony. He wrapped up this revelation by adding that if you are not willing to let God make an ass out of you, you will surely make an ass out of yourself. Dad spoke about the truth of this word applied to his own life by saying, "I asked God to make an ass out of me. I moved in all the fivefold ministry but I had never been broken until He appeared to me in my room and I sought for Him to make out of me an ass. Not an apostle, not a prophet, not a pastor, not a teacher, not an evangelist but an ass. God told me He doesn't need any more preachers what he needs is asses."

~

"Humble yourself in the sight of the Lord and He will lift you up" James 4:10 (KJV)

~

Dad understood how without God we are nothing and when we comprehend that truth He will increase our value. Someone who considered themselves my Dad's enemy called one day to tell him that they were praying he would be brought to naught. Naught means nothing or zero. This man spoke to declare his desire that Dad would be brought to destruction but Dad had a keen way of taking what was meant for a curse and knowing how to turn it around to be a blessing. He said in reply to that man, "Keep on praying brother!" Dad wanted to be nothing. He wanted to be nothing so that God could be everything in him. He wanted to be made a zero because when a zero is placed next to The One it becomes a ten. If you are the one, in your flesh you can never be more than a one but if Jesus is The One and you are the zero next to Him you become more. He multiplies you and exalts you when you humble yourself before Him, and if you die daily and are made to be zero, then everyday a zero is added to the right of that One. Before you know it He has lifted you up because of The One.

~

"I've seen the flesh elevated in every revival. As soon as man gets to the place where God can use him, he tries to use God. And so almost as soon as the revival comes, it ends. Because God will not contend with the flesh having its way. Only the Holy Spirit can have its way if homes and cities and nations are to be transformed by the power of God!" -Virgil Johnson

~

Dad had another visitation that I must tell you about but this time it wasn't Jesus who appeared. While ministering in Cape Town, South Africa for three nights straight he cast demons out of several different people who had come up for prayer. After those meetings concluded he was invited to the house of a nationally renowned medical doctor who believed he was cursed by a tribal witch doctor. When Dad arrived at this mans house he knew by discernment that the doctor was losing his mind but he also noticed voodoo paraphernalia in the room that the doctor was keeping in his possession. Dad began to pick up each of these items and throw them in the trash. As he began to throw them away someone else who was there tried to stop him by saying, "Aren't you afraid of the devil?" He replied, "No, he's afraid of me!" He prayed for that doctor and saw the doctor instantly delivered from the demon that was tormenting him.

The night after all this transpired Satan appeared on the balcony of the apartment Dad was staying in. The Prince of Liars walked into the room and pointed his finger at Dad and said, "Virgil, you've been challenging me." Dad responded, "That I have." The devil replied, "I'm going to show you how real I am. I'm going to walk up and touch you." The devil started towards Dad with his arm outstretched and when he came near he touched Dad on his arm. As soon as Satan touched him Dad began to chill like he had a high fever and every muscle in his body began to jerk. It took him a few moments to get his mind focused enough to say, "Yes, you've touched the flesh. You are real. But that which you have touched is dead and that which is alive is my spirit. And you are a spirit and I will defeat you in the Spirit!" With that declaration, Satan disappeared.

~

"There are two deaths. I have been crucified with Christ and yet I live and yet not I but Christ that lives in me. (Galatians 2:20) Why do I need to die again if I have been crucified? Sanctification is second death. I've already died to sin through the crucifixion of Jesus but I have to die to self to be sanctified, to be made into a vessel of honor and fit for the Master's use! (2 Timothy 2:21) I must be sanctified with the word of truth so that I will no longer live after the flesh but the Spirit. So that I may be made alive in the Spirit and justified in the Spirit. So many people are dead to the law and you couldn't get them to sin because they know it's wrong, but to no longer even have the desire to sin is to be sanctified or dead to the flesh. If you are dead to the flesh then no devil can make that flesh come back to life." -Virgil Johnson

~

As I was growing up we traveled from one state to the next. Ministering all over the country and seeing the sights if we had time in-between meetings. We ministered out west a lot and so many miracles happened in the farm lands of Nebraska. Once a father came to a meeting carrying with him his little girl that was about eight years old. He laid her on the platform and asked if Dad would pray that she receive a miracle. The girl was skin and bones with her eyes rolled back in her head, literally at deaths door. She had been diagnosed with brain cancer and two weeks prior the doctors had sent her home from the hospital to die, giving her only two weeks to live. Dad knelt down by the child and prayed. He soon heard the voice of the Lord say, "Three days and I will heal her and she will go back to school and be an A student." Dad told the father of the girl what the Lord had said. The father then gently picked up the limp body of his child and replied, "That's good enough for me", and he went home. Three days later the child's grandfather came to church and stood up to testify. He said, "This morning I got up early to go over to my sons house, before I had to milk my cows. As I went into the house it was full of commotion. I asked what happened and my son told me that my grand baby woke everyone up this morning, fixing her own breakfast!" Praise God!

While living in Louisville Jeremiah accidentally shut my tiny two year old finger in a door. Like most little sisters I was trying to play with my big brother and he didn't want me in his room. He went to shut the door to his bedroom, not knowing my hand was on the frame, and the next thing he knew I was screaming at the top of my lungs. Then he saw the tip of my middle finger on the floor. He carefully picked it up and brought it to Mom and she very nearly passed out at the sight of it. After overcoming the initial shock, she got on the phone to call for help. Dad was out of the country at the time so Mom called my godfather Drummond. He and his wife came to pick us up and take us to the hospital. Louisville had one of the top surgical hospitals in the nation and they were able to sew my finger tip back on. They did such a good job with the surgery that you cannot tell it was ever detached. Though God was working through the entire situation, the big miracle in this story is when we received a letter in the mail from the hospital a few weeks after the surgery notifying us that the hospital was forgiving all of the debt from the surgery without us ever applying for aid or leniency. We never had health insurance but God never failed and He always made a way!

After about a year of living in Kentucky we relocated to Lafayette, Louisiana. There we would meet lifelong friends and ministry partners. We were invited to Louisiana by a pastor who had a church and wanted Dad to partner with him in ministry. This church had a Christian school and Jeremiah and I would attend school there for the next few years. We all made many friends but Mom found one in a rather peculiar way. One evening while Dad was out of town and Jeremiah and I were in bed asleep, Mom heard a knocking at the front door. It was around ten o'clock at night and Mom answered the door in her robe, as she herself was about to go to sleep. A woman was standing at the door and she said, "Please, I need help." Mom replied, "What can I do to help you?" The woman answered, "First I want to tell you that I am a Mormon. My husband and I are having problems and he just left me." There was a sadness and desperation in her voice as she continued, "I know you are a Christian, I've seen you in your yard and seen your joy. I've heard you singing and you must be a Christian. You're a Christian aren't you?" Mom smiled and answered, "Yes I am, come on in and we can talk."

Mom had never met this woman in her life and yet this woman had observed the love of God inside of her from just watching her from afar as she was living her everyday life. The lady came into our home and sat with Mom that night as Mom willingly opened up her heart to listen. Mom spoke life and truth as she encouraged the woman to trust God in her situation. The woman asked Mom to sing to her and Mom played a tape cassette of the background music she sang with and sang to the woman three songs. She breathed hope into this woman's heart and prayed with her before she left to go back home around midnight. The next morning this lady came to the spirit-filled church that we attended and she set out on a new path to being transformed. The presence of God drew this woman in and she not only found help that night but hope and love and a friend. She and Mom established a good relationship and remained friends for many years.

In South Africa God not only gave Dad the idea for How To Discern Spirits but his second book as well. When we moved to Louisiana Dad put into book form his mustard seed revelation which he titled Beyond The Faith of Man. This book is about Mary the mother of Jesus. It is only two chapters long but became almost as big a seller as How To Discern Spirits. It beautifully describes the faith of Mary. Mary was just an ordinary girl who chose to believe the word of the angel and the confirmation of the Holy Spirit. She had to walk out her faith the same as all of us. She even had to accept the price Jesus paid for her salvation at the cross. Mustard seed faith has always been preached as the size of one's faith being as small as a mustard seed but the Holy Spirit revealed to Dad that it is not the size of the mustard seed that was being highlighted but the persistence of the seed. It is powerful, unstoppable and will grow anywhere under any condition. By 1989 this new book was being printed and How To Discern Spirits on its second printing.

Here are a few excerpts from Beyond the Faith of Man.

"The time has come for the church to face its lack of power. All our witty inventions and 'higher theology' have not brought forth the true and glorious manifestation of Christ that the world is dying without. We cannot bring forth from our mere selves that which will lift humanity out of its tragic situation. Like Mary we must conceive, carry, birth, raise, and release to the world that Holy One which is not from the earth. We must be over-shadowed and overwhelmed by the Holy Spirit. We must be able to say to the Lord, 'Be it unto me according to thy word.' The word of faith which produces real Christianity is beyond the faith of man."

"I cannot prove to you by any natural credentials that I am a Christian, that I have been born again. Nevertheless I am a part of the family of God. The Bible tells us that signs shall follow the believers. I have my inheritance and the Word of God tells me, 'Freely you have received, freely give:' (Matthew 10:8). You can only give away what you have. Thank God, I have my birthright. The world may not always accept it but I know I am a son of God, not THE Son, but a son nonetheless."

"It is imperative to any ministry that the approval of the Holy Ghost be upon it. Mary may not have fully comprehended her situation but she knew she had a relationship with God through the power of the Holy Ghost. This should be the number one priority in every believer's life. I believe that after Mary experienced this no one could talk her out of it. After standing in the shadow of God why would one want to stand in the shadow of man and his institutions and ideals? I have looked into the eyes of prominent people with outstanding ministries who knew they had compromised for the acceptance of man. There I saw emptiness, a tormented soul, and I knew that through their comprise, they had missed God's blessings and settled for second best."

Once Dad preached the sermon on Beyond the Faith of Man at the Immaculate Conception Catholic church in Washington, PA. It was one of the only times he was ever invited to a Catholic church to minister. Many, many of the different denominations would invite Dad to come and preach and he never refused any of them based on their doctrinal beliefs. He would say that the name on the church didn't make a difference because no matter where you go people are all the same. Many Catholics who heard the message of Beyond the Faith of Man could really identify with the word about Mary and her faith because they revered her faith so much. After he preached the sermon at that church in Washington most of the congregation lined up for prayer and the first ones in line were the priests. Each one of those men asked for the baptism of the Holy Ghost! Forty people received miracles that night and in addition to the priests thirty others received the baptism of the Holy Ghost with the evidence of speaking in tongues.

While visiting a church in Louisiana my brother was introduced to praying for the sick in a very similar way to how Dad was introduced to believing for healings and miracles. Jeremiah was around the age of thirteen at the time while we were ministering at a church with a large congregation. The prayer line was so long that Dad had to split them up into two lines and ask Jeremiah to help him pray for the people. Jeremiah said, "I don't know what to pray." Dad spoke words very similar to what his mother had spoken to him when he was just an eleven year old boy learning how to pray for people. He answered Jeremiah and said, "Just take their hands in yours, ask the Lord to heal them, believing. Then stand back and watch it happen." Don't you love the simplicity of God? Jeremiah did as he was told and two people in his prayer line received instant miracles. The first was an older lady who had become blind from cataracts. After Jeremiah prayed the way he had been instructed to, the woman was instantly able to see with perfect clarity! The second to receive an instant miracle was a young man who was almost completely deaf. Jeremiah prayed for him and they tested his hearing to confirm that his hearing had been fully restored! The young man was so thankful for Jeremiah praying for him that he brought him a skateboard the very next night as a thank you gift for Jeremiah's faith and courage to step up and do something he had never done before. This gift made an impression on Jeremiah's heart because at that age he was quite the avid skateboarder. It spoke to him of how much God loved him. The skateboard was special but temporary. The experience of seeing the miracles will last him a lifetime.

~

"Train up a child in the way he should go: and when he is old, he will not depart from it." Proverbs 22:6 (KJV)

~

(Photo of my family from 1987)

I will tell you of one more miracle that took place while we were sojourning in Louisiana. It happened while we were ministering in Ft. Lauderdale, Florida. A Cuban man and his wife came to the prayer line together for prayer and the husband told Dad that he had been in a life of drugs for many years. Just a year prior the man had given his life to the Lord and been completely set free from that life, but there had been an unforeseen consequence as a result of it. While living his life apart from God the man had contracted AIDS from a contaminated needle. He only became aware of the disease six months after he married his wife, thus unknowingly passing the disease to her. They felt as if they had been handed a death warrant by the doctors but they were believing God to intervene. Dad agreed with them that the Lord would give them both a miracle and after he laid hands on them to pray the Lord spoke and said, "I have healed them both." Dad relayed the message to the couple and a week later they had a doctors confirmation that both of them were completely healed of AIDS!

We didn't stay very long in Louisiana but our years there were full of the goodness of God. After about five years of living in Louisiana the Lord directed us to move to Greensboro, North Carolina. Dad's invitations to speak on Christian television increased and the word about his books got out even more. The owner of Whitaker Press in Pittsburgh, Pennsylvania happened to see Dad on television one day and contacted Dad to order a book. The same day the man finished reading How To Discern Spirits he called Dad to tell him that he believed the book was best seller material and proceeded to order twenty-five hundred copies to begin to distribute in Christian bookstores around the nation. The book was even made available for purchase around the world in every country where Whitaker Press distributed books.

During that year we lived in Greensboro my Papaw came to live with us after he had had a massive stoke and needed full time care. My Dad did not want his dad in assisted living so he offered to help by having him live with us, but my Papaw missed Indiana too much and stayed only for a few months before going back home. Shortly after he went back to Richmond his others sons admitted him into an assisted living facility and he lived there until he passed away on November 28, 1992. He was a man whom Jesus loved and was faithful to stand beside a wife who had a calling and supported her through it all. Though through the worlds eyes he may not have been an important man, he was key to the legacy handed down to me. I look forward to seeing him again soon.

I would also like to mention the passing of my Grandpa Burdette who passed into glory on February 13, 1995. I unfortunately didn't know him well because we didn't visit Richmond very often as I was growing up, but I know he was a good and kind man. In his last years his memory had begun to fade and the last time we visited him he remembered my parents but not Jeremiah and I. On the day he died he was found in his favorite easy chair and dressed in his Sunday best. Apparently in the middle of the night he had gotten up from his bed and dressed himself in a suit to sit in his chair to wait on the Lord to come and take him home. My Dad said that he wouldn't have been surprised if Grandpa had packed his suit case as well. I look forward to getting to know him better when I see him again in heaven.

~

"There is a reality. There is a relationship that is meant to be between us and God, a closeness. We must learn to hear His voice and stay close to Him so we can continue to hear it. His sheep hear His voice. I know my wife's voice and I could pick it out of a crowd. It's the same with me and Jesus. We need to be able to hear His voice over all those demons that scream lies like 'He's not coming!', 'It's not going to work!', or 'You're going to die!' Whatever the lie is, you need to be able to hear that Voice that says, 'I love you, I'm with you, stand fast!" -Virgil Johnson

~

# 5

## Blank Slate

~

"With the nine spiritual gifts we can outvote the carnal mind. Jesus said we would do the works that He did and greater works. Conquering this carnal mind is the greater miracle! Jesus was born with the mind of His Father and I was born with the carnal mind that must be overcome to take on the mind of Christ. It's how Moses could face Pharaoh. It's how Daniel stood in the lion's den. It's how the Hebrew children walked through the fiery furnace. It's how Peter walked on water. They all overcame the carnal mind and broke into the other side where the Spirit reigns over the flesh. You can live in the reality of the Spirit of Truth that makes you free. Who rules the mind, rules the body." -Virgil Johnson

~

By the end of the 80's things within the church world were shifting. The Charismatic Movement, also known as the charismatic word renewal, had peaked and almost died out. Our lives were also in transitioning and Dad sought direction from the Lord on where He would have us for the next season of our lives. We had a small group of brothers and sisters in the Lord in Greensboro that Dad ministered to, but the Lord did not want Greensboro to be our permanent home just yet. The 90's began a transition of entering into what the Lord would later reveal to Dad as a time of being "stripped down and remade". Dad's ministry would now enter into yet another recreation. This next chapter in our lives would be a season of testing and preparation for our entire family. Without the testing you can't be proven and without preparation you'll never be able to walk in the blessing.

During our last few months of living in Greensboro Dad was invited to speak at a church in Pennsylvania. It was a good sized church with some property and a small congregation of maybe five people. This church had no one to lead them and had been given over to the control of three women. These women offered the church in its entirety to Dad after they heard him minister. The offer had no strings attached, no board members and the property would be his to do with as he saw fit. The ladies offered him the property in hopes that Dad's ministry would bring new life into their own lives and the community by bringing a fresh word and revelation. Dad consulted the Lord and had peace in his heart about taking over this church. Before we knew it we were called to the small town of New Bethlehem, Pennsylvania, a place known as "the town that is twenty minutes from nowhere".

During the 80's the finances of our ministry had increased greatly but during the 90's we had a different experience. From our year in South Africa having been a great time of provision it carried on for the next seven years as there was an explosion of people within the churches hungry for more of God. This resulted in an increase of meetings for Dad as the teaching of how to discern spirits was in high demand. When that Charismatic revival began to come to its end, so the hunger of the church dissolved. Don't get me wrong, people still wanted to know God but by the end of the charismatic word movement the flesh had taken charge of how things should go and the Holy Spirit was quenched. As it has been with every great revival that has preceded it. A fresh outpouring of the Holy Spirit comes in power and begins to renovate and transform until man's carnal thinking gets in the way. Man plans and plots and structures to build its own tabernacles out of the great move which inevitably crowds out the Spirit's ability to have His way.

Within the first few months of Dad taking over the church in Pennsylvania, all but one of the original members left and a whole new group of people came in. We forged many strong friendships with several families and Dad did a lot of one on one mentoring. My Mom also started a women's group that would meet at the church for fellowship to cultivate deeper relationships through fun activities. I was the only child in attendance at every ladies meeting but all the ladies loved me and made me feel welcome. It was at this church I first began to help my Mom lead song service. It was named Lion's Den Church. Not long after leaving Richmond Dad changed the name of the ministry from Living Word to Lion's Den Ministries because it was in the lion's den where miracles happened. It seemed that with every transition his ministry went through a new name was just an outward declaration of the change.

We found a house to buy that was way up on a hill in the middle of farmland. This three acre property was surrounded by corn fields and sold to us by the farmer who kept the crop and cattle on the surrounding property. It was a two story house with a basement. The top floor had four bedrooms and one bathroom and the property came with natural gas rights and its own spring for water. Which meant we didn't have to pay for water or heat. Dad found the house one day while driving by and seeing a for sale by owner sign in the front yard. He contacted the owner who offered to let us live in the house for the first year while paying the entire down payment in installments over the duration of that year. The house was being sold at a very good price and Dad agreed to the deal on the contingency that the seller would guarantee him a loan for the purchase when the end of the year came.

As I mentioned before, we did not have a lot of money at this point in history, but God sent us to Pennsylvania so Dad was confident the Lord would make a way for the purchase of this house. The time came for the purchasing of the house so Dad contacted the seller to find out what the closing costs would be, which was a sum of $3,000. Dad was honest with the seller and told him he was $800 short of having enough money to cover the closing cost. The seller had come to know and trust Dad, as he was faithful to make the down payment installments and proved that he was a man of his word. Dad also had personally ministered to the man and helped him by counseling him during at time when he needed direction. The farmer really wanted us to buy his house so he told Dad that he would loan him the money needed to cover the rest of the closing costs! As always Dad sought God with the situation of not having the full amount of money for the closing costs. The Lord had assured him that He was in the deal and it would all work out and God never failed before so why would He now? It turned out that someone had sent Dad an offering in the mail that was meant to arrive before the day of the closing. That offering was delayed by the postal system and arrived instead three days after the closing. So three days after we purchased the house Dad paid the seller off and had yet another testimony of God's provision.

Twenty miles from nowhere is where I did a lot of growing up. I was just coming into the age of understanding and the middle of nowhere is a good place to establish who you are. The less input a young person has from the world on the subject of who they are or should become means they are more likely to look to God for the answers they seek. In this place that seemed to be the far reaches of the earth we had no cable TV, no kids next door to play with and a forty-five minute drive to the closest Wal-Mart. It was a drastic change from living in the big city of Greensboro where most modern conveniences were essentially right at our finger tips. As I look back, I am so thankful I didn't have as much time spent in front of mindless television. Most of my days outside of attending school were spent exploring our three acres and the land around our property. Being secluded also developed in me a passion for reading which in turn created in me a love of writing. We may not have had a lot in those lean years but we sure had enough and every need was always met. I look back on it now and I can only see the goodness of God raising me up exactly where and how He knew I needed to be raised.

I know it was a struggle at times for my parents and my brother who was a teenager that felt like he had been snatched from paradise and dropped in the barren wilderness. Not getting what you want is not so easy on the flesh, but in my experience it made me appreciate what I had even more once I was mature enough to understand it. I may have struggled less in those years only because I was young and didn't know what I was missing. We were not completely sheltered from the world, as no one can be, nor should be. If we are not exposed to the realities of living in this world we would never have something to compare the good life with. Walking with Jesus is a choice and a life long journey that begins with one step off the path that leads to destruction and onto the narrow way that leads to life. There are many happy accidents that occur on that trail that leads to the top of the mountain and the influences of the world will try to deter the journeyer. But if we are determined to get to the end, Jesus will be with us every step of the way encouraging us to climb higher and we will make it!

Like I said, money was scarce, and if it had not been for the faithfulness of those dear brothers and sisters in the Lord who would give offerings every month, many times we would not have had groceries or paid the bills. Dad was never a salary pastor, so when evangelizing decreased the funds did as well. Dad was on the phone a lot when he wasn't out traveling, constantly keeping in touch with every person who sincerely wanted his guidance. Maintaining those relationships by counseling them or just calling to say he loved them was so important to Dad. A good friend and financial supporter named James Hagerty would often send love offerings or have us to come to his house for home meetings. Jim lived in farm country Ohio and had a large family, as well as a large heart for giving. His generosity often paid the house payment for us. Jim saw the value of the word Dad had been given and connected us to his son Steve in hopes that Dad could help him. Steve soon came to see that same value his father saw in Dad's ministry and through Dad reaching out to him in love Steve was set free to walk on a new path. Through Dad's mentoring Steve trained in the ministry and was greatly helped by Dad. Steve and his sweet wife Lisa, along with their four children, became our close friends.

In the summers we spent a lot of time outside during those times when we weren't traveling. We went to the river to swim and tube, we had a friend who owned horses and would let us ride. We had a four wheeler and a dirt bike for a while, both of which were given to us, and I loved driving the four wheeler while trying to keep up with my big brother on his dirt bike. We picked wild black raspberries and concord grapes that grew on our property that we would make into jams. We had a large vegetable garden that was kindly plowed for us by the farmer who sold us our property. As a family we planted and tended a garden that produced a bountiful crop allowing us to put up preserves which was a great source of provision for our family to eat. Jeremiah was given a pedigree golden retriever by Lisa Hagerty and that dog produced a few litters of puppies, of which Mom was able to care for and sell so that we could have extra income. Winters in Pennsylvania are miserably cold and snowy, but for a kid that meant fun to be had outside sledding and skiing, of which we did both. There were hard times, yes, but the good far outweighed them.

Many of the good times we experienced were during meetings at our church. I loved going to church and being with our family in the Lord. We also had many dear friends who came in as guest speakers to minister from around the U.S. and the world. We heard such good word and saw many miracles. Evangelist Greg McKim, a faithful minister of the gospel and a friend of our family, came to preach at our church when I was suffering from chronic ear aches. I went up for prayer that night because my ear was aching during the service. Brother McKim put his finger in my ear and prayed and spoke to the pain to be gone. He then asked me if it was any better, nothing had changed, so he prayed a second time and still my ear was aching. He prayed a third time and instantly the pain from the ear ache left and I never had another ear ache again!

Dad became a father in the Lord to several men and women that he mentored throughout his ministry. As I have mentioned before, we made lifelong friends in Lafayette, Louisiana. Including a few young men who wanted to be trained in the ministry by Dad, Jerry Dueitt was one of those young men. When we left Louisiana he followed us and lived with us in Greensboro and in Pennsylvania for over four years. Jerry was so determined to be trained in the ministry by Dad that he was willing to make a drastic change and move from his lifelong home of Louisiana to come live with us, knowing that being close was the best way he could learn from Dad. He was assistant pastor at our church in New Bethlehem, until he went back to Louisiana. And he was also a travel companion for Dad when Mom had to stay home with us kids because of school. Jerry became like a second big brother to me and today continues in the ministry as a preacher of the gospel with his lovely wife Roanne.

One adventure Jerry had with Dad while they traveled together in the ministry was while out west. On a cold snowy day in January they were driving through Colorado on Highway 50 when they topped the Colorado Monarch Pass, which is at an elevation of over eleven thousand feet on top of a mountain. It is a high and curvy road that you would not want to have any mishaps on because directly over the guardrail is a steep drop off the mountain. Just as they got to the top Dad opened his mouth to tell Jerry to be careful of ice, and as soon as he said it, they hit a patch of ice and lost control. Jerry shifted in to second gear as the car went spinning out of control and then he accidentally went into reverse which made things even worse. Dad was in the passenger seat saying, "Jesus!", over and over again. Finally they came to a stop in the oncoming traffic lane. It was a miracle they didn't go over the mountain but even more of a miracle that there were no cars coming as they were spinning out of control on the road. Dad instructed Jerry to move the car so they would not be in the oncoming traffic lane, trying to get Jerry to come out of his state of shock. Jerry was so tense he had to have his hands pried off of the steering wheel. Afterward Jerry asked Dad why all he had prayed was the name of Jesus over and over. Dad laughed as he replied, "I was praying up a storm in my head but all that came out of my mouth was Jesus, Jesus, Jesus!"

"Whoever calls on the name of the Lord shall be saved." Romans 10:13 (NKJV)

I will never forget the testimony of the day we were down to $25 in the bank account. Not only were the bills coming due but we needed to buy groceries because the fridge and pantry were almost bare. Dad decided to get himself ready to leave the house and Jerry asked where he was going. Dad replied, "I'm going down to the church to beg God." Jerry laughed and said, "That'll be the day!" Dad left with the purpose of getting alone with God. He had already asked God to intervene weeks before but God had not yet spoken to him about the situation or caused the provision to show up, and now he was down to the wire. While driving to the church Dad had a conversation with the Lord and just before he got to church the Lord spoke and told him to go to the post office instead. Dad obeyed and then immediately drove back home. Jerry greeted him at the door and said, "You came back fast." Dad grinned, showed Jerry a check written for over $2000 and said, "My God will never see me forsaken or begging bread!"

During those years in Pennsylvania we stayed a little closer to home but we still did a lot of evangelizing together as a family. Attending public school was usually the only thing that kept us from going with Dad. In 1994 we were invited to travel to Australia and minister for seven weeks. Jeremiah had already graduated from high school and I would be starting sixth grade during the time we were to be in Australia. Mom knew she couldn't take me out of school for seven weeks straight so she decided she would homeschool me, but there was still a hurdle to overcome. The state of Pennsylvania requires that a parent have a high school diploma or a GED in order to teach their child from home. Mom had just barely missed her graduation from high school because she had chosen to get married a few weeks before receiving her diploma. She made the decision to go back to school to get her GED to be able to teach me. My Mom was always a bright student in school and would have earned her diploma if she hadn't chosen to marry instead. But I know it was not an easy thing to go back and learn and be tested after having been out of practice for so long. But she did it and I will forever be grateful for her determination to do whatever it took to further my education and keep us together as a family. She was my most favorite teacher ever! It turned out that I loved being homeschooled and from then on it gave us much more freedom as a family to travel together. I was homeschooled until I graduated in 2000 and finished high school with test grades well above college grade averages.

With my schooling taken care of Dad scheduled our trip to the land down under and acquired four round trip air plane tickets purchased with accumulated Holiday Inn reward points, (that's a lot of points, I know) and he made arrangements for us to leave the country for seven weeks. With all the preparations in place we set off for the destination of Brisbane, Australia with $75 to our name. After a day layover in Hawaii we arrived in the country with $27 and seven weeks of evangelizing ahead of us. My parents walked in unwavering faith and I am an eyewitness of this truth, it is with joy I do testify of the goodness of God toward us and how He showed up every time, just in time! It may seem like a crazy notion to leave all you have and go to a foreign country with a family of four and no money, but crazy is often what faith looks like. Faith like that can only be produced in a life that is willing to lay it all on the line for the opportunity to live in the reality of the unlimited provision that God is. If He speaks and directs you to go, then He will provide, and you can stake your life on it because God cannot lie.

Upon our arrival in Brisbane we were welcomed with open arms by our dear friends David and Amanda Patch. David was very close to our family, as he had come to live with us for about a year while we were living in Louisiana. When he was called into the ministry he wanted very much to learn what he could from Dad, so he took a year away from family and home to be mentored. His time with Dad dynamically changed David and his ministry, to this day they have a thriving outreach in Brisbane. Our hosts while staying in the Brisbane area were Brad and Glenda McKenzie, members of David's church. They were gracious hosts and became good friends of ours as we spent a few weeks getting to know the couple and their five daughters.

Our first morning in the country, while suffering from jet-lag, my parents woke up at four in the morning and could not go back to sleep. So they decided to go out for a walk to watch the sun rise and admire the many varieties of wild birds that adorned the trees all along their walk. Suddenly a voice came calling out Dad's name, "Brother Virgil!" Mom and Dad both turned to look and saw a man on his morning run coming towards them. Dad recognized the man as one of David's church members and he greeted him with a smile. The runner came to a halt and said, "I heard you were going to be in the country. It is so good to see you again. You know Brother Virgil, the Lord woke me up this morning and told me to give you a thousand dollars." He grinned and continued, "I said to God, if this is You Lord then let me meet Virgil on my morning run. I honestly didn't believe I would and here you are!" They all laughed and marveled together at how amazing God is, as that faithful man counted out ten one hundred dollar bills into Dad's hand. If it hadn't been for the inconvenience of sleep being disturbed by jet-lag, Mom and Dad would have never met that runner. God truly does work all things for the good of those who love Him and are called according to His purpose.

And so began our time in Australia. We traveled for about six weeks from Brisbane to Cairns and from Cairns all the way down the eastern coast of Australia and back to Brisbane. Traveling about two thousand miles total. Then we finished up the trip with about a week in New Zealand. We saw some of the most beautiful of God's creations, from crater lakes surrounded by ancient banyan trees, to the Great Barrier Reef and pristine beaches. We visited an animal sanctuary that sheltered many of the different species native to Australia, where we fed lorikeets and petted wallabies. We ministered at many churches throughout the journey, preaching and singing and spreading the good news. In New Zealand we saw lots of sheep farms and kiwi fruit vineyards, this country has some of the most beautiful landscape in all the world. My favorite memory of New Zealand was the evening we drove up to this little open air building where the people met to worship and we were greeted by the sound of a congregation of mostly indigenous Māori people singing. There were no windows or doors on this building because the climate in that region of New Zealand is nearly always ideal. As we approached we could hear them all singing and they were all on pitch, in perfect harmony and in perfect timing together. If you have ever heard people singing together in church you will know how truly amazing it is when everyone is on key and in sync! I always think of that experience as being my glimpse of what it will be like to hear the heavenly choir.

(Photo of me petting a wallaby)

We returned home from our trip overseas happy, but tired! Seven weeks away from home is a long time to be away from creature comforts but it was so worth it. 1995 was turning out to be an exceptional year for me as it was my first opportunity ministering down under but it was also the year I made a real commitment in my heart to follow Jesus. Like most children raised up in church, I had given my heart to Jesus in a Sunday school class when I was very little but it wasn't until that year I turned thirteen that I felt I fully understood the weight of salvation. After I asked Jesus to renovate my life and truly have all of my heart the Lord spoke to me and said, "I have called you to preach My gospel. If you will follow Me, I will send you around the world." After hearing His voice so clearly for the first time I understood that from that moment on the only way I could respond to the call was purposing to pursue Him. It was a word given to me that would take a lot of trusting and faith on my part to stay the course until it would come about but I have never once doubted that word. Less than a year later, while I was alone in my room praying, I received the baptism of the Holy Spirit. Many life changes happened in that town twenty minutes from no where, in an old farm house on top of a hill. Dad was being stripped down and remade, and I was being called.

On July 19, 1996 a disaster hit New Bethlehem. A dam broke and caused Redbank Creek to swell over seven feet above flood stage. Most of the downtown area was underwater resulting in catastrophic damage. Our church property abutted that creek and the building filled up with seven feet of flood water destroying everything inside. We watched from afar looking down on the valley from on top of a hill as we witnessed the town flooding. It didn't take long for the water to recede and the very next day we were able to go inside our church. Everything inside was covered in several inches of thick mud that was almost as slick as ice to walk upon. The podium and sound equipment were displaced. Jeremiah's drum set was here and there in pieces. The piano and organ were ruined and all the sound equipment was made useless. The offices were in utter disarray, all the printing and audio duplicating equipment was trash. The majority of the tape cassettes were ruined, including all of Dad's masters for the sermons he recorded and sold. All of the vinyl records were destroyed. Many things were lost forever in that flood. Two of the very few tape cassettes that were salvageable were Mom's second and third recorded albums. One entitled From The Cross To The Crown, which was recorded in the early 80's, and the other entitle Jesus My Rock, recorded in the late 80's.

Brother David Patch was visiting at the time and as we stood from afar looking at the church filled with water he looked at Dad and said, "Don't you feel bad Virg'? Aren't you worried or upset?" Dad smiled and said, "No, my heart is not in earthly things." David replied, "Is it alright if I feel bad for you?" Dad laughed, "It's your privilege, go right ahead!" You see, Dad was not tied to the things of this world and stuff is replaceable. He knew anything that was not repeatable that had been lost in the flood was just something that the Lord saw fit to remove. He had no fear of how God would provide for all that was lost because God is Provision, so how could He fail? He knew it would be hard work to rebuild the church but he didn't have a vision of failure. Instead he had a vision of the great opportunities and blessings that God would bring about due to the disaster. What was about to happen could not have happened if the church and all those things in it had not been destroyed by the flood waters. When he looked at that devastation he couldn't feel sorrow. For his heart was full of the joy that comes from the expectancy of the good God would work out of it all.

It took a lot of work cleaning out the church of all that had been destroyed and we did it as a family working together. My Mom's sister Debbie was in town visiting us on vacation when the flood came and she even helped with the clean up. Church members and theirs families pitched in as well and even though we only had a small group of people that attended, as we came together with one purpose we were able to rebuild. After the church was cleared of all the debris inside, the pews that were nailed down to the floor had to be removed. It took several strong men to get the carpet up, as it was so saturated in mud it felt as though it weighed ten times its normal weight. The building underwent a complete gutting but little by little it became a usable space once again and soon we were having church inside, now sitting on those stackable chairs Dad bought so many years ago.

Right before the flood hit Dad had returned from a trip to South Africa, and the Lord had blessed him finically through the offerings given to him. Though money was still not in a great abundance he wanted to be the first person to give money towards the church rebuild. We did not have flood insurance, and though we applied to FEMA for aid, they denied us. So it was left to us and the few people who attended to raise money for the supplies needed. Dad said, "I wanted to be the one to give the first dollar that went into the rebuilding of the church. I was the pastor and so I should be the first partaker." With that purpose in his heart he went to the lumber yard and bought $500 worth of floorboards to show the people his faith in what God would do and to encourage them to not lose hope in a situation that seemed hopeless.

A few months prior to the flood we were given a Dodge van and that van just happened to be downtown in a mechanics garage for repairs when the flood hit. As you can imagine everything in that garage was destroyed. Dad went to the shop a few days after the waters receded to talk to the shop owner who said he didn't have any flood insurance. The owner also said it was very doubtful that he would be able to give Dad any compensation for the lost van. Dad began to thank God for taking care of the situation, and a week later he went back to the garage for an update and was given the same story. On the third week after the flood he went back again and the shop owner greeted Dad by saying, "Has my insurance company gotten a hold of you?" Dad replied that they hadn't and then the man said, "They have already settled with two other people. Here's the number of my insurance company, call them and they'll get you a check."

This is how Dad would tell what happened next, "The van was worth $1800 and the insurance company gave me $3400. This was a van given to me but I didn't particularly want that make and model. I was content with it and never complained to the Lord about it but He knew I would have rather had a different van for traveling. So when that one was destroyed I found the very van I wanted that was valued at $5000 and bought it for $1150, clearing $2200 in the deal. That was five days after I bought the $500 in materials for rebuilding the church. You think that giving that $500 didn't come back to bless me? I didn't get afraid or anxious or depressed, I got challenged. My faith was challenged and I knew I had to lead by example by sowing that money. I didn't know how God would bless me, but I knew that He would and He did!"

Just a few weeks after the flood, Dad was off to Australia again for missions. This time we stayed home and he took a team of preachers with him. It's so amazing to me how even in a time of not having a lot of money readily available, God always made a way financially for the ministry. The Lord provided time and time again because of Dad's faithfulness and the faithfulness of those who partnered with him in giving so that Dad could bring the gospel around the world. God even made a way for our next trip overseas as a family, this time to South Africa again. I had traveled there before but now I was old enough to appreciate it and would actually be able to remember it. We spent some time in London, England before we made it to South Africa and I got my first taste of Europe. While in London we visited West Minister Abbey, Big Ben, the London Tower and the magnificent lion statues in Trafalgar Square. We traveled in an iconic London cab and a double decker bus seeing all the sights.

My Dad passed along to me his love of history and geography. So from a young age I discovered a passion for adventures and a love of traveling. When we traveled we didn't just go to a place but we experienced the culture, this was a better education than any school could have ever offered me and it helped to expand my understanding of just how vast this world of ours is. Reading about a place cannot compare to the education of experiencing it. In South Africa I got to see where the Atlantic Ocean and the India Ocean meet at Cape Point. We traveled from Capetown across the beautiful country filled with wild animal herds to Johannesburg, the largest city in the country. The land scape would go from amazing diverse natural lands to towering sophisticated cities with all the modern conveniences. Many of the people we met during our times of ministering in South Africa became precious friends. I am blessed to have family in Christ that spans across the globe.

On our last week in the country Dad's knees began to swell, one worse than the other. The worse of the two became swollen to about the size of a cantaloupe. The pain was so bad that he could not put his weight on his legs for very long. He was still scheduled to preach meetings and Dad was never one to back down from a spiritual fight. That night when the attack came he preached sitting down in a chair on the platform. He told the people he was just going through a bit of battle and confidently assured them he would get the victory. What a testimony it was for all those people who attended that night, including me. He lived his faith out in the open and was never ashamed of the gospel of Jesus Christ, even when faced with a battle.

Earlier that day the pastor of the church had invited a doctor who was a member of his church to come and visit Dad. Dad let him look at his knee but the doctor couldn't tell for sure what the issue was unless he took an x-ray and ran tests. Dad declined his kind offer. You see, Dad lived by a word he used to speak to many people, "If you give the devil a name you are much more likely to live with it." Now that does not mean you should never be diagnosed, but it was something he believed and so he would rarely ever seek out a doctor to help with a physical issue he was going through. The doctor could have diagnosed the issue but Dad believed it would not help him fight the battle, so he chose to believe that God knew the problem and had the answer to that problem. The doctor sent over pain killers for Dad, though he had not asked him to, and as Dad laid in bed that night the image of that pain medicine sitting on the counter in the bathroom kept coming to him. He woke Mom up and asked her to flush the medicine down the toilet. He said it was beginning to tempt him and he didn't want his mind to be on anything but the Lord.

We went to the airport the next day to fly home and I watched my Dad as tears rolled down his cheeks from the pain of walking. Thankfully we were able to get a ride on a golf cart through the airport to our terminal. The devil had spoken to Dad that morning and said, "The only way you are making it out of this country on that plane is in a box." So no matter how it hurt or what it would take, Dad was determined to prove who God was and push through the pain to get back home. When the devil spoke it was a confirmation to Dad that he would make it home and the miracle was just around the bend. We did fly home and the pain continued but it was at least a bit more bearable as long as he didn't put his weight on his knees. For two weeks after we got home he would wake up and ask the Lord, "Is today the day for my miracle?" And he would get no reply. So he would walk as much as he could and rest as much as he had to, all the while thanking the Lord for the miracle that he had not yet seen.

After two and half weeks he decided to go for a walk, although his knees had not improved. I watched as he labored to walk out the door and heard my Mom ask if he needed help, he replied no. But he did need help, that which only Jesus could give. I watched my Dad hobble outside in severe pain so that he could get alone with his Healer. He walked about a quarter mile by the time he made it to an unpaved back road on the property across from ours. He must have looked really bad off as he was walking because a driver stopped to ask if Dad needed any help. He kindly told him he was alright and the driver went on.

Once he was alone again he cried out to the Lord, "God, if you have stopped using your Son to heal, then give me the name of the doctor you are using to replace Him!" Dad's declaration was not a cry of defeat but a challenge for God to prove Himself yet again. Dad was faithful and he endured the battle as he held onto the knowledge that God had not changed. He reached heavenward for a miracle as he shouted to the sky out of his dissatisfaction for still being in that state of pain. Out of the still quietness of that country road God replied, "I still heal by my Son." That was all Dad wanted to hear. With that confirmation he turned around and started walking back down that gravel road and with each step he took, the pain became less and less. He made it back home and told us that he had gotten the victory. Within three days all the swelling was gone and there was not even a hint of soreness from that devil that had attacked his joints.

Not long after he received this miracle, the Lord gave him a dream directing him to leave Pennsylvania. The small group of friends that we continued to fellowship with in Greensboro had asked Dad if he was willing to come back to start a home church. We had been consistently holding house services in the home of our dear friends Paul and Ava Brewer who were being mentored by Dad. They even traveled overseas with Dad throughout the years, Paul going with Dad to South Africa and Ava going with a group a preachers that Dad took to India. Dad kept this invitation in his heart during all that had happened with the flood and began to seek God on the matter. The dream was given by God to confirm that we were to move to North Carolina once again.

Shortly after the miracle of his knees he returned to South Africa to minister. Dad was a walking testimony and he wanted all those who had witnessed his affliction to be able to see the miracle with their own eyes. So to South Africa he went, to testify and evangelize and it was a great encouragement to so many! While in the country he had several meetings but the main purpose was to go with Drummond Thom and hold a seminar specifically for pastors. Together they did a week of classes at no charge. The main subject of teaching was on the gift of discernment. Dad knew if he could reach the pastors then they could in turn transform their congregations with the revelation he had to share. He believed that this strategy would be much more effective than going to each and every individual church to minister.

In Pretoria, the capital of South Africa, Dad ministered at a church where some of Dad's friends who were also preachers were in the crowd. After he finished preaching he prayed for many people in a prayer line until he had ministered all that he could physically do that night. As he began to walk off the platform towards the door a woman who had not yet been prayed for stood up and asked for prayer. Dad told her he had done all he had strength to do and that he was finished. She replied, "I couldn't make it to platform for prayer because my legs are in such pain it is very hard for me to stand or walk." Compassion swelled up in his heart as he remembered the pain he had in his knees not so long ago. He said, "Honey, you just made it in!" He turned to the crowd and said, "Do you see this woman? I'm going to guarantee you she gets a miracle!" He looked over at where his friends were seated and spoke again with great authority, "Do you hear me? I tell you, I am guaranteeing you this girl gets a miracle before I even pray!" He felt the pastors react in their spirits with apprehension as their faith wavered. Surely you cannot guarantee a miracle, can you?

With boldness and confidence Dad looked at the woman who had stood up in her seat, pointed towards her and said, "You just got a miracle!" Suddenly a look of surprise came into her eyes and then a wave of understanding hit her. She began to shout for joy and she knew that she was healed! She stepped out into the stair-stepped aisle of the auditorium and began walking up and down the stairs to prove to the crowd that all the pain was gone. The crowd burst out in praise to the Lord for His marvelous works! When you know God as well as my Dad did you will find yourself being bold in the authority that He gives you. We say we have authority but we don't always know how to operate in it for lack of confidence in the understanding of who He is. When we have the understanding of who He is and who we are in Him we will speak with power and boldness through faith and witness signs and wonders and many kinds of miracles!

Shortly after Dad's return from South Africa we sold both the church and the house in March of 1997 and moved to Greensboro once more. It was the year I turned fifteen. Barely a few weeks after we had settled into a little basement apartment that we rented, we headed west. We ministered in Alabama, Oklahoma, Colorado, Idaho, Wyoming and Nebraska. From the time we moved to Greensboro our traveling in the ministry together as a family increased and we almost always went with Dad wherever he was invited to speak. Shortly after returning from our three week trip out west we moved to a two level house that we rented and held church in for two years. It was our family and four other families that soon grew with two more additional families. The Hagerty family moved from Ohio to Greensboro not long after we did, so that Steve could continue to learn under Dad's ministry. Their family became part of our family and their daughter Sarah, the only girl out of their four children, became my best friend. To this day she and I still share a deep and precious friendship. It was not much longer after that the Duiett family came from Louisiana with their two children to live in Greensboro as well.

We actively started looking for a house to buy instead of rent, one that would have a large enough living space that we could hold worship services in. We found just the right house for us in a quiet neighborhood just outside the city limits on a beautiful lot at the end of a dead end road. The real estate agent actually brought us to the neighborhood to look at a different house but before we left the neighborhood another for sale sign caught Dad's eye. This house was empty and ready for immediate viewing. A few weeks prior to this the Lord had given my Mom a dream in which she was standing in a large kitchen and to her back was a wall of glass through which you viewed the back yard. As soon as Mom saw the kitchen in the house she recognized it to be just like the one in her dream. Both Mom and Dad new right away that the house on Panners Trail was the one the Lord had for us. All they had to do now was believe that God would bring in the down payment.

The owner of this house was a widow who was very eager to sell the property, so Dad made a very low offer. The real estate agent protested by saying that the offer was so low it would offend the seller but he replied, "Go ahead and offend her." The agent did as she was told and to her surprise the seller agreed to the price without making a counter offer. Dad and Mom were approved for a loan and the money for the down payment came in the day before it was due. When you live for the God who cannot fail, your part in the relationship is to just believe in faith that He will provide for you as you trust Him to do so. He doesn't bless His people because they are good, He blesses His people because He loves them.

After moving from Pennsylvania the Lord spoke to Dad that the time spent there was so that God could, "strip him down and remake him", but He also said that Pennsylvania was "a safe harbor during the storm". Dad had walked through so many different moves of God from the 50's to the 90's and those eight years in Pennsylvania were full of testing. There was a lot of waiting, a lot questioning, a lot of learning to trust even more, all for the purpose of being prepared for the final chapter of his story here on earth. Dad was being separated from what the church world has established as what success in the ministry should look like. So many ministers of that era, and even today, equate the size of their church or congregation, or its outreach to success. Having reached what their flesh believes the Lord expects of them by religious standards. Many see success as having buildings, airplanes, wealth, dozens of published books or programs and telecasts. Once again the way God was leading Dad seemed opposite of how things were being done in the church world. He already knew he was a Christian who went against the grain but God was searching inside him to make sure there was no flesh there that could sway him to do anything but the work He had planned for him. In Pennsylvania what little desire Dad had left inside of him to make things happen for his ministry was completely removed. He then began to see God creating all around him the circumstances, provisions and abundance that flows out of the throne of heaven to pour out on a life that is completely submitted to God's will. He would say he had truly dealt with his flesh and overcome it.

~

"I have often heard young preachers say that when they received their calling from God and they shared it with their friends. Instead of being accepted and encouraged, they would be rejected. When this happens, we must deal with our flesh so that our ministries may mature and God may be manifested in our lives. When Joseph and Mary took Jesus into Egypt it became a type of the flesh, or bondage. In other words, Jesus was reared in the flesh. There He dealt with the flesh. The scripture asks, 'Can any good thing come out of Nazareth?' The seed had begun to grow. It came out of Egypt through Nazareth so that the flesh would be totally rejected and Jesus could become the first man to walk in the new day of the Spirit. Man really doesn't want the flesh but so many times that is all he gets from the church. I believe we are living in a day when we are going to see the spiritual man manifested."
-Excerpt from Beyond the Faith of Man

~

My Dad would say that he truly learned the importance of letting the Holy Spirit help him deal with his flesh when the Lord gave him children. He said that my brother and I were his blank slates, minds that had nothing in them at all and he and my Mom had been given the ministry of filling those minds. Parents can only give to their children what it is they have. He realized that many of the things he had to deal with in his own nature could be avoided for us, if he was only willing to let the Lord transform him. If Dad could become more like Jesus then Jeremiah and I would see Jesus and be able to learn of Him through Dad's example. Dad wanted us to have as much of an advantage as he could give to us for overcoming the carnal mind.

My parents made a conscience decision to let God transform their minds so that they would expose me to the Spirit of Truth and as they taught me they filled up my mind with liberty and the love of God, not fear or the law or denominational doctrine. I like to put it this way, they protected us from the church world and the carnal as best they could while projecting us into a life of Godliness by being a living example of the love of God. Many people let the legalism of the church world create for them a template by which to rear their children. This template is steeped in the fear of man's opinion, and chokes out the liberty all children long to be free to grow in. Once those children are adults they find themselves trying to reconcile this hard handed legalistic God who says He is love but has shown very little proof of it through the reality of living life. Who wouldn't reject a God who is hard and full of restrictions, controlling His children through fear of retribution via the enforcement of the law? But God does not demand holiness of His children, He recreates us to be holy through the revelation of who we are in Christ Jesus and His love for us as His beloved children.

Growing up I was free to make mistakes but I was taught to think before I would speak or act, to consider others and to consider the heart of God and how He would react in a situation. I was made to see Jesus in His simplest form so that as I grew up in my flesh and would do many things wrong, I would always look to Him to help make it right. Children are fleshly creatures who don't need to be made aware of sin and the ugliness of the world but made aware of the heart of God so that they may learn to dwell in the beauty of His holiness and freedom of His Spirit. In understanding His heart I could more easily turn to Him when I sinned and not fall into condemnation. Condemnation produces unhappy, anxious, depressed children who lack self confidence and have very little confidence in God's love for them.

Dad said, "My mother was my God until I was old enough to seek God out for myself. She was the standard by which I learned." As my Grandma was my Dad's standard, so were my Dad and Mom for me. More than anything they did their best to raise me without fear. So often a parent's fear causes them to try to control their children's lives through that fear. To not only keep them from harm but from experiencing life in a way that can only be experienced by making mistakes. This may be from a motivation of what the parent believes to be love, but ultimately it puts a handicap on children from a very young age. It takes the Holy Spirit in a parent to recognize how to love a child into discovering who God made them to be. I was told over and over that I was a precious individual, that there was no-one else on earth like me and God wanted it that way. He created me to think, feel and act like only Angel can and He knew how to take my individuality and combine it with His transforming power to make me into something even more beautiful than I already was. Love is both spoken and acted out, love is discipline in reasoning with a child to do what is right and teaching them the difference between God's heart and their own Adam minds. Sometimes reasoning is not enough and love comes in the form of a swat on the bottom to get that little Adam mind's attention and say, "No, don't do that because it will hurt you." Love will have no part in anything that brings condemnation or belittles someone by making them feel inadequate due to what makes them unique.

My parents love for me was based on the knowledge that I was not really theirs but I was God's and He saw fit for them to have me for a while. They new if they could instruct me in what was right that I would grow up to make right decisions. But they also knew that there would be many things I didn't get right on the first go around and gave me lots of mercy because of it. I was made to believe that all things are possible with God and that no matter how many times I might fall, He will pick me up. Not because I am a sinner but because I am His beloved. Perspective makes a world of difference. The story of every child is that Jesus loves them and He is working with them to make them who He wants them to be and mistakes are a part of that story. If you make sin the focus through the law, then they will grow up to either turn their hearts away from God, or just become semblances of themselves while constantly living under condemnation within the confines of a doctrine of man. Being blinded to ever fully coming to know the true nature of God or who they are in Him. Perhaps they may become good church members, but a follower of Jesus with an intimate knowledge of the heart of God, they will not be. Show them who God is by loving them like He does and they will never be powerless against the enemy, or their Adam nature. And they will grow up to be overcomers.

I was that blank slate. Out of all the men and women Dad trained for the ministry I was the only one whom he never had to help to unlearn anything. One day, when I was about sixteen years old, I earnestly asked Dad when he was going to start training me for the ministry. He smiled at me and said, "Angel, I've been training you since we were born." My heart could have burst with the love I felt as he solidified that truth into my heart with one simple statement. I had seen him train so many different people and so I imagined there was some formula or a certain way things had to be done to be considered one who was in training. Like people who believe they must attend a Bible college if they are truly called into the ministry, an outward approach to something that can only be done with an inward transforming. I knew I didn't have to go to Bible college, but at that time I thought there was something more formal or outward to prove that I was being trained. Truth is, I was being trained up in a quiet, steady, diligent, every-day-of-my-life process that would project me into the things of God. I was never told a certain way it had to be or that I must perform a certain way to appear holy and good. I was never even told I would be a preacher, but because of their example a desire was put in my heart to live a life of faith like my parents did. I was loved into running with all my might into the arms of The Father, and so I have.

My parents showed me the importance of working on the flesh and partnering with Holy Spirit to take on the mind of Christ, not by preaching it but by being a living example of it. I saw the battles and the victories. I witnessed the shortcomings and the overcoming. They raised me by the Spirit so that by that living example I would grow to have my own hunger to seek Jesus for that same relationship. As for them and their household, we would serve the Lord. I still had family nature in me that had to be dealt with, but I was given the tools at such a young age that by the age of accountability I could begin the process prepared. To this day I let the Holy Spirit deal with my Adam nature and that is greatly because of the example lived before me by my parents. If they could do it, so can I. My understanding of that truth inside of me is almost inexpressible.

Dad would say to parents, "What you choose to not deal with in yourself shows up ten times greater in your children." Parents would often come to him for help with issues of their children being rebellious, or disobedient, or even in trouble and he would say, "I don't have any trouble out of my children because I don't give God any trouble. My obedience to the Father draws out of my kids the desire to want to be obedient to me." Obedience is better than sacrifice. I have seen many people work out of the carnal and then demand out of their children righteousness. Preacher's kids usually get the worst wrap amongst them all. Those who carnally pursue ministry end up religiously working themselves into a place of forgetting to minister to their own families first, which is the most important calling every parent has, no matter their profession. My Dad would say that he refused to sacrifice his family on the altar of religion. He wasn't about to raise us the way the church told him to, but rather how the Holy Spirit led him to. He knew that through the fruit his life produced by living in obedience to God, we would see Jesus. That intimate relationship with God proves who He is in you and in turn draws others closer to Him by you simply living what you believe. My examples for how to live life were full of the glory of God because they laid down their own wills for the taking up of His. I share with you how my parents raised me not so that you will feel like you have to do things exactly the way my parents did, but to know that in Christ there is a better way. God created every single one of us to be unique and we will all have a different story. If you have been doing things wrong up until now, it really doesn't matter, if today you choose to do it His way.

If we focus on what is wrong and the mistakes we have made we can never move forward into living life fully redeemed from the old. Every individual who's life is found in Christ has a beautiful story because of that liberation that comes from redemption. Every life that follows Jesus gives Him glory. I believe the telling of the stories of those lives is what should bind us together. The testimony we have is what we have to share with others that they may know the reality of who God is. Your story can add to my story by sharing that evidence of the presence of God in your story. It is the blood of the Lamb and the words of our testimony that make us overcomers with a story to tell. What if we saw the true image of the body of Christ as being incredibly diverse stories all woven together to be the greatest story ever told of how Love came in and renovated us all? What if instead of comparing each others lives and generating condemnation, we instead boast of the work He has done in and through us and embrace our uniqueness for the pursuit of unity? What if we came together with the purpose of provoking one another to love and good works? What if that is what the true body of Christ looks like?

~

"Let us hold fast the profession of our faith without wavering; for He is faithful that promised; And let us consider one another to provoke unto love and to good works: Not forsaking the assembling of ourselves together," Hebrew 10:23-25 (KJV)

~

My life, my parents lives, my grandparents lives, and your life, are all apart of the gospel of Jesus Christ. Bound together by the Spirit. That epistle, or story, written daily as we all live and move and have our being in Him connects us in ways only the Spirit can. Our stories would not be complete with out each other. For too many years people have come together under the same denominational banner and instead of looking at life as a multitude of stories meant to converge to become unified, it has been a congregating of comparison. Comparison and miscommunication bred by the flesh that has created ignorance and division amongst those who are all called to be one body.

What do you believe church looks like? Gathering together in one building and saying you agree with the congregation on doctrine? I believe the idea of assembling was always meant to be so much more simple and free than the church world has created it to be. Have you read about the life of Paul the Apostle? Have you ever noticed how life was so fluid for the early church and how it was never about a specific building erected as a tabernacle to God? Paul would visit a group of people who had become a community of believers that held fast the profession of their faith and provoked one another to love and good works. People of different minds and ideas all coming together to proclaim a common love of Jesus and a desire to encourage and uplift one another. No memberships or dress code, no expectation of everyone being at the same level of learning. If someone had a need then someone else in the assembly would fill it, all things were common among them because they were equal and they understood how their stories were interconnected through Jesus. The day of Pentecost did not mark the founding of a church organization, it was a new way of walking that was released to bring unity among the children of God. If the Holy Spirit and His true purpose in us is eliminated from the gospel, then a church becomes nothing more than a club. So what if assembling simply looks like just living life with Christ-like believers?

The early believers were very diverse people bound to one another by the Holy Spirit alone, no denomination necessary. Paul would come and fellowship when he could and he would write letters when he couldn't be there in person. He understood just how human everyone was and how without love and encouragement they were at risk of falling into the old mindsets of Adam or even the law of Moses. It was not about a sect of people who looked the same, spoke the same church language, or were subjected to one man teaching them. Paul could teach others because his foundation was so sure that he could really help those who were young in the growing process of their walk. He encouraged them to do life together that they might know another facet of the heart of God which speaks of how much God loves when we love each other. Paul edified those people with his own experience, yes, but he was ever encouraging them to look to be taught by the Holy Spirit instead of himself, so they too might know God in a way they could only comprehend by obtaining that revelation for themselves.

~

"But the anointing which you have received from Him abides in you, and you do not need that anyone teach you; but as the same anointing teaches you concerning all things, and is true, and is not a lie, and just as it has taught you, you will abide in Him."
1 John 2:27 (NKJV)

~

Do you believe you need only One Teacher? The only way a Christian can ever truly be Christ-like is by walking in the power of the Holy Spirit. He was given to be our Teacher, the Revealer of God's mysteries. He comes to reside in every person when they accept Jesus into their hearts but He is not activated in a life to transform it until we are baptized in that Spirit of Truth. Completely submerged and purified in that fire, which is the only power to transform our Adam minds into the mind of Christ. There is no natural understanding that can bring us into the things of God, it is a supernatural work. The flesh separates, but the Holy Spirit unites. If a people who are called by His name come together in the perfect bond of unity in the Holy Spirit, free in the words He has spoken into our lives, that is an assembling of an army of warriors that will take the land for Him! That is a people who's relationships are so forged in love that they walk together as one in the Spirit and bring about the will of God. Strength lies in unity, not in numbers, and I have personally experienced what it is like to assemble with Christ-like people and see the Spirit move.

I believe this understanding of people coming together in unity is very different from the reality of what the church world embodies today. Carnal thinking has projected an image of God's church that barely even resembles a spotless bride. Scripture says wherever two or more are gathered together in agreement they will touch heaven and signs and wonders will be the result. Most church members can't even agree on when to start services or what type of music to sing, much less be willing to put aside their own wills to work together and bring about God's will. Imagine if congregations could actually agree for God's will to be done! The gates of hell would shake with fear! It's not about professing to agree with one another, it is agreeing with one another in the Spirit that makes us one body and of one mind, that is the mind of Christ.

May these words that the Holy Spirit has given me go forth like a two edged sword to cut through the lies of the enemy and to bring to ruin the kingdoms built by mans hands. Out of the blood and dust may a new hope rise that there is a new way that He has paved for us, a deeper understanding that we must have proven in our lives to show the world the hope of His glory and the way of life in Him. It is time that His people, His body, His bride, the true worshipers arise and show this lost and dying world what His church really looks like!

# 6

## Few Are Chosen

~

"The God of our fathers has chosen you that you should know His will, and see the Just One, and hear the voice of His mouth. For you will be His witness to all men of what you have seen and heard." Acts 22:14-15 (NKJV)

~

The new millennium came and the world and the church world showed their lack of being able to hear the voice of the Lord by giving into the Y2K fear. Many churches around the world were stocking up on emergency food supplies and preaching the end of the world being near, because they believed all the computers worldwide would stop working at the dawn of the year 2000, which would result in society as we know it being completely devastated. Suspicion leads to gossip and breeds panic, discernment allows you to identify the spirit that is working behind the scenes so that you can know and be prepared. The Lord gave my Dad a revelation that explained what Y2K was all about. The Lord said it was the devil testing the waters. Satan wanted to see if there was enough fear on the earth to send in the Antichrist. Then came a second test with that fear-o-meter on 9-11-01, and though the attack was on the U.S., the shock was felt around the world and the fear was almost tangible. The Lord revealed to Dad that these two tests of the worlds fear were like unto when Satan came to Jesus in the wilderness to see if he could tempt Him. Satan tempted Jesus three times to test and see if He could make Him doubt who He was and to distract Him from what God had sent Him to do. Dad prophesied that there would be a third world wide event that would be the final test to prove whether or not Satan could release the Antichrist into the earth. One last test to see if people's fear could be overwhelmed.

If people have no fear they cannot be controlled, and Satan knows it. A defeated, depressed, powerless church is full of fear, and the only difference between it and the world is that God is the subject of their conversation. The Lord showed Dad that the third test upon the earth to be released would have to do with pharmaceuticals. The majority of people worldwide are dependent upon drugs. Many without even considering an alternative route will automatically turn to medicine for the answer. There is a dependency upon science, vaccines and mans imperfect ability to find cures. Though taking medicine is most certainly not evil, if one is dependent upon it they could be strongly tempted to do whatever they were made to do to obtain it. With this hold pharmaceuticals have on so many people, the Antichrist will be able to deny people their access to what they have become dependent upon, and quickly sift between those who depend on God and those who depend on man. Would fear grip your heart if you couldn't buy your drugs?

~

"Men's hearts failing them from fear and the expectation of those things which are coming on the earth. Then they will see the Son of Man coming in a cloud with power and great glory. Now when these things begin to happen, look up and lift up your heads, because your redemption draws near." Luke 21:26-28 (NKJV)

~

Prescription drugs are in most every home and commonly used by the majority of people. Today we are faced with a crisis in our nations having what they call opioid epidemics, as more and more people are addicted to prescribed painkillers. If you're sad you take uppers, if you're to excited you take downers. If you want to live longer after a major organ surgery you take drugs that sustain you. Dependency upon the arm of the flesh. Man is knowledgeable and has made advances in science that improve life and can even lengthen it. To take advantage of the advances made through medical science is not wrong. But so many are looking to everyone and everything except for God as the answer. Yet the Great Physician stands and beckons you come and partake of Him, ask of Him, trust in Him, for He is willing and He is able. You are free in His love to choose and even if you choose the way of the flesh you will not be separated from the love of God for it. I want to stress that doctors and medicine being the right or wrong way to do things is not the point here. It's depending upon a substance or man's carnal knowledge over the Truth of the Word of God that could ultimately lead to people being snared by the enemy.

~

"And be not conformed to this world: but be ye transformed by the renewing of your mind, that ye may prove what is that good, and acceptable, and perfect, will of God." Romans 12:2 (KJV)

~

By now you have noticed how I make a distinction between "the world" and "the church world". Let me explain why. The Lord spoke to my Dad that there are three different worlds, or spiritual realms, that are on this earth. There is "the world", "the church world" and "God's world". They are each separate places to walk or dwell in. "The world" is that of fallen man, the carnal and Adam way of living and those who are not reconciled to God through Jesus dwell in the world. The "church world" is a realm between the world and God's world. After salvation we are invited into God's world but most often we step into the church world which is the domain of man's knowledge of God or a carnal minded understanding of who He is. The church world was created by looking to man to explain to us who God is instead of depending upon Him to reveal all we need to know by the Holy Spirit. Our individual faith ushers us into God's world when we believe that Jesus is the Son of God. But then in, our naturally ability, we turn from the Holy Spirit as being our Teacher and seek man to explain to us the mysteries of the Spiritual realm. This understanding is why I have consistently made throughout this book a distinction between the church as described as the Body of Christ in the word, and "the church world". I believe this distinction must be made and it is crucial to understanding how God is moving in this day. I see a clear distinction between the three worlds because it was a revelation given to my Dad so that I might understand what the Lord was bringing me into now. Seeing these three worlds and being able to make the distinction was a precursor to the path I am now on and I believe it is right that I share it with you. May the Holy Spirit open the eyes of your understanding to receive it.

~

"If the world hates you, you know that it hated Me before it hated you. If you were of the world, the world would love its own. Yet because you are not of the world, but I chose you out of the world, therefore the world hates you." John 15:18 (NKJV)

~

"God's world" is the reality of walking in heavenly places with Him on a daily basis, having one mind and one heart with Him. It is the realm of all things are possible to him who believes. It is separate from the world and the church world because there is no carnal thing allowed in it. It is the kingdom of heaven that Jesus preached and gave us access to because He now sits on the right hand of the Father and He sent another Comforter in His place to bring that reality alive in us. It is a place where we can dwell only once our hearts and minds are conformed to His through the Holy Spirit opening the eyes of our understanding, our spiritual eyes. We may live in the natural in the world and may even sojourn in the church world for a time but it is in God's world where we walk in the cool of the evening with Him like Adam did in the garden, where we hear His voice effortlessly. This relationship is established through our wills becoming one, it is attainable and it is possible to dwell in that world. My Grandma did, my Dad did, I do. The writing of this legacy is the evidence of that reality.

It was in the year 2000 that God spoke to Dad about how things would be changing for his ministry and how it would be quite the opposite of his Pennsylvania experience. God specifically said, "Millions will flow through your hands", and Dad began to believe for it. Not so he could obtain a personal jet plane, or a mansion, or a Rolls Royce, or to build a mega church, but for the sole purpose of the ministry being funded to the point that whenever he would be invited to go, the money would always be there and in abundance. Many people within the church world abuse the idea of prosperity because their understanding of it is carnal and not Spiritual. God does want His people to prosper, but their motives must be pure, and their hearts right to walk in that blessing. Because if the motivation of your heart is not right, prosperity will become your god and destroy you. Many Christians want blessing without testing but the only way to truly walk in divine prosperity is to be tried to the point of knowing there is no flesh left inside. With no fleshly motives in the way you can be assured there is no desire for money for self, but solely for the purpose of the Kingdom. When your will has become His will, you will never desire something outside of His will. I don't believe that heavenly prosperity looks like a mega church, it does, however, show the glory of God upon a life that is sold out to minister the gospel in the most effective way possible. People used to think we were rich because we traveled around the world and had every need met in abundance. But when we had money in the bank it was quickly spent on furthering the gospel, so the majority of the time there was very little in the account. Money that is being used for it's true purpose is actively being put to use and doesn't stay in one place for very long.

~

"But seek ye first the kingdom of God, and his righteousness; and all these things shall be added unto you." Matthew 6:33 (KJV)

~

From the time the Lord spoke about the increase of finances to Dad we began to see every single need for the ministry and for personal expenses to not only being met but provided for in abundance. It was truly a time of having the provision even before the need arose. It was not that God had changed, but Dad's understanding of Him had changed, and He saw that God was beginning to move in a new way in his ministry because he was now prepared to walk in that blessing. All he had walked through his entire life would now produce fruit from all that co-laboring he had done with the Holy Spirit. As this transition began to take place, Dad was given all new messages to preach and God began to send him to hungry churches who longed for the meat of the word. The word was brought forth in a new way and confirmed by God leading him to places where it was not only received but transforming the lives of those who received it.

~

"Ye have not chosen me, but I have chosen you, and ordained you, that ye should go and bring forth fruit, and that your fruit should remain: that whatsoever ye shall ask of the Father in my name, he may give it you." John 15:16 (KJV)

~

As Dad walked into this transition he knew it was time yet again for a changing of the ministry name. The Lord spoke to him to rename the ministry to Well of Salvation, inspired by a scripture in the book of Isaiah. A new way required a new name.

~

"Behold, God is my salvation; I will trust, and not be afraid: for the Lord Jehovah is my strength and my song; he also is become my salvation. Therefore with joy shall ye draw water out of the wells of salvation. And in that day shall ye say, Praise the Lord, call upon his name, declare his doings among the people, make mention that his name is exalted." Isaiah 12:2-4 (KJV)

~

A shift began to take place in the church world and the response was more invitations for Dad to speak. God closed off many of the church connections from decades passed and began to open up new churches and even more house meetings than before. I began to notice how the focus was beginning to move from church buildings and being concentrated on ministering to people in small groups, or one on one in home gatherings. Florida was one of the states we began to frequent and during a visit at a church in the Jacksonville area we met a woman named Lois Burrell. She is the quintessential southern lady and a joy to have as a friend. Like I said before, this story is full of so many other people's stories because without them this story would not be what it is. I would like to tell you about a few of the faithful I have come to know and love, who have impacted not only my parent's story but mine as well. We have come together as members of One Body and have been given to each other to share our experience of Jesus with one another. These are some of those Christ-like brothers and sisters that I recognize as the Body.

Lois is a follower of Jesus who lived a life time in the church world and had finally reached the point of being tired of not seeing the reality of God within the church world. A hunger began to increase inside of her and cause her to begin to seek for that proof of Jesus completely working within a life. She knew the word was true, but very few were living in that reality. She cried out to the Lord and the Lord answered her cry when her sister Beverly convinced her to come and hear Dad preach. Lois didn't want to go and hear yet another preacher claiming to have the goods only to be disappointed yet again, but her mind was changed when she heard the sermon series of my Grandma's preaching. She was so impressed by the faith that was preached in those sermons, that if this man was anything like his mother, she knew he would be worth hearing. Lois saw right away how genuine our family was and felt the Holy Spirit so strongly when she heard Dad preach and saw him pray for the people. She knew we were the real deal and we also recognized that Spirit within her. Though Dad did not do this frequently with church goers he had just met, he offered to come to her house and visit the next time we were in the area. She was so excited that she said she felt just like Zacchaeus in the Bible, because she knew Jesus was coming to her house. Not only did Lois recognize how important it would be for our families to be connected, but her husband Charlie did as well, and we are to this day the best of friends and close family in the Lord.

Lois began to learn from Dad all that she could about how he had become an overcomer. She saw the evidence in him and wanted to know how to obtain it for herself. Not long after she met us the Lord spoke to her very clearly that she was to come out of the church and begin to learn directly from the Holy Spirit. She was to be, not only separated from the church world, but raised up for a specific ministry God had for her. She and Charlie decided to open up their home for meetings in which Dad could minister, and they gave us a place to stay in their home. Charlie became close to Dad as well, and he even went on a mission trip to South Africa with him. The Burrell family expressed their love and support to us in so many ways and were faithful supporters of Dad's ministry. They continue to partner with Well of Salvation as co-laborers in our ministry outreaches to this day. We even assemble together on occasion, though we are several hundred miles apart. Distance cannot keep the Body of Christ apart because the bond created by the Spirit is too strong.

God was creating opportunities to forge new friendships with people who wanted a partnership with what the Lord was doing through Dad. People who would be so connected to us in love, that we would strengthen one another and form a bond that makes little sense in the flesh but perfect sense in the Spirit. I share with you about these relationships to speak of a unity that has been forged in the Holy Spirit and to testify of the faithfulness that unity in Him alone can produce. We are all very different and from different walks of life, and yet the Spirit has made us one, and we have not forsaken the importance of coming together or assembling in Him for the edification of one another. Yes, it looks a whole lot different than the church world model, but I see it as being the Body. One thing I have done in my life is gotten used to being different. I don't want to be what the church world considers normal because the supernatural can't fit into a box.

At the end of 2001 we were invited to speak at a church in Massachusetts, here we met more of His precious Body. The New England states were just opening up to Dad for evangelism and up until the new millennium he had not done much ministry in that region of our country. While ministering in Ashland, Massachusetts, before the morning service, we stopped at a coffee shop to get some breakfast. Dad didn't know it but it would be his first encounter with one of the church members at the church we were about to minister at. As he ordered our food from the express lane in a very un-express like manner, the person behind him in line was getting very impatient. Dad could have discerned that spirit from a mile away! So he decided to "try" that spirit and after trying the man's patience to the utmost he finished ordering and walked out with our food and a smile. This impatient man was in a hurry to get to church so he could do parking lot duty, an obligation which is of the utmost importance in the church world. God forbid we be late to our duties! And what an important duty it is to make sure the guest speaker could find his designated parking spot. Oh to be used of God in this incredibly important way! (Please note the sarcastic humor implied.)

We ate our breakfast on the way to the church and we entered the parking lot. We were ushered to our preferred parking spot by that very impatient man, who managed to arrive before us. We did not recognize him from the coffee shop but he recognized us. We parked the car and as Dad emerged from the driver seat, that parking lot saint saw Dad's distinctive goose down winter hat rising above the height of the car. Suddenly the man realized he had been behind the guest evangelist in line at that coffee shop, and he knew he was busted for his impatience, because this preacher was known for his ability to discern spirits with precision. To hear this story told by Stefano Piardi would make you laugh a lot! His frustration and annoyance with Dad in the coffee shop was from a motivation of doing the appointed task that was given to him by his church. One can justify one's flesh as long as it is out of the reaction of service to the church, right? Why not get mad at the crazy slow man in front of you before going to church to worship God? He was totally responding in his flesh to the very man he was excited to get to meet and learn from in the Spirit. Stefano knew his lack of patience was blatant and there was no way he could have hidden his carnal response from this man of God.

Stefano's wife Dawn had a different introduction to Dad. That morning during worship the youngest of the Piardi family named Coby, who was just shy of two years old at the time, saw Dad sitting in the front row while most everyone else was standing and singing. Without hesitation Coby left his parents who were worshiping and went to Dad and climbed right up on his lap. His mother Dawn watched Coby as he toddled over and found his way to Dad. She was happy to see that Dad gladly welcomed Coby on his lap and she knew immediately that there was something very special about this preacher. Children are sensitive to spirits and even at that young age Coby was drawn to the kindness and love in Dad. He knew right where the best seat in the house was! So began our friendship with this family who would become our family in Christ in ways we could not have comprehended on that day.

Stefano and Dawn had been looking for something more of God for their lives at that time. What Dad spoke that morning resonated in their spirits and they were deeply touched by the message. They wanted to know more from this man of God. They were so hungry for the supernatural and for Jesus to show Himself in a deeper way to them. They found themselves at a place where they could no longer be complacent with how the church world insisted things must be done, and here came the man that broke the mold. They had seen the supernatural in their own lives, and glimpses of it within the church world but they were seeking for a message that would reveal to them how they could dwell in God's world. So after service Stefano went to officially meet Dad and give him a special love offering. Stefano was taken back by how nonchalant Dad was about receiving the gift, because in Stefano's experience, most ministers he had known would latch themselves onto you the moment you mentioned giving money. But Dad simply told Stefano to go to the literature table to meet Mom and she would give him the contact information for the check to be sent. This reaction set Dad apart in a way they had never experienced with other spiritual leaders and he was a bit of a conundrum that intrigued them to want to get to know him better. Is it possible someone could be like Jesus?

Several revivals had broken out from the mid 90's and into the 2000's that were affecting the Spirit-filled churches. This, in part, increased the desire of many church leaders to have the same experience as was in Toronto or Brownsville. The hunger for revival was sparked once again and as a result many churches opened their doors to the message Dad was carrying. The Piardi family wasn't just looking for another revival, but for something completely new. It was the cry of their hearts, even if they didn't quite know how to explain it at that time. They were not just looking for miracles or people laid out on the floor drunk in the Spirit, they were longing for Jesus in His fullness and the evidence of a life transformed to be like Jesus. It was Dad's sermons on conquering the mind, which was a word given to Dad to expound upon discerning of spirits, that began to set the Piardi family free. When Dad spoke of his heart's desire to not be the one that people saw, but for Jesus to be who people saw in him, they really knew they had met a man who had no hype and had given himself over to the leading of the Holy Spirit completely. He was a man they could learn from and what may have surprised them beyond this was, that he was a man who would love them, no matter what.

Not long after we met the Piardi family, God called Stefano to preach. The day it happened he was very excited and called Dad to confirm what he had heard. Dad's response was, "That's good. Many are called but few are chosen, find out if you're chosen." Stefano was a little stunned at his response but knew it was probably the one he needed to hear. Being called into the ministry is something many people experience. Sometimes it is their own fleshly desire to be used of God that leads them, and that is not bad, but that motivation leads people to get discouraged and they either end up giving up the ministry or just push on in the flesh and build their own tabernacle. Then there are those who are not only called, but chosen for a specific purpose within the Kingdom. It is a much harder path than being called, but if you are chosen by God, then He knows you will be a vessel He can fashion and use for His purposes. He knows no matter how long it takes He will be able to mold that clay and recreate you into the likeness of His Son.

Soon after meeting Dad, Stefano and Dawn were led by God out of the church they had been attending and began being taught, not only by Dad, but by the Holy Spirit. They started a home service in their carpet store for a while but soon realized that wasn't what God was doing either. Their services would soon end as the Lord lead them into the new. They had left church but had one foot left in the church world and were now being shown the path into God's world. That Holy Ghost appointed meeting of our families began to unfold its purpose and is still unfolding to this day. Stefano would travel to be in Dad's meetings whenever he could, he even traveled from Massachusetts to Florida to be a part of services, and he never missed a service when we were in the New England states. He redeemed the time well, not knowing it would be short. Like the apostles who knew there was nowhere they could go to hear the words of life, but to travel with Jesus, so the Piardi family understood that if they wanted to have a radical change they should glean what they could from Dad whenever they had the opportunity.

~

"So then faith cometh by hearing, and hearing by the word of God." Romans 10:17 (KJV)

~

Around this time our supply of How To Discern Spirits books was almost completely depleted and Dad began to seek God for the provision for a third printing to be done. There was a minimum amount of books required to purchase from the publisher and it would cost almost $1700 to do it. He had told no one except the Lord about the need that he had, and unbeknownst to him, Dawn was awakened the night before by the Lord speaking to her concerning this very thing. At this point in time Dawn was still establishing her relationship with Dad and was even unsure if she should call him and come right out and say what was on her heart. Sometimes it is not always an easy thing to boldly speak what you know God spoke, especially when it is to someone you really respect or might not know very intimately. She even tried to get Stefano to reach out to Dad and see if there was a need but Stefano knew that if the Lord had spoken to her, she was the one who should make the call.

Dawn resolved to call Dad and she began by saying, "I believe the Lord told me you have a need. I couldn't even sleep because of it stirring inside of me." Dad replied, "Well, maybe you should ask Him exactly what it is He is wanting you to do." He spoke in this way perhaps to encourage her to be sure of what she had heard and speak it boldly. Dawn replied, "No. I believe He said you had a need and whatever that need is, you tell me and I will meet it." Dad paused for a moment and then said, "Huh. Funny it should be you. I had four different people in mind that the Lord might move upon to use. But He chose you." Dawn decided to step out in boldness to establish her hearts determination in carrying out what the Lord would have her to do and to let Dad know she was resolute in being instrumental as a source that was willing to meet the needs of the ministry. She said, "Maybe this is the new way of doing things Virgil, but I want you to know that this is how it will be between us. If you ever have any need, I want you to tell me, and I will fill it." Dawn was establishing a covenant that declared she was willing to believe that no matter what, God would provide for her to be a provision for the ministries needs to be met. All Dad had to do was ask. Dad spoke again and said, "I have a need for $1681." She was being precise and so was he. She told him the check would be in the mail that day. When she went to write out the check she was going to round it up to $1700 and the Lord stoped her and told her to write the exact amount Dad had requested. Both she and Dad were learning a new way the Lord was showing them about giving and receiving.

In the New England states we met many people who became friends and faithful partners of the ministry. There were countless physical miracles during these years but what was even more, was that people were being set free from self or the prisons that they were held in within their minds. The word brought forth during those last years came with such power that those who heard it were not only hearers but doers. So many people experienced strong holds being torn down in their lives and began to walk in the fullness of what God had for their lives. Dad even changed the way he prayed for people by no longer having prayer lines. Instead he ministered in all of the gifts in a new way. Instead of asking someone to come up for prayer for whatever their issue was, he would listen to the Lord to direct him to an individual, and then God would speak a word for them or give them a miracle. Dad would find the person in the crowd and minister to them in that personal way as they were simply sitting in their seat.

One of the miracles that happened and transformed someone's understanding of the love of God towards them happened to my friend Stefano. It wasn't in a church setting but during a simple conversation that he had with Dad on a phone. I want to share in a direct quote from Stefano of this testimony of how God released a word through my Dad.

It is in Stefano's words and with his whole hearted approval I share this with you, "By now it was January of 2003, and we had been with Virgil since December of 2001. I remember that fateful day he came to preach at the church we attended at the end of 2001 right after 9/11. In January of 2002 we started following him in earnest and by February or March 2002 we left the church we had been attending to start a small bible study/church in our carpet store in Shrewsbury, Massachusetts.

We had a good size carpet store at the time, but any good sized business needs 'feeding' all the time. It is a beast that provides well in good times of economic expansion and will cripple under a mountain of debt when things don't quite go right, this due to the high level of fixed costs such as labor and rent. It was a very snowy beginning of January and whenever it snows business falls off the cliff, as nobody goes out shopping. No one wants new carpet being installed when the weather is this way. Walkways are not cleared and ice, salt, mud and slush are not usually things we want to associate with brand new carpet. Snowstorm after snowstorm our checking account was buried like the driveway outside our store.

One Friday afternoon toward the end of January I got a call from my wife and she said, 'I paid all the bills.'

'Good', I said and she replied, 'No you don't understand, I really paid all the bills.'

!?! 'What do you mean?' I said not believing what I had just heard.

'I paid all the bills and I sent them out in the mail, and now the checkbook is overdrawn by $24,000.' She said with finality.

'What have you done??? Are the envelopes still out in the mailbox?' I said in hopes that it could be reversed.

She replied, 'No I went to the Post Office and they are gone, they are all gone. You need $24,000 in the account or they will all bounce.' (It was a steely, hard voice born of resolve and had a finality to it that was very intimidating.)

This was no time for a half baked faith response! I was outmatched by the sheer size of the amount and the time constraint, and the devil was all too happy to remind me that by Monday I would be out of business and out in the street in the cold, literally. I hung up the phone with my wife and called Virgil.

'Hey Virgil.' Pause. 'I need prayer.' Pause. 'I need help.' Pause. 'I need a miracle!' Pause. 'The business is in big trouble and I need $24,000 by Monday or I am toast. Toast with a capital T! My wife decided to believe God at the most inopportune time and now there is nothing I can do!'

There was silence. 'Virgil? You there?' More silence. Then the silence broke and Virgil spoke, 'Yeah. It has been snowing quite a bit over there, we saw it on the news.'

-My thoughts- Really??? Tell me something I don't know! Snow and ice everywhere, shopping is nonexistent, people are depressed and my wife has the account overdrawn by $24,000! Maybe you did not hear me properly, *I need a miracle and not the weather report Captain Obvious!* -End of my thoughts-

'Let me call you back in a bit.' He says and ten minutes later Virgil called me back with this word, 'This weekend you will have a breakthrough and none of the checks will bounce. You will increase in sales every weekend. Weekend after weekend it will continually increase.'

Saturday came and there were good sales, close to $10,000, really good but nowhere near what I needed. Sunday we did a bit more, a couple thousand more. Monday also was unusually good, I think we reached $17,000. Tuesday sales continued to come in and we were around $20,000. I think we went to the bank every day to make deposits and the checks never bounced and sales never ceased! New weekend, new snowstorm, more sales. New weekend, new snowstorm, more sales. This pattern continued well into March through 2002 and 2003 and was the fifth snowiest year in hundred years with one hundred and twelve inches of snow and yet that was our breakthrough year. We got tested and we didn't even know it! A stubborn unmovable wife put faith to the ultimate test. A simple preacher who knew God had delivered the promise and the ability to believe God for anything. Today I know better than I did then, Virgil did not hear from God in any particular way but He declared the Word as he knew God had given him authority to do it. And so it was!"

Around this same time Dad and Mom had to walk through a test of their own. While ministering at a church in Connecticut after the service ended, He was suddenly aware that Mom was coming under an attack. When she stood up from her seat one of her legs did not want to work properly and she felt very weak. Dad had already identified the spirt and began to rebuke it. He told her, "Melonie you're going to have to walk down the aisle to the back of the church by yourself while I tell the pastor we are going to leave early. I'm not going to hold you up but you can do this on your own." He was encouraging her to help her build up her faith and he spoke healing with every word. Mom didn't know exactly what was happening but she made it to the back of the church to wait for Dad. He soon joined her after excusing themselves for leaving so quickly after the service. He helped her to the car and as they drove back to the hotel Mom asked Dad what was going on. He answered, "It's a stroke." Once they made it back to the room he said, "You just get in the bed and sleep."

That night while she slept, he didn't. He didn't sleep, but he also didn't let his mind run with thoughts of worse case scenario, and he never once thought of calling a doctor. But oh how he prayed and stayed His mind on the Lord! As she slept he declared, "By the morning I will have the miracle!" He used the word of the Lord and stood on his experience of knowing who God is. He prayed out of confidence that he was directly in the center of God's will. Dad stood his ground against the devil and refused to let him have any room to make a home in his wife. The devil even spoke to him when the sun began to rise, to see if he could get Dad to waver. Satan put a thought in Dad's head saying, "The sun is up, maybe you should wake her and check to see if you really did get the miracle." In that moment Dad knew he had the victory and he let Mom sleep on, all the way until ten o'clock! When she woke up the signs of stroke that had been on her face were completely gone and she had full strength in her limbs and her entire body. She received a miracle! Praise God!

~

"Husbands, love your wives, even as Christ also loved the church, and gave himself for it;" Ephesians 5:25 (KJV)

~

Why didn't he get the church to pray for her, you may be wondering? Remember how we touched earlier on how getting people to agree upon something is not an easy thing? Dad, through wisdom, knew that the fight had to take place in an atmosphere of total faith and peace. Not that the church people were completely faithless, but more often than not, when people are faced with sickness they will react in fear. A long time ago in his walk Dad realized most people viewed his way of walking in faith as being radical and strange. They didn't fully agree or understand, and that was ok with him. But from that experience he learned that when crisis would happen it was to Jesus alone he could turn and not to man. It is one thing to say you believe God heals, it is another thing to actually lay your life, or even someone else's life, on the line to test that faith. That afternoon Dad shared the miracle with a lifelong friend who was also a faith teacher, that friend reacted in fear when Dad told him the testimony. He suggested that Dad should take Mom to the doctor to make sure she got a miracle. Which was not only absurd to Dad, but broke his heart to receive a reaction like that from someone that he knew believed that faith works. When God gives you a miracle, you will know it and you will need no man to confirm it. When Jesus healed someone in the Bible he didn't follow it up with, well, you better go to the doctor and get yourself checked out, just in case. No! He said, take up your bed and walk! It is done! Go in confidence and know that God has touched you this day! You are forever made whole!

In 2002 Dad wrote his third book. As I have mentioned before my Dad's level of education was not very high and he actually wrote his first two books with the assistance of ghost writers, who were my Mom and my Uncle Gary. This time I was the ghost writer for the project entitled Grow Up Or Keep Repenting. This book is about the differences in the ministries of John the Baptist and Jesus. It is about how John came to bring us a message for repentance, to pave the way for Jesus, while Jesus taught us how to overcome through Him and walk without sin-consciousness and in His righteousness. The message of repentance, although essential, is not the message we are meant to embrace. Repentance is needed only once to bring us to Jesus and once we are in Him, we are made overcomers. After that we should begin to grow up and no longer walk in our Adam nature which makes sin the focus instead of the finish work of the cross. It is the mature Christian who has put away childish things and learned to walk in confidence, knowing through the Holy Spirit we have power just like Jesus did.

Here are a few excerpts from Grow Up Or Keep Repenting:

"Repentance is easily abused when you continue to commit the same wrong over and over again. It becomes a crutch in your life that you lean on. Instead of seeing the error of your ways you continue to hold onto repentance. Without overcoming being the key to your Christian walk you allow the devil to use condemnation against you. And condemnation becomes an open door for depression to enter in. Do not allow the devil to steal your joy! Stop repenting and start overcoming in you life today."

"Change. Find out what is causing your problem and deal with it. Is it tradition? Is it your position in your church? Have you been at ease in Zion?' (Amos 6:1). Have you become depressed, bored, or complacent? Then it is time for you to get on your knees before God and seek out a new challenge, begin to strive for something more. CHANGE! You cannot dwell in one place forever and not expect to become restless. To change is to become different, to transform."

"John said, '...he shall baptize you with the Holy Ghost and with fire.' (Matt. 3:11) The Holy Ghost is power to overcome any obstacle in your life. With the Holy Ghost you can overcome any oppression. With the power of the Holy Ghost you will be able to overcome any demon. The fire purges us of impurities. It is a consuming fire and once our trouble is consumed it is no longer in our lives. Thus we are overcomers!"

"Here is yet another solution. Let the church be led by the Holy Ghost. Balaam began to write his own rules and defy God. How many pastors today write their own laws to ease the flesh, rather than obey the will of God? Once we obey the will of God He will give us to eat of the hidden manna (Revelation 2:17). He told us He would keep the best to the last and that He would reveal the fullness of His Son to them who will hear what the Spirit has to say. He will reveal His fullness to those who overcome."

Meetings continued to increase and we were on the road more often than we were home, sometimes it even felt like we lived in hotels more than our house. We traveled up and down the eastern coast of the country constantly evangelizing while also continuing to have a house meeting. Even if we were not present Jerry or Steve would faithfully step in to minister in Dad's absence. We would travel again to South Africa in 2002 and Australia in 2003. I believe it is fitting that Dad's last trip overseas would be to South Africa because it was a place that he had such a burden for in his heart. In 2004 Mom and I would go with him and it would be our last opportunity to do so. I praise God that He made a way for us all to go together.

It was in mid-September of 2004 when Dad started having severe chest pains and suddenly called for Mom, Jeremiah and I to come into his room and pray for him. We all began to pray in the Holy Ghost as Jeremiah laid hands on him. Dad stood with his back up against the wall to help him stand straighter, because that position seemed to bring a little relief from the pain. We didn't pray for very long but the chest pains left and he was alright again. Later that month he spoke at a church about how proud he was that his family would come to him and pray when he needed us. Looking back now I know it was on that day that we prayed for him that he knew in his heart he could leave this earth assured that we would be able to go on without him here. He knew we had the faith it would take to depend on God for ourselves.

It was about a month or so of fighting this battle over his heart but he never stopped believing or traveling and ministering for the Lord. In fact, the last weeks of his life were spent traveling from North Carolina, to Georgia, to Florida and even all the way up the coast to Massachusetts. Mom and I were with him on this last journey. At the time none of us saw it as the last battle, because we had seen him go through so many battles before and win them all, so we had no doubt whatsoever that this one was any different from the others. We had great confidence in his faith and that God would give him the victory, and He did. Just because the victory looks different than what your carnal understanding may perceive it to be does not mean that it is anything less than victory. This man had run a spectacular race and he was about to cross the finish line!

In a Holiday Inn in Marlborough, Massachusetts Dad was resting in the bed after a sleepless night. He said that if he could just relax enough to get some sleep, he would be doing better. Mom and I had been praying all night and into the morning. I decided to massage his feet to help him relax, something I had never done, and after I had done so he said, "Thank you baby, Daddy loves you." The next thing I knew a great exhale of breath left his body and he went very still. Earlier that morning our dear friend Stefano had come to pray with us over Dad, but had to leave for a short while to take care of some business. So Mom immediately called Stefano after Dad's breath left his body and Stefano hurried back to join us. We prayed fervently for resurrection. An hour went by and it literally felt like five minutes but it wasn't until the Lord spoke to me and said, "It's time to let him go", that we stopped praying. He spoke and we accepted the Lord's word. I believe Dad had already settled the matter with the Lord but he chose not to tell us about it. Whatever the final outcome, he was willing to walk it out. Both ways led to victory and he knew it. From that day that Jeremiah, Mom and I prayed for him when the heart attacks first started, he knew his time to be with the Lord was at hand. He had submitted himself to the victory of gaining heaven if a miracle for his body was not what the Lord had in mind, and on October 13, 2004 he died believing and received his prize.

~

"Work out your own salvation with fear and trembling. For it is God which works in you both to will and to do of his good pleasure. That ye may be blameless and harmless, the sons of God, without rebuke, in the midst of a crooked and perverse nation, among whom ye shine as lights in the world; Holding forth the word of life;"
Philippians 2:12-16 (KJV)

~

Words cannot describe the weight of the importance of the legacy handed down to me from my father. I do not boast in myself but in the Lord who chose to set me apart. The word of God says in Luke 12:48, "To whom much is given, much is also required." I am aware that although I have been raised up in these wonderful revelations and truths, that I still have the free will to choose what I do with it. I do not choose to squander it, neither do I take it lightly, but I have let it be my foundation for which God has built upon. Perhaps you would say that I have been conditioned to walk in faith, but this walk still takes a willing mind and steadfast heart. God has promised me an even more abundant blessing than the generations before me have experienced, if only I choose to lay down my life for the purpose He has chosen me for. It is a choice, and I choose Him.

Because He first loved me and called me according to His purpose it was such an easy choice for me to lay down my life in exchange for His. He reached out to me to forge a covenant because He wanted me, and I believed Him. Because I have had the privilege and honor of being a third generation follower of Christ my foundation was made sure. Because those who went before me did not merely preach the gospel, but lived it to the letter, and were faithful covenant keepers. I was weaned on faith, brought up on miracles and healings, taught the importance of speaking in tongues, speaking in prophecy, giving words of knowledge and interpretation and how crucial discerning of spirits is. And above all these I was taught the utmost importance of learning the voice of God. I was shown that the proof of God working in your life is displayed in you being able to hear His voice and respond to it in obedience. To hear is to obey, or in other words, obedience is the fruit of hearing His voice. Not because we must obey but because our heart longs for nothing else besides that very obedience. A willing mind and steadfast heart in God's hands translates into a confidence that doesn't only come from being the descendant of great men and women of God, but from comprehending what it is to be a daughter of The King.

In November 2005, almost exactly a year after Dad went to be with Jesus, my Mom suffered a severe stroke. I came home from work one evening to find her on the floor in our living room unable to get up. Jeremiah and I worked together, but had driven separate vehicles to work that day, so I was the first to arrive home. I went to her side and down on my knees at the same moment. I knew instantly what the battle was. You see, my Dad had left me with a great gift, the victory that he had won over the first stroke Mom had suffered was the ground work for the confidence with which I would walk in for this second battle. His faith gave me the faith to believe God for another miracle, because I knew if God did it before He would do it again. Jeremiah and I began to pray and we called on our close family in Christ to back us up. Jerry and Steve came to the house right away and joined us in prayer. After an hour of prayer and Mom still not being able to get up, the three men carried Mom to her bed. She slept without waking all through the night and through the next day and night. I never left her side.

The battle was on and we were believing for a miracle, but this one would be progressive. Mom awoke and could not get up, so I prayed and then she could. With my help we made it to the bathroom and then to her chair. She couldn't speak, so we prayed and then she could. She couldn't drink very easily or chew properly, so we prayed and soon she could drink with a straw and eat solid food by the end of the week. Her stroke was a massive stroke, it made her unable to speak, write, eat, or walk, and if I had focused on the outward evidence of the circumstance I would have been hopeless. But everyday we pressed in and pressed on and little by little she was being made whole!

Our dear friends and family in Christ were not only praying with us but actively doing everything they could for us, such as making meals, helping around the house or coming over to spend time with us. I could never, ever thank the Duiett and Hagerty families enough for the love they poured out over us during that time. The Piardi family came to spend a few days with us for Thanksgiving, not long after the stroke happened. By that time Mom was walking, eating and speaking a lot better, but there was still evidence of a stroke. I also owe the Piardi family my thanks for their love and all they did to support us through that time. Many other brothers and sisters in the Lord lifted us up in prayer from around the world and we could feel their love for us through it all. I have been blessed with an amazing group of people who love the Lord and love me.

Before this took place we had already planned a family vacation on a cruise to Mexico for myself, Mom, Jeremiah and his wife Katie. We were scheduled to fly to Florida and sail on the ship during the first week of December and we decided we would go, even though Mom was not yet one hundred percent. It was not a time to back down from the devil and we took steps forward in faith every day. We were all planning on sharing a little cabin with four bunk beds, and when we checked onto the ship they told us we were receiving an upgraded cabin. We went from one of the smallest available rooms to the second largest suite on the ship. That was the favor of God and something special that He gave us to encourage us to keep moving forward in faith. The upgrade included two bathrooms, three queen beds, a living room, a huge balcony and perks throughout the cruising experience. We pressed in and obtained a blessing!

When you are gaining ground is the best time to advance on the enemy, so at our first stop in Mexico we booked a 4x4 tour excursion. We knew it was a choice within wisdom, but one that would be yet another step of faith. Mom wanted to wear sandals that day because we were going to the beach and they were comfortable for her to wear. As we walked down the hall from our room to disembark from the ship, one of her sandals kept falling off of her foot. I would stop and help her get the sandal back on, naturally this began to frustrate her. I realized that the sandal was falling off because she didn't yet have the muscle strength to keep the sandal on. After a third time of the sandal coming off I looked at her and said, "This sandal will stay on your foot, and today, this will be our miracle!" She smiled and said amen. That sandal never fell off again and I believe the muscles received perfect strength in that moment. They stayed on as we walked from our cabin, off the ship, and to the dock where we would get in our Jeep. We took a crazy, bumpy, off road adventure with Jeremiah at the wheel, and he really knows how to have fun off-roading. We got in and out of the back seat of that Jeep several times, walked on the beach, played in the water, went back to the ship and to the room. Never ONCE did her sandal fall off her foot again!

My Mom was such an amazing warrior. It takes a steadfast spirit to walk through such a battle as she was faced with. She was surrounded by those who loved her and lifted her up in faith, but her healing came about by refusing to give up and exercising her own faith in believing God would heal her. She had learned much from walking with Jesus since she was a little girl and every step towards Him brought her closer to comprehending His power within her. She was constantly built up by a faith filled husband, but even more so by her own establishing of who God was in her life. Dad was not there for this battle and she was challenged within herself to really believe that she was an overcomer and victorious, because God loved her and had a purpose for her yet on the earth to be fulfilled. Sometimes she would compare her faith to Dad's, which is a natural thing we all do when we are met with someone who has radical bold faith, but God established in her through this battle that her faith was more than enough. I saw an incredible confidence that she gained through her victory. Dad passing away left in her a little bit of unsureness of what the Lord was doing and how He would continue to use her. This victory gave her the second wind she needed to carry out her own ministry until Jesus called her home.

During Mom's healing I took off about of month of work to be with her around the clock, but by the end of that time I was able to start work again as she was almost one hundred percent back to being in complete health. She had always had an issue with high blood pressure and not long after her full recovery, she found out her blood pressure numbers were normal. During the healing process she also dropped three dress sizes. She had received a complete miracle from a massive stroke and there are many who can testify to this and glorify God for His miracle working power!

Soon after this victory I began to act on the call on my life and preach the gospel of Jesus. I knew I was called but I still hadn't learned what it meant to be chosen. At first I set out to do exactly what I had seen my Dad do, travel and evangelize to churches and home meetings. For the next few years I would travel to evangelize up and down the east coast with Mom as my travel companion. I still maintained my full time job as a residential painter working with Jeremiah's painting company, a trade at which I had become a master of at this point in my carrier, having excelled at this job since I was seventeen. My brother was a wonderful boss and always gave me any time off I needed when it came to traveling in the ministry, which allowed me freedom that most full time jobs never would have afforded.

It was in August of 2007 when we made a trip to minister in Pawtucket, Rhode Island at the church of Pastor Charles and Sue Cabral. This wonderful family had become very good friends of ours from when Dad ministered at their church, and this would be the first time I would have the privilege of ministering there. I was scheduled to preach a few services over a week's time and on the very first day we met together for dinner. Brother Cabral invited two young men from his church to join us that evening and one of the young men was Brendan O'Malley. He was one of the youth leaders at the church and the saxophonist in the worship band. Brendan began fellowshipping with the Cabral family around the time Dad had passed away. From my previous times of visiting, I became good friends with the pastors daughter Diane, and Brendan had become good friends with her as they worked together in the youth and music ministries. This connection between the three of us resulted in a week of fellowship together.

And, as providence would have it, Brendan happened to be a mechanic and I happened to need a mechanic, as I had driven into town on a bent rim. I didn't know what exactly was wrong, but I knew the vibration I felt when driving wasn't right. So the first day I was there I shared this with the group and Brother Cabral volunteered Brendan's services. Out of love for his pastor Brendan willingly took my car and fixed the issue, not knowing that sacrifice of love would lead to him receiving an even greater love.

It wasn't love at first sight, but it was close. At the end of the week we both felt something growing in our hearts, so I decided to find out if there was something more than sparks and extended my stay for another week. At the end of the second week we were head over heels in love. We agreed to having a long distance relationship and continued getting to know one another during our many phone calls and visiting each other for the holidays. Barely two months after we met I received a call while I was ministering in Tennessee. It was Brendan, and he was so excited because the Lord had spoken to him. During a church retreat, at which he spent days on end of alone time with the Lord and fellowshipping with like believers, he sought direction from the Lord about the possibility of our future together. God spoke to Brendan very clearly, giving him that direction he sought. He said to me, "I've heard from the Lord! I'm moving to North Carolina and I'm going to marry you!" I laughed and cried and gave him my whole hearted approval. I thought it was funny how my Dad had proposed to my Mom on the phone and my future husband did the same thing with me! Brendan was true to his word and flew down to surprise me with an engagement ring on Valentine's Day 2008. We were married on April 12 of the same year in the backyard of my family home.

(Photo of Brendan and I on our wedding day)

Although Brendan having a motorcycle was a very big plus for me, I was truly drawn to his servants heart. In the natural we shared many like interests but it was his heart that was set on God that won my heart over. In the natural he reminded me of my Dad in many ways and to me that was the best thing in the world possible, after all there was no man that I more greatly respected or loved than my Dad, until I met Brendan. I knew Brendan would be a help mate to me as much as I would be for him, and that we would grow up together with the Lord in the center of our marriage. We certainly didn't know everything, but we knew love was more than a feeling, and the first expression love always makes is committing to one another for life. We are the very best of friends, and life has been not only a learning process of togetherness, but an absolute delight! Many things about him drew me in, but the most important things were that he loved the Lord, he was Holy Spirit filled, and he was willing not only to commit to me but to having Mom in our lives, which in turn showed me just how deep his love was for me. By being willing to let Mom love him like her own son, compounded with letting me love him as his wife, he began to grow exponentially in the knowledge of the love of God towards him. What amazing faith he has! Few men would have welcomed a bride's mother into the very beginning of his own relationship with his wife.

Mom asked only one thing of Brendan when he asked for her blessing to marry me, "Will you love her like Jesus loves the church?" He answered in honesty, "I don't know if I can love her as much as Jesus loves her, but I sure am going to try!" That was the right answer and she gladly gave us her blessing. She could not have loved him better if he had been her own biological son and she was so very proud of the man he became over the years. She would tell me all the time just how proud she was of him and how glad she was that we were so happy together. She recognized every sacrifice he made for her to be such a close part of our lives and she daily asked the Lord to bless him for it. And incase you were wondering, Brendan has done an excellent job of loving me!

Not very long after we were married we decided to buy the house from my Mom so that she would be completely debt free. She had already decided that the house was mine and my brothers inheritance that she was intending on leaving to us when she passed away. So to settle this, she gifted Brendan and I half of the fair market value of the house and we bought my brother out for the remaining half. The house and all that was within it that belonged to her passed to me in that deal and she never so much as had to worry about having a last will and testament. Oh the preciousness of a woman of wisdom! She was indeed a virtuous woman whose value was far above rubies.

When Mom and Dad were first married they signed waivers exempting them from paying into social security, which in turn disqualified them for collecting social security money. This waiver also made them ineligible for medicare. They had no safety net, as the world terms it. No guarantee of money in their old age from the government. Shortly after we moved to Greensboro Dad decided to buy a life insurance policy that would pay off their debt when he passed. He only paid about three years into the policy and it did indeed pay off almost all the debt and lifted that burden from Mom. The only debt left was some equity debt on the house, but when Brendan and I purchased the house, she become totally debt free. God told Dad shortly after he bought the house on Panners Trail that the house was his "retirement package", a gift from the Lord to enjoy in his older age. He did not live to see it paid off but that's the thing about faith, sometimes we must believe and never see the promise ourselves, knowing God will still be faithful to fulfill the promise.

Things seemed to be changing so quickly in such a few short years. Just about the time I met Brendan the Lord had begun to deal with me on many things within my flesh that were not yet conformed to His heart. He lovingly brought me to a place of brokenness one day. He showed me myself as a piece of pottery that was shattered and how He was taking those pieces and retransforming them into clay to remold me into the vessel of His choosing. The main thing he brought to my attention at that time was how full of myself I really was. It wasn't until then that I began to learn to let Him have full control. That included opening my eyes to see that I was chasing after a ministry that was only what I had seen my father do. It was not wrong or bad and God had honored every effort I had made within my own understanding, but God not only had something different for me in mind, but something greater.

It was within that revelation I began to yield to His will and began to understand being chosen, though it has taken me until the writing of this book to fully comprehend what that means. There is a higher price that must be paid by dying to self in a way that leaves no room for the will of the flesh. I must decrease so that He may increase, so that His Kingdom is built and not my own. When the Lord spoke to me that day He got my attention and I stopped traveling in the ministry. Soon after He spoke again, this time calling us out of the church world. I say "us" because the Lord spoke to me to end having home church services in our house, but I brought this word to both Brendan and Mom to hear their counsel and find confirmation. They believed the Lord had spoken and it was right that we should do so, so that Sunday was the last Sunday services were held in our living room. We loved our church family so fiercely that we were willing to do whatever it took to live in the fullness of God, may they always know how much we still love them. It was perhaps not easily understood at the time but a radical change was what God needed to begin to prepare us for the new. It isn't always easy to be the first to speak up in the crowd, but someone must do it.

It was time for the rubber to meet the road, it was time for the Holy Spirit to have my full attention and not be looking to man's opinion for what God had for my life. Over the past ten years God slowly but surely worked on my focus, so that it would be on Him alone. Then He began to open my eyes to see how the church world was so far from what He had always intended and that's why I had to be separated from it. The heart of man wants a formula to follow to come into the understanding of who God is. There is no formula to how the Holy Spirit moves in us, there is only us giving Him freedom to do in us as He wills. Does this mean God is a God of disorder? On the contrary! Perfect order in Him is only found as the Holy Spirit is given the freedom to lead us in the way He sees fit. The religious spirited church has become a body of people with the inability to see beyond the confines of their own system of belief, holding tight to the traditions of man. Hearers but not doers.

~

"But be doers of the word, and not hearers only, deceiving yourselves. For if anyone is a hearer of the word and not a doer, he is like a man observing his natural face in a mirror; for he observes himself, goes away, and immediately forgets what kind of man he was. But he who looks into the perfect law of liberty and continues in it, and is not a forgetful hearer but a doer of the work, this one will be blessed in what he does."
James 1:22-25 (NKJV)

~

Structure and discipline have replaced the Holy Spirit governing and because of it people forget what they have heard for themselves directly from the mouth of God. But isn't structure the foundation of the church? Surely you cannot expect people to just be full of the love of God and walk out into the world to spread that love because they are allowed to be free in the perfect law of liberty, can you? It would be chaos if we did not convene at a certain time and sing a certain set of songs and be told what to do by someone other than God Himself, right? Wrong. This misrepresentation of the Holy Spirit has gone on far too long! How long do you think He will stand for it? Believer, He dwells within you, and according to Colossians 2:9, in Him dwells the fullness of the Godhead bodily, so why do you continue to look to man to teach you? You are His creation that was fashioned for His purpose which is to know Him and be known by Him, to be loved by Him and love Him, to hear His voice for yourself. That relationship is all it takes to qualify to hear His voice and be brought up by Him into all things spiritual and see Him manifested in your life.

The Lord spoke to me after He called me to come out of the church and said, "Your ministry will be one of reconciling the church to Me." At that time He spoke that word I was only just beginning to understand what it meant to be able to discern between the church world and God's world. I didn't fully understand what that ministry He spoke to me of would look like, but I believe He said it and so I was willing to find out what it meant. First I had to be separated, then learn to sit and be still at the feet of my Savior, so that I could better hear and respond to His voice and His voice alone. He called me out of the church world for a purpose and it has taken years for the understanding of that purpose to develop. He has been taking those broken pieces of pottery and making them moldable again, then reforming that clay into a new vessel and that is no a simple process. The only way I can describe it is that I have been saturated in the things of His kingdom and shed off of the things of the flesh and this earth. Little by little and step by step I have been made into a vessel of honor that He fashioned to pour out His Spirit from. The past fifteen years of being set apart were crucial to me for establishing confidence in the power of Christ in me. I am no longer who I once was but can now say, as He is so am I in this world.

~

> "And we have known and believed the love that God has for us. God is love, and he who abides in love abides in God, and God in him. Love has been perfected among us in this: that we may have boldness in the day of judgment; because as He is, so are we in this world. There is no fear in love; but perfect love casts out fear, because fear involves torment. But he who fears has not been made perfect in love. We love Him because He first loved us." 1 John 4:16-19 (NKJV)

~

Know who you are and the devil can't talk you out of it!

# 7
# When Your Will Is His Will

As I was called out of the church world I began to look back and see how my Dad was the precursor for this new way. He was my example of someone who truly walked in the things of the Spirit. I began to recall many things the Lord showed Dad that could help me understand this change that was taking place. After stepping out of the church world and into something completely new, I honestly didn't know what was going to happen. The first few years of this transition were full of growing up while still not knowing what it was I was being prepared for. The one thing that stood out to me the most was when Dad himself was shown something new in the last few years of his life. God gave him a revelation about a new move that was beginning to take place and Dad called it "The Be Like Jesus" move.

This new understanding came shortly after we met the Piardi family. Dad said he saw God doing a quick transformative work like he had never seen in anyone before. He said that he was amazed at how when the revelations he was given by God were presented to them they immediately applied them to their lives. He could only describe it like the Bible does as a "quick work" because of the speed of which the change was coming. He saw how they were willing to lay it all on the line for the deeper knowledge of who Jesus is because they truly believed the message of becoming one with the Lord through taking on the mind of Christ. This rate of speed with which the changes were happening alerted Dad to knowing something great was about to happen.

~

"For he will finish the work, and cut it short in righteousness: because a short work will the Lord make upon the earth." Romans 9:28 (KJV)

~

In January of 2002 Stefano was visiting us in Greensboro and he and Dad were sitting at a local national park fellowshipping with one another. As they sat observing a statue of General Nathanael Greene, the man for whom Greensboro is named, Dad began to share with Stefano the details of when Jesus appeared to him and what God said to him. After retelling that amazing encounter Dad added, "Today God showed me the fulfillment of what He said when He said I am going to show you a new way". Now, after over thirty-five years since Jesus appeared to him for a second time in that hotel room in Ohio the Lord brought him into the full understanding of it. Stefano was curious, although oblivious to what Dad was talking about so he asked, "What is it?" Dad answered, "It's you."

It was too profound for Stefano to have understood at that moment, but Dad was excited to see what God was doing and he knew the time was near for radical change within the church. What Dad believed he was seeing was a true desire within a believer to break free from the constraints that man had created through the church world organization. Dad had lived a life of oneness with the Spirit to a level that scared most people and he desired nothing more than to communicate to others that the same oneness He had found in the Lord was available to all who thirsted for it. Through over fifty years of being in the ministry he was shown that no amount of church or preaching could get people to comprehend God in His fullness, only the Holy Spirit having His way in them could do so. Many wanted what Dad had but I believe he was a man before his time. Though he may not have known exactly what the new would look like as it unfolded, he certainly knew that it had begun, because the Lord revealed to him that the time was at hand for that new way to be activated. I believe Dad began to see just a glimpse of what was to come for the time you and I are in now.

Dad said it like this, "The healing movement had power, but power without a real understanding of Truth will not produce change. So the word movement came and it was like a rediscovery of the word of God. Once we came into that knowledge we had to begin applying this knowledge of Truth with the power and begin to become like Jesus. So now we are in the Be Like Jesus movement. If we are to become like Jesus the next step is understanding the power of the Holy Spirit being the One who not only teaches us all things, but that He alone is the power to transform our minds."

We can be like Jesus. The church world has robbed God's people of this truth by diluting the truth of the written word and attempting to circumvent Him with their manmade doctrines. Dad was beginning to see something he had never seen before in all his years in the church world. He could see it because he no longer dwelt there, even though he still actively ministered to those who did. Let me be clear, Stefano himself was not the new that Dad was having revealed to him. The new way was in how God was working in Stefano. Dad saw the beginning of something that would come about in the future. He called it a "new dispensation". I don't believe he could define it because it wasn't for him to do so, but I believe this revelation has been unfolded for me so that I may share it with you.

I believe this new dispensation of the gospel is a new application of the way the gospel will be presented and it is completely without formality. A totally unreligious, straightforward, practical, effective and easily applied way that is without any preconceived ideas. Without format and without ceremony. A true form of ministering by letting the Holy Spirit work in whatever way He wants. No more dead letter or ministry of condemnation as spoken of by Paul in 2 Corinthians 3, but a pure representation of the ministry of righteousness which is the glory of God. This new way is quite the opposite of the current church world order and will lead to the revealing of the spotless Bride, the Body that was always meant to walk in God's world and no other place. A true radical way of walking, just like Jesus. Jesus was misunderstood by the majority of people but embraced by those who could see true love in everything He was. It is a new way of delivering the gospel of Jesus Christ without mixing in tradition or carnal and it will cause rapid change with lasting results. If you have no preconceived ideas of how God should move, then the Holy Spirit has freedom in you and He will move!

Dad spoke of this new dispensation and believed that it would be activated just before the trumpet sounds to call the Bride home. He explained that we would first have to go through a process of the old giving way to the new. The last word from the Lord that Dad left us, just before he went to heaven, was that there would be an exodus of people coming out of churches world wide. God spoke this to Dad and then confirmed it with the word in 2 Kings chapter 7. Dad said people would become starved for the reality of God and fed up with not receiving teaching that would allow them to be a spotless and perfect Bride. He believed God would raise up a people who sought to be taught by the Holy Spirit, to learn of Him and take on His nature so that they would be like Him and be ready for His return.

Dad ministered this revelation with these words, "What happened to the man at the gate of the city? He was trampled. I want to leave you with this, I'm going to tell you what's getting ready to happen. The man at the gate is a type and shadow of the majority of pastors in the church world today. The pastors who hold the gates of the churches, keeping the starving people inside are going to get trampled to death. I believe we are going to see the greatest exodus out of the general church world that we have ever seen. They are going to look for the Truth. They are going to look for men and women who live it. They are tired of hearing about it, they want to see it! They are even tired of hearing the scriptures being read and telling them that 'God can do this and God can do that' but they have nothing to show for it. The man who kept the gate didn't believe Elisha when he spoke the word of God, and that man was trampled to death as the people came out of the gates of Samaria. The city represents the church. People will be hunting the reality of God so intensely that revival will break out, one like we have never seen before. I remember when revival broke out in 1948 and 1949, so many ministries had thousands of people just start coming to their meetings over night. They were people leaving the churches and meeting in tents or open air meetings. They came to see the reality of the blessings, the miracles, the salvations, the power of

God that was being released in the new move of God. Those people never went back to the churches they came out of. But this time there will not be a chance for flesh to build tabernacles out of the great revival of God. How many major changes have been in the church world? From the very beginning you had the people without the law who had prophets and judges and then a radical change happened when God gave Moses the law. When Jesus came there was another radical change in how things were done and one more radical change must happen for the return of Jesus, amen? This change will be so radical that the church world will be astonished and they won't even be able to identify it. Like the Pharisees who could not let Jesus preach in the temple for not understanding who He was and why He preached like He did."

That quote is from the last recorded sermon my Dad preached before he went to be with Jesus. Dad fully believed he would be here for the last move of God because the Lord Himself had spoken to Dad that his ministry was reserved for the end times. In 2002 while traveling through Connecticut, Dad stopped at a gas station to fill up the car and received another confirmation of that word in a strange way. Dad and Mom walked inside the convenience mart of this gas station to get something to drink and to pay for the fuel. The person behind the counter was a short Hispanic man who spoke broken English and he looked at Dad keenly for a moment before saying, "You're a preacher." Dad replied, "Yeah." The man spoke again, "I see on your forehead the Holy Spirit." Dad again replied, "Yeah." The man continued, "I also see written on your forehead, Sealed For The Last Days". Dad grinned and agreed by saying, "Yeah." Mom said her jaw dropped as this stranger spoke with power. They paid for the drinks and gas and then said thank you and good bye. Once outside Mom said to Dad, "Didn't you hear what he said Virgil?" She was blown away and he, as per usual, was quite laid back about the whole thing. He replied, "He didn't tell me anything I didn't already know." This was a confirmation about something he had established in his heart a long time ago because when Jesus appeared to him that was one of the things He had spoken. You may be curious as to why he is not alive today if this is the case. I believe God has the power to raise whomever He sees fit for His final purpose that is to be brought about in the last days. Just like when Jesus was raised from the dead and many saints who had died came back from the dead to proclaim the victory, it's not so far fetched to believe that God will do something similar again. I don't know exactly what He will do, but I do know He is a God of His word!

~

"And the graves were opened; and many bodies of the saints which slept arose, And came out of the graves after his resurrection, and went into the holy city, and appeared unto many. Now when the centurion, and they that were with him, watching Jesus, saw the earthquake, and those things that were done, they feared greatly, saying, Truly this was the Son of God." Matthew 27:52-54 (KJV)

~

The true church is a living breathing Body of Christ and not a denomination or people who agree on a certain doctrine of man. The church world projects an image of an organization and its doctrine being the center of all things. Don't get me wrong, the church world has always had nothing but good intentions and has had glory. Countless amazing things have come about because of organizations who reached out to the world with the gospel and it has all been instrumental in God's plan. So many lives have been changed and there are so many people who would have otherwise not heard the story of salvation if it had not have been for people coming together with a plan on how to get it to the world. People have been impacted and nations changed over the thousands of years that have passed. The old dispensation was good for a time, but now the old must make way for the new, for its glory far exceeds that of the former. The Body of Christ, the true church, has been called to be a people who walk only after the things of the Spirit and fulfill only the things of the Spirit. He who is the very definition of purity cannot be mixed with flesh. Jesus told us that it is possible for us to live with the flesh being in submission to the Spirit, if the mind that was in Him is also in us.

~

"Let this mind be in you, which was also in Christ Jesus:" Philippians 2:5 (KJV)

~

In John 17 Jesus states His desire for His people to be in the world but not of it, to be sanctified through the truth so that we may all be one and perfect in that unity bringing glory to God! We are called to be a Spiritual people whose will is His will. Could this be said of current churches around the world? Is there a oneness in the body of Christ? Is there unity and unselfish love? Is there even agreement on who Jesus is? If all of these things be lacking, then the carnal way of doing things is yet abundant. Jesus told Nicodemus in John 3 that what is of flesh produces flesh and what is of the Spirit produces that which is Spirit. Jesus isn't coming back to marry the church that has the most accurate interpretation of His gospel but those who are living and moving in the Spirit that He sent to transform us. His power is missing because the ability to hear His voice is not being taught. If you can't hear from Him for yourself you will never be made to comprehend His will and have yours conformed to it.

~

"These words spake Jesus, and lifted up his eyes to heaven, and said, 'Father, the hour is come; glorify thy Son, that thy Son also may glorify thee: As thou hast given him power over all flesh, that he should give eternal life to as many as thou hast given him. And this is life eternal, that they might know thee the only true God, and Jesus Christ, whom thou hast sent. I have glorified thee on the earth: I have finished the work which thou gavest me to do...They are not of the world, even as I am not of the world.

Sanctify them through thy truth: thy word is truth. As thou hast sent me into the world, even so have I also sent them into the world. And for their sakes I sanctify myself, that they also might be sanctified through the truth. Neither pray I for these alone, but for them also which shall believe on me through their word; That they all may be one; as thou, Father, art in me, and I in thee, that they also may be one in us: that the world may believe that thou hast sent me. And the glory which thou gavest me I have given them; that they may be one, even as we are one: I in them, and thou in me, that they may be made perfect in one; and that the world may know that thou hast sent me, and hast loved them, as thou hast loved me.' " John 17:1-3 & 16-23 (KJV)

~

This lack of hearing God's voice may be the current state of the church world, but I will tell you one thing, the word of God promises it will not be like that forever. For He is returning for a Bride who is without spot or wrinkle, an image of perfection. She who is in agreement, who is one, who is powerful and full of the glory of God. Jesus prayed for our perfection and told us we could be perfect in the Spirit. He didn't say that you must wait for perfection until you get to heaven. We are invited to come into that oneness in Him so that when He looks at us He only sees Himself and He is perfect. To be perfect is to reach completion and the word says we are complete only in Him. This perfection Jesus teaches us of is not something that can be comprehended through carnal thinking, and we may never fully understand it until we get to Heaven, but believing His word that we are complete and perfect in Him unlocks God's world for the believer because it is the only way we can ever see us as He sees us.

I believe that during this Be Like Jesus move, that has been quietly taking place, He has been raising up a people that are so codependent upon God that all they know is hearing and responding in obedience to His voice. Where the carnal is self-sufficient, in contrast the spiritual is totally dependent upon the presence of God in you. So, this people He has chosen no longer depend upon operating by the carnal mind. These people are people you have most likely never heard of. They have stepped out of the church world and are being led by Him alone, for His purpose that is soon to come about. Perhaps you are one of them who has been prepared for such a time as this. When you look into the lives of these people you will not be able to give them an ounce of the glory because the evidence will speak of Him doing the work and not us. It's not about transforming people into people who have it all figured out, but to have a people who have been so radically changed by His love and the power of the Holy Spirit that they have been transformed to be like Him! A people who have boldness and confidence by faith in who they are in Him.

~

"Whereof I was made a minister, according to the gift of the grace of God given unto me by the effectual working of His power. And to make all men see what is the fellowship of the mystery, which from the beginning of the world hath been hid in God, who created all things by Jesus Christ: To the intent that now unto the principalities and powers in heavenly places might be known by the church the manifold wisdom of God, According to the eternal purpose which he purposed in Christ Jesus our Lord: In whom we have boldness and access with confidence by the faith of him." Ephesians 3:7 & 9-12 (KJV)

~

It is a good thing that someone reaches out to the world so that the world may know it is lost. It is a good thing that once the lost have been found they have an example to live by. It is not a good thing that those born again believers be made to become like a church and their doctrine. Flesh wants to identify with flesh, but Jesus came so that flesh would be done away with and the Spirit of God would be made alive in us. Jesus is the only example we were ever made to pattern ourselves after. Some people have a hard time seeing Him because of the filter of the flesh and have taught others who He is through that filter. It is a pattern that has been perpetuated for thousands of years within the church world. A veil over the eyes of those deceived by a religious spirit.

~

"Therefore, since we have such hope, we use great boldness of speech, unlike Moses, who put a veil over his face so that the children of Israel could not look steadily at the end of what was passing away. But their minds were blinded...Nevertheless when one turns to the Lord, the veil is taken away. Now the Lord is the Spirit; and where the Spirit of the Lord is, there is liberty. But we all, with unveiled face, beholding as in a mirror the glory of the Lord, are being transformed into the same image from glory to glory, just as by the Spirit of the Lord." 2 Corinthians 3:12-18 (NKJV)

~

I have known so, so many people who go to church to find God with hopes of becoming like Him by osmosis. They ultimately end up not very much at all like Jesus but exactly like who the church dictates they should be through specific doctrinal laws. I have yet to know a church that did not have its own set of laws by which the people were made to adhere. It is like a mold by which a congregation must pattern itself to be like whomever is leading it, or to be like the great man or woman of God who has gone before them and laid the foundation for the doctrine. How is that any form of the freedom and diversity which the Spirit embodies? It is not liberty but law and death. This new way is a higher way, a more Kingdom way. The way to living free from the flesh and the condemnation brought by the law. That which cannot be obtained within the confines of the man made tabernacle. Jesus said He came to establish the Kingdom of God. His entire ministry was based on preaching that one message of what the Kingdom of Heaven looked like and how we could obtain it, the only way to live in God's world. Jesus is the only example that God ever intended people to be conformed to, and Jesus never built a church, but He did tear one down!

I am not telling anyone to walk away from what they believe. What I am doing is encouraging you to reexamine what you think you know by pressing in to hear God's voice for yourself. Don't take my word for it, ask God! All I want to do is share this beautiful revelation He has given me and let everyone who is looking for freedom know that I have found it and it is obtainable. This is not a fairytale or something unreachable, it is how we were always meant to live, one with Him. It is the confidence of knowing that we are His and exactly what it means to be His. The Holy Spirit longs to be the One you turn to and be taught by. He eagerly awaits for you to tap into the power He brings so that you can live free from self, the Adam mind, brokenness, hurt, fear, depression, anxiety, the need for control and all the lies of the enemy. If the church should find out what power they are inheritors of they would not only be a Bride without spot or wrinkle, but they would shake the gates of hell and set this world on fire with the glory of God! Like those who have gone before me, I want to make known the realities of living and moving and having our being in Jesus. I believe people are so sick of being told they must learn of man, that they are desperate enough now to believe what the word says about the Holy Spirit being our teacher and that it is actually possible.

~

"But the anointing which you have received from Him abides in you, and you do not need that anyone teach you; but as the same anointing teaches you concerning all things, and is true, and is not a lie, and just as it has taught you, you will abide in Him."
1 John 2:27

~

I have gleaned from my Dad's revelations my entire life. I have grown up in the knowledge of who God is because he was faithful to live it and to give it away, but just as he was made to realize that his own vision could not be the same of his mother's, I too had to walk with Jesus and begin to press in for myself to hear His voice. He speaks and then waits to see if we will respond and how we will respond. If we hear and obey, then He becomes more confident in that fact that we are listening and will speak more. Not only will He speak more often but He will begin to reveal more of Himself to us through every word. As I have drawn near to Him, He has placed in me a vision, and one that I am willing to lay down my life to be made fit for.

This book has been an evolving story. I will honestly say it has not always been easy to put into words what the Spirit is revealing. It is, after all, a story that is still being written and will continue beyond the pages of this book. But I believe with all my heart the words that God has spoken to me. I also believe that those who are hungry are walking into a freedom like there has never been known before. I have not given every detail of our every day lives in the telling of our stories, because this story is not as much about us as it is about who God is in us, and what is being brought about through us. In the beginning of this book I told you that God gave me a revelation that changed everything for me. It was truly a turning point, and now that I have told you about my foundation, I can tell you about the day God renovated my life with that revelation. All which came about because of a desire to help my Mom.

(Photo of my Mom and I)

In 2017 I had this great idea to try to increase my Mom's quality of living. She was having some issues with her knee being stiff and aching, and this on and off again pain was giving her some limited mobility. We prayed often together for this issue, and sometimes there would be weeks of it feeling perfectly fine, and then some days it wasn't. We did senior exorcises together every day in which we would do aerobic motions while being seated in a chair. That was good and seemed helpful, but I thought we could do more by helping her increase her exorcising. So I came up with the idea of getting a stationary bike, a well intentioned idea that was from a heart of concern. She couldn't get out and take walks like we used to do, so this was another way of keeping her active and feeling good, or so I thought. So I presented the idea and she agreed to give it a try, we even went to a second hand sports equipment shop to see how much a used stationary bike would cost.

The next day while I was going about my daily tasks the Lord spoke to me and said, "You are imposing your will on your mother. It is not in My nature to impose My will on you, so why are you imposing your will on her? When you impose your will on others it creates a burden and condemnation upon them." He spoke and I heard it loud and clear. I didn't cry but I was very quiet for a while as I sat and absorbed the fullness of what He said. Dad had always told me, "Jesus is a gentleman, He never forces Himself on anyone." That came to mind, as well as many of the instances throughout my life of when I had tried to impose my will on others. Like trying to force my husband to not drink diet soda because it is not as healthy as drinking water, or arguing with someone to have my opinion be heard and overriding theirs. Even if the motivation of my heart was from genuine care for the other person, the truth is, it isn't a facet of Christ-like love to impose your will on someone else. He gives us the freedom to choose and the opportunity to be ourselves with liberty and joy, and He calls us to do the same for everyone.

God truly never makes anyone do anything against their will, that's why it's called free will! He loves us into a place of wanting to do His will, which is the very best for us. But He couldn't force us to do anything, even if He wanted to, because that would go against His nature as a just and righteous God. He invites us to let Him love us and for us to love Him in return. He gives us a choice to believe Him or reject Him. He wants us to do His will from a heart of always letting us be the ones who want to do it. That is the perfect relationship with Him that He died to give us. He wants friends, not servants.

~

> "No longer do I call you servants, for a servant does not know what his master is doing; but I have called you friends, for all things that I heard from My Father I have made known to you." John 15:15 (NKJV)

~

As soon as I repented for what I was unwittingly doing to my Mom, I immediately went to her and told her what the Lord had said to me. This time I wept as I felt the weight of the word God had spoken. Speaking it out loud woke my heart to understand fully what it meant to realize I was unknowingly placing a burden upon Mom. My Mom, the woman who loved me so deeply and so well my entire life! I told her I was sorry and asked for her forgiveness and as all this poured out of me she smiled with tears running down her cheeks and replied, "Thank you baby, it's alright. I forgive you." I cried in her arms for a while and then we began to laugh as joy welled up inside of us from the goodness of God and how He reached us in such a way to change the situation for our good. I hope the fullness of this revelation can reach everyone who reads this.

I can't stress enough how my intentions were good, but they were based in my fleshly knowledge and the self-righteous assumption that I knew what was best for her. I thought exercise would be the answer for Mom when she was at a time in her life when her body was naturally slowing down, and yet all the time she was willing to submit to my will because she loved me so immensely! How often do we burden those we love the most just because we think we know what is best for them? How often do we crowd them with our good intentions and drive out the will of God from a situation? She was willing to try for my sake, to please me because she fully trusted me and my leading, but in her heart she didn't want to do what I was asking. Not only did she not want to do what I proposed, but she knew she couldn't. If I had imposed my will on her and made her try, it would have emphasized her inability to do so, and in turn made her feel less than she was because she couldn't do it. Is that love?

The Holy Spirit in me made me aware of all these things after the voice of God spoke a word. I heard His voice and then I responded. He has come for this purpose to teach us! I was being taught in that moment something that was radically opposite of the carnal way of thinking. That which only could have been comprehended in the Spirit. It is inside of us to want to make people see our point of view, in fact it is only natural. But I have not been made only natural in Christ Jesus. I was crying out for more of Him but first He had to help me decrease, or deal with my carnal way of thinking. This revelation has given me the key to loving others like Jesus does. Not only is condemnation no longer present in the life of one who walks in the perfect love of Jesus, but that life in turn should not cause others to come into condemnation. Not imposing your will on others will lead to unity in the Spirit among the chosen. It will create a sensitivity of our oneness as a body of brothers and sisters. In this revelation we will become slow to speak and quick to listen. It will create an unbreakable bond that is not based in fleshly relationship, but viewing one another as equal in the Spirit.

Imposing our will on others is the very essence of our Adam nature. And it has caused division and discord, while being the major point of hypocrisy within the church world to the world who is looking from the outside in. People always striving to be better than the other denomination or arguing to prove that their doctrine should be the one that is deemed truer than another. The Holy Spirit is the Unifier and without Him there will always be division. Not imposing your will on others is the very definition of meekness and being meek is not only a fruit of the Spirit but an attribute of Jesus. In Matthew 11:29 He tells us that He is meek and lowly of heart. He who has all the power in the universe never once imposed His will on anyone. He presented the truth in meekness and love giving them all the freedom they needed to make the choice for themselves and it set people free! And it has been setting people free ever since. How can we understand the heart of God unless we can understand Jesus? And how can we fully understand Jesus without the power of the Holy Spirit operating in us to reveal His nature to us? The word says the Holy Spirit is the revealer of the mysteries of God. It is a false doctrine of an angry God mixed with the keeping of the law that drives out the need of the Holy Spirit moving in and through us. He is meekness, therefore without Him we cannot be meek. Being meek is not being shy or introverted but the opposite. It is understanding the power you have and not overpowering someone else with it.

Not imposing our will on others is radically opposite of what we are taught to believe in the carnal. The carnal minded person must make others understand what they believe and they are determined to have their will done whatever the cost. The spiritual minded person lets the Holy Spirit bring forth revelation from their hearts to share with people with the purpose of touching the other persons spirit. This in turn causes that person who is being ministered to to open up their hearts to the leading of the Holy Spirit. So it shouldn't be about my will or me getting my point across, but about letting Him pour out of me so He can do that transformative work that only He can do. That takes the pressure off of not only me, but the one whom I am hoping to reach with the truth. If I don't have a hunger to feed you but to see you fed by Him, then it is not my will but His that is done.

Man so often starts off with the best of intentions and then brings people into bondage with his ideas and ways of doing things that become laws to live by. We learn best not by having things explained to us but by experiencing them for ourselves. If you impose your will on others you are not walking in the Spirit, of that I am sure. But I believe this revelation of the nature of Jesus not lording His power over you but lovingly inviting you to become a part of Him, will help you to comprehend who He is in you. That comprehension brings maturity and the power to overcome. And, if you will let it, you will be made to be able to edify the Body in love.

~

"Till we all come in the unity of the faith, and of the knowledge of the Son of God, unto a perfect man, unto the measure of the stature of the fulness of Christ: That we henceforth be no more children, tossed to and fro, and carried about with every wind of doctrine, by the sleight of men, and cunning craftiness, whereby they lie in wait to deceive; But speaking the truth in love, may grow up into him in all things, which is the head, even Christ: From whom the whole body fitly joined together and compacted by that which every joint supplieth, according to the effectual working in the measure of every part, maketh increase of the body unto the edifying of itself in love."
Ephesians 4:13-16 (KJV)

~

As we speak the truth in love may we grow up into Him in all things! This will bring about the unity of faith that is lacking within the church world. Where I can sit down with you, and even though we may do life a little differently, we can come together in the Spirit to love and edify one another with the words He gives us and the words He has written for us. Then it's not about me or you, it's about each of us understanding the others value through the eyes of God. In the unity of the Spirit you may be able to provoke me to understand something I might not yet be able to see on my own because of my perspective from my walk. The Spirit functions this way to allow us to help one another. This is how we become stronger together. As the Holy Spirit in me identifies with the Holy Spirit in you, I can know that what you are saying is good and right because it is of the Spirit of Truth. This is what it truly means to minister one to another. When the carnal understanding is removed, then the Spirit Himself ministers through us to one another perfectly. Through this ministry we become one in the unity of the faith and the knowledge of God! As one heart, one mind and one Body in the Holy Spirit. Flesh will always cause division and the Spirit will always bring us together as one in the Lord.

It has so very little to do with us and everything to do with Him! It brings Him delight when we remove any restraints from Him having His way in us. He does not impose His will but He presents it in such a way that we can do nothing but yield to its goodness! Where our will is totally imperfect, His is totally and completely perfect in every way, with our ultimate good at the heart of it. Can you see Him in this way? Do you feel His love breaking through all of the lies you have held onto for so long? Do you feel it washing over you like water rushing in a mighty river to clean off that old dead flesh? Not your will, but His will be done! The beauty of it is that you don't have to kill your flesh, He did that for us on the cross, all you must do now is identify with what He did and come to know who He truly is to walk in New Life. The Holy Spirit allows us to take on the mind of Christ and as we yield to that power working in us, the flesh, or carnal mind, gets overtaken. Thus we become hidden in Christ.

As you purpose to open up and let the Holy Spirit have His way, before you know it your will becomes His will. When you comprehend that His will is your will, you will know what oneness with Him means. The word says in Philippians 2:5 "let this mind be in you that was also in Christ Jesus." That mind that gave Jesus oneness with the Father despite His living in a fleshly vessel surrounded by a carnal world. I don't know about you, but I am living everyday to dwell in a place of oneness with Him! Some days I may operate in the world, but while living in that carnal realm I choose to not be carnal in my thinking and limit God. This means I'm dwelling in God's world, in the Kingdom of Heaven. In this world I must work, I must have relationships, I must live life as any other human, but if I am one with Him, I am walking in God's world of no limitations. He is apart of everything I do and experience, if I am in Him. I just have to let the Holy Spirit renew my mind so I can become aware of His presence on a moment by moment basis. If I walk in that way, then His world overrules the carnal world and that is where miracles happen. That is where the blind see and the deaf hear and the dead are raised! That is how the harlot is satisfied in Jesus, the fishermen become fishers of men, and the Pharisee can understand revelation that fulfills the law. THAT is where we hear His voice loud and clear!

It is time that the church world be exposed for being an imposer of its will. As good intentioned as it may have begun, there is now a new way in which we must administer the gospel of Jesus that will finally break through the barriers between the world and God's world. Imposing your will on someone else does not provoke them to love, or edify them spiritually. It has proven itself an ineffective way to raise up people who are righteous in word and deed and pureness of heart. If the administration of the gospel we are using is working then we should not be producing church members but full grown Christians who come to church to learn and in turn go back out to apply what they have learned. Then they should go and show others who Jesus is without having to return again to the church. Fellowship is essential but sitting next to each other on a pew is not fellowship. Fellowship is partnership and active participation in each others lives. I believe if people who heard from God were sharing what it was they were given then the whole world would know who He is. Once you learn something it should not have to be taught to you over and over and over. Church should be a living, moving flow of coming in and going out, if it is efficient. Instead of a people being born in the church and dying in the church, what if they were born again because of Jesus revealing Himself to them and then set on fire to go out and take the world for the Kingdom? But gaining and keeping members has become the goal of most every pastor in every church, and so their flesh clings to this long held belief.

Remember, we are all created equal in Him and He wants to teach us. Not one of us is greater than the other, though some may know Him more intimately than others, simply because of where they are in their own walk. He is our Father raising up His children as He sees fit. He doesn't compare us one to another, so why do we do it to ourselves? A life with Him will inevitably change us but He does not demand we change. He draws us out of darkness, out of sin, with His love. And that love with which He first loved us, loves us just as we are. What if we saw each other this way? What if we gathered together for the sheer joy of being in each other's company because of our common love for Jesus and our love one to another? What if we could fellowship with the common goal of seeing His will done, whatever it takes? A united people that gather together with one heart and mind and spirit are those who give the devil nightmares!

God desires a sensitivity within our spirits through the operation of the gifts of the Holy Spirit, so that we can know when someone else needs Him and be a light in their darkness. That can only be done through the operation of the gifts of discernment and word of knowledge. Without the Holy Spirit working in us, then all we are left with is our feeble carnal ways and ideas that we implement in hopes it will help. It may help some but it does not hold the power to transform a life. If we are one in Him then we will have His perfect words to say and His perfect will to pray. It is the Holy Spirit alone who can intercede for us and if we let Him do the work it will always turn out for our good and for the good of the people that we love. His will is always done through us when the Holy Spirit has His way in us! His Spirit operating in us and through us is the glory of the new covenant ministry that Paul spoke of in 2 Corinthians 3, and that glory alone is what transforms us into the image of Christ and takes us from glory to glory!

If you are walking without that glorious power then you have not submitted yourself to the Holy Spirit. Because in Him is all the fullness of the operation of the nine gifts of the spirit, the five-fold ministry and the ability to produce the nine fruits of the Spirit. Without Him we can do nothing but with Him only having a little bit of control we will only make ourselves more miserable than before we were saved. But with Him completely having our tongues, our minds, and our hearts, we will be made overcomers and more than conquerors in Christ Jesus! In this we will have confidence and boldness to let His will be done on earth as it is in heaven!

# 8
## Not Imposing Your Will

Is His will your will? Mine is and I know it. Because I know Whose I am. I am a daughter of the Most High King. If you knew my parents before me you would see a bit of both of them in me because it is from them that I learned how to think. So in the natural I may think like my parents, talk like my parents or act like my parents. So it should be in the spiritual. If we have been adopted into the family of God by being born again by the Spirit then we should think, talk and act like our Father. No longer am I only natural but through the adoption into the family of God I am a daughter of God. A rebirth took place as I became born again into this supernatural family. Being fully aware of who I am in Him, I have been able to grow up spiritually so that now I am able to think like God, talk like God and act like God. Some people will have a hard time understanding this truth, but it is key to living a victorious life here in the natural. This door to freedom can only be unlocked by establishing your identity in Christ. I was shown the possibilities of living in God's world by my parents and as soon as I could make the choice for myself I began to walk after the things of the Spirit. To quote a song my Mom used to sing, "It's not because of who I am, it's not because of what I've done, it's because of Whose I am!"

It has taken thirty-eight years to come to this place I now dwell, with a whole lot of partnering with the Holy Spirit who dwells in me, so that He could empty me of myself and fill me up with Him. I am now only an extension of Him, like a branch connected to a vine. I abide in Him and He abides in me. His words spoken to me have become my reality and I guard them in my heart at all costs against the lies of the enemy and the naysayers of this world. This confidence is often put to the test, and sometimes I get it right the first go around, and other times I need another chance to prove it. But it always comes out as victory, no matter how long it takes to get it. The proof of this power in me is that my life produces fruit. It not only produces fruit but that fruit remains in me so that I can operate in Him on a daily basis.

If I am emptied of myself, my will is His will. If I no longer have control, He has full control to work all things to my good. If I am rooted and grounded in His love, then I am confident in who I am in Him. That confidence allows me to live in this world while not being of it. I do not make myself righteous by any means. I am not strong enough or smart enough or disciplined enough to make myself righteous. But I believe the word that says I am made the righteousness of God through Jesus, and therein lies my assurance of being in right standing with the Father. I cannot pass on to you my experience or make you understand anything of my own natural reasoning, but if I speak (or write) the truth in love, then I believe the Spirit that is behind it will reach you and breakthrough any barrier.

Knowing who I am means I can love you, because I love myself, because I know how much He loves me. And if I do not love like Jesus loves, then I am like sounding brass or tinkling symbols. In other words it's all nothing but noise that makes no melody. I can do nothing with out Him and I know it, so I choose not to do anything without Him. That is living a life free from condemnation and full of the power of God to do what He has chosen me to do. Like my parents before me, I have learned to walk in God's world, in the reality of all things are possible. First to edify me, second to edify my family and third to edify everyone else the Lord causes to cross my path. This oneness with God not only allows my life to be full of and overflowing with all the fruits of the Spirit but it makes me an excellent wife, daughter, sister and friend. I am not boasting in myself because I have not done this work! It is the power of God through the Holy Spirit who has transformed my mind to be one with His and that makes me who I am. Being Virgil and Melonie's daughter gave me a great advantage in this life, but being God's daughter is what has enabled me to reach out to the hurting and lost and bring them hope in a hopeless world. I do not need to prove to you a single thing because the proof is in the fruit. You may be able to find faults in my natural way of thinking or doing things, but when it comes to the supernatural, you will not. Because it is not my mind that is active, but the mind of Christ in me, and His way of thinking is perfect in every way.

What my parents handed down to me in the natural is not important, what is important is that my parents taught me how to deal with that nature. They brought me up to know I had a choice to press in for change through pursuing Jesus. I could have chosen to stay in my natural mind, that was influenced by the human traits passed down from my parents and grandparents, but I chose to pursue the mind of Christ. Neither one of my parents ever told me that I had to follow a religious outlined doctrine, but they always pointed me to Jesus. I had to overcome my natural fear to gain my own confidence in Jesus, and that's something that they couldn't do for me, but they could let me know it was obtainable. I praise God for parents who got me hooked on hearing God's voice!

I have known a life of miracles and it has been proven to me that miracles are a facet of God's nature. From the time I was little, before I could comprehend what a miracle was, I was exposed to them. No matter what happened, going to God was always the first option, and usually the only option. How else could I come to believe that miracles are a part of a life lived with Jesus, except that I saw it proven again and again? This was all I knew growing up, His word and it being true. I tell you all these testimonies in hope that you will be encouraged to not walk through this life on your own. Walking by faith is full of trial and error, don't be afraid to fail. Because even though it may take you time to comprehend who He is in you, He is not disappointed in you for learning how to grow up. Without Him we can do nothing, and with Him there is no limit to what we can do, if we only believe. He is a great God and a merciful loving Father! I know there will most likely be more things I will have to go through to have my faith tested again. But I also know I will make it through whatever may come because His track record is perfect!

I want to be real with you and tell you there are times when I have chosen to step out of the Spiritual and work in my flesh. Sometimes I forget or I revert back to some things that I thought were already dealt with, but I am of the belief that it is ok to make mistakes. It is in the making of those mistakes that we learn to not repeat them. So if I do forget who I am in Him, which has happened from time to time, then all I need to do is be reminded. To go back to the words He has spoken to me and stand firm on that truth because it is unfailing. I get in that quiet place with Him, hear from Him, talk to Him and refocus. The more and more I focus on Him, the less and less the world or the flesh will be able to take my focus off of Him. I can do all things through Christ who strengthens me, as long as I don't forget with Whom my strength lies.

~

"And Jesus looking upon them saith, With men it is impossible, but not with God: for with God all things are possible." Mark 10:27 (KJV)

~

I know a little and I'm still figuring a lot out. I may not get it right every single time but I'm believing for the impossible. What I do know for sure, is that I want to have unshakable confidence like those who have gone before me and I'm willing to do whatever it takes to receive it. Sometimes mistakes are the only way we can come to know that our flesh is in the way, or our minds have not yet fully conformed to His way of thinking. There will always be an answer as to why our faith didn't work and we must be diligent to seek it out, so that by learning, our faith may grow.

As you read just a few of my experiences, I hope that you will not look at my life and want to pattern yours after it. But that you would examine your life and see the good that God has already done for you. I want you to know that my heart is this, that in the reading of this book you will not only read stories and testimonies, but that the Spirit behind the words will touch your heart. I want to tell you the hard things and the wonderful things so you will know that my life, and my parents lives, and my grandparents lives are stories full of overcoming, and that all of the overcoming is through the power of the Holy Spirit working in us. May you never, ever compare your life to someone else's. Because comparison is the thief of joy. Read about these realities of God and become encouraged that you too can know Jesus in such a way that your story will be just as amazing as ours.

~

> "As newborn babes, desire the pure milk of the word, that you may grow thereby, if indeed you have tasted that the Lord is gracious. Coming to Him as to a living stone, rejected indeed by men, but chosen by God and precious, you also, as living stones, are being built up a spiritual house, a holy priesthood, to offer up spiritual sacrifices acceptable to God through Jesus Christ. But you are a chosen generation, a royal priesthood, a holy nation, His own special people, that you may proclaim the praises of Him who called you out of darkness into His marvelous light;"
> 1 Peter 2:2-5 & 9 (NKJV)

~

The church world has kept people in a shroud of dimness, it may not be complete darkness, but it is not fully being in His marvelous light. They have created an idea of conformity to their ways and called their ways God's way. When God comes to dwell in you, He must demolish that which is of the Adam mind and of the corruption that has been sown into you through living in the world. Not so you can conform to a church but so you can be transformed into His image. We need only to be taught of Him how to become like Him. Captives, slaves, or servants are not shunned from the Master. They are even a part of the work but servants are not invited to know everything the Master is doing. The Master makes all of His ways know to His friends. I know what it is like to not only be a daughter but to also be a friend.

~

> "Henceforth I call you not servants; for the servant knoweth not what his lord doeth: but I have called you friends; for all things that I have heard of my Father I have made known unto you." John 15:15 (KJV)

~

I believe He is separating those who genuinely want to be transformed into His image from those who just want to be conformed to an image within the church. The word speaks of a sifting, of a falling away of those who are not His, so that He can take those that are His to the place that He has prepared for us. This sifting is a time of revealing the hearts of people. I also believe this separating is happening because there is a controlling spirit within the church world that must being exposed. It is a spirit that is not of God, for He is not an imposer of His will. This exposure caused by the sifting is what will set apart the faithful.

~

> "He who is faithful in what is least is faithful also in much;" Luke 16:10 (NKJV)

~

Why don't you see miracles? Why aren't more people's lives touched by yours? Where is the presence of God in everything you do?

I don't pose these questions to condemn you but to get you to think! It's in the little things that He shows us how He is able to take care of the big things. God is in the details of our lives first and then the expression of Him becomes more and more evident so that others might see His glory. There should be proof in each and every believers life, just like there was in Jesus. We are not glorified on the day we sign up as members for a church, we are glorified by Him when we fully comprehend we are His and we are one with Him. If we want the world to see His glory in us we must be bold in the knowledge that we are the carriers of His presence.

I have witnessed that a great majority of those within the church world still have their understanding darkened. Being born of the world and our Adam nature, we have been conditioned to hide who we are for the fear of being rejected. Unity among the brethren breeds openness and understanding, but so many church goers never fully reveal themselves to someone else for fear of being known as they are in their imperfections. Because they assume they know how others will react if they were to know the truth of who they are, and so they hide. The keeping of the church world laws breeds this fear, and the church world continues to operate in this lie. Transforming into a group of people living double lives. People who on the outside may appear righteous while on the inside have fear, doubt, fleshly desires, disputes against one another, hurts, shames, depression, anxiety, and addictions. Are we not called the redeemed? That doesn't mean we won't have flesh to overcome and issues to deal with, but being redeemed means we are new creations and should reflect Jesus in every way. If we have learned who Jesus is we are renewed in the spirit of our mind and able to then live like Him. Those who have not put off their former conversation have not learned Christ and it is very evident in the church world that perpetuates dependency upon flesh.

His people are meant to be built on the Living Stone and fit together by the Holy Spirit, who is the Unifier. We should be bound together in love, not membership, and I believe He is bringing us into this unity so that we may be the Body of Christ that He has fit together. We can know the difference between flesh and Spirit, we can judge what is righteous and unrighteous, once we comprehend the power in us. That is what separates us from the world yet allows us to reach out to them so that they too might know His power and love. No church and no man can give you the power that the Holy Spirit alone can give. Knowing I am dead to self and risen with Him makes me seek those things which are above, because all that He is, as He sits on the right hand of God, is available for me to obtain, if I know who I am.

~

"If then you were raised with Christ, seek those things which are above, where Christ is, sitting at the right hand of God. Set your mind on things above, not on things on the earth. For you died, and your life is hidden with Christ in God. When Christ who is our life appears, then you also will appear with Him in glory." Colossians 3:1-4 (NKJV)

~

Is your affection on things above or things of the earth? Do you desire to be accepted by a congregation of similarly opinionated people or bound through unity in the Spirit to brothers and sisters? Are you willing to die for that person you sit next to every Sunday? Because there is no greater display of love than being will to lay down your life for another. The brotherhood of Christ followers must be forged in that very Love.

Flesh separates us from God and living in the Spirit. The carnal mind is enmity between us and Him, keeping us from being one with Him in the Spirit. We all have flesh but I have seen living proof that flesh can be made subject to the Spirit! We can have a life that is so hidden with Christ in God that wherever we go, we go with His presence being on display. If you are willing to die to the flesh and your carnal way of thinking, you can be made like Him. It is the power that works in me by His perfect will, not me that does the work through my will. Collaboration with the Holy Spirit is how we are made into the image of His glory and able to truly love one another.

~

"You did not choose Me, but I chose you. And I appointed you to go and bear fruit, fruit that will remain, so that whatever you ask the Father in My name, He will give you. This is My command to you: Love one another." John 15:16-17 (NKJV)

~

I am His friend. I do what He says to do. He has made His ways known to me and now my will is His will. Jesus, my Friend, will give me whatsoever I ask in His name. Christ, who my life, has appeared and I also will appear with Him in glory. I didn't choose Him… He chose me.

~

"Then He (Jesus) told them, 'For this reason, every scribe who has been discipled in the kingdom of heaven is like a homeowner who brings out of his storeroom new treasures as well as old.'" Matthew 13:52 (NKJV)

~

The Spirit of wisdom must go hand in hand with the knowledge of the fullness of Christ. I would not share everything I have experienced about Christ with you now, because many things can only be revealed to you through Him revealing it to you. Coming into the fullness of Him, as you walk with Him, is far more beneficial than me telling you everything I have learned. But there is yet one word I have been given that I must share with you. The revelation of not imposing my will on others has set me free to love like Jesus does. It was even the main purpose for this book until this book was actually written. As I said before, it has been an evolving project that through researching my heritage has opened my eyes to a timely message that could have only come forth by writing this book.

I may have bypassed a lot of struggles that living in the carnal causes many to experience, but I have done so by the grace of God alone. People could read my story and accuse me of having an easier life, but truth is, I've just been shown a different way of living. I was taught to seek the Kingdom of God and all these things have been added to me. Not that I know all there is to know, far from it. But I do know He is good, and I am loved, and that is a revelation that has projected my life into an entirely different way of living and believing. In this book I bring to you treasures that are both old and new. I want you to know that I have walked through many life changing experiences that have brought me to where I am today and been through many circumstances in my life that caused me to grow up.

This knowing who I am in Him did not happen overnight. There has been stubbornness and anger to let the Holy Spirit work out of me. I was conceded and full of pride in my nature. I used to be so strong willed and opinionated that I could argue my point fervently, so much so that people used to tell me I would make a good lawyer! My Dad once laughed and said I could argue a black man white. I also had a strong complaining spirit, until it was recently revealed and removed by my kind and loving Savior. Before I spiritually grew up, I always wanted to prove myself better than someone else and I was not always kind. I lacked greatly in wisdom and actively tried to impose my will on others. I was, as I mentioned before, full of myself. I smile as I write this because I am no longer who I once was and do now stand as a testimony of the power of God to come into a person and completely renovate them. Not because I somehow disciplined myself into change, but because the power of God through His Son and Holy Spirit has made me new.

I barely recognize myself anymore, if I look back at who I used to be. I am slow to speak and quick to listen. I have an understanding of this power He has given me, but I do not lord it over anyone else. I can not remember the last time I lost my temper. I am so full of joy it cannot be measured and it is quite infectious. I am kind and truly love other people with out expecting to be loved in return. Which allows me to be slow to offense and to suffer long with hope in my heart. He has replaced my stubbornness with willingness to do what He says is necessary. I don't need to argue an opinion any more because I know the Truth and that He does not force Himself upon others. I am more circumspect in my walk, more open to letting others be who they are and loving them without ever expecting them to change. All the while having great hope that God will work in them to transform them the same way He transformed me. I will not push you to change, I will encourage you. I will not make you to see my way but point you to His. I am no longer full of myself but full of Him and overflowing!

And He is still working on me. He and I are still walking this thing called life out together. I know that what is to come is far better than what I leave behind. I have grown up in Him spiritually in the way only He could have raised me, and I no longer struggle with not having confidence in who I am in Him. If He speaks, I listen and He is speaking more and more. I am not the only one who hears His voice, and I know it, and that keeps my heart and mind open to receive from others of Him. I see clearly now the path which He has laid for me and I am walking in it daily. I want you to know that you have the same inheritance that I do, if you are in Christ Jesus.

The revelation of not imposing my will on others was a preparatory word for the ushering of my Mom into Heaven. By the time she was on her way to be with the Lord I had already had over a year to meditate upon and actively apply the revelation of not imposing my will on others. He showed me what needed to be done and I changed. But tests must come after revelation to confirm in you that you are indeed walking it out and living in the understanding of it.

In 2018 we planned a vacation to go on a cruise in June of 2019 for Mom's birthday, when one day we received a call telling us the cruise was canceled because the cruise line had rented out the entire ship to a large undisclosed corporation for their private use and our room was no longer available. We were told we could reschedule another cruise or get our deposits refunded. So I decided to pray and ask the Lord what to do, and He spoke to me that we should cancel and in place of the cruise have a big birthday party for Mom's 70th birthday. A party to which we would invite all of our friends and family from around the world. I told Mom about the plan and she agreed that it was the Lord and that it was a wonderful idea. So I began to reach out to over fifty families that we loved, some of which we had not been in contact with for many years. We invited them all to come and celebrate with us in June at our home. We reconnected with many of them and I know it was truly divine in its appointment because of the way everything unfolded. Even if many of them could not come to the party, we were able to reach out and let them know we still love them and we hadn't forgotten about them.

We began to plan for a party while God had already long been working His plan in the background. Mom was actually a pretty healthy person, and hadn't had any sicknesses or illnesses after her stroke. But suddenly, one day she began having fainting spells when she would stand up from a seated position. We didn't have the full understanding of what was going on when it began, but we knew there was a battle ahead.

As I looked back on the weeks prior to this sudden fainting, I realized she had started eating less and she complained of loss of appetite. When she fainted a second time I still didn't fully understand what was going on, but I called again on my Jesus on her behalf. She and I were by ourselves that day and I was not strong enough to get her up off the floor, so I put an air mattress on the ground and helped her onto it. I told her to just rest a little while and while she slept I laid next to her and prayed for hours. The Lord spoke to me just before she woke up and He simply said, "When she wakes up, it is going to be good." Oh the words of a loving God! A God who knew what I was about to walk through but comforted my heart by letting me know the outcome was ultimately going to be good! To me this is the epitome of His ways being higher than ours!

When she woke up I told her what God had said and she was happy that He had spoken. She was strong enough now for both of us to get her up to sitting on her recliner and we sat together all day until Brendan came home from work. Jeremiah and Katie had left that same day on a flight to Nevada for vacation. I communicated what was going on to Jeremiah before he left and he was considering staying, but Mom insisted she was alright and that they should go because she did not want to be the cause of them missing out on their trip. Little did we know, but it was all for our good. When Brendan came home he helped me get her to bed and this time when she got up we knew it was serious. Her blood pressure was drastically dropping every time she would get up because her heart was beginning to fail. We didn't fully understand this aspect at the time because none of us could have possibly known.

That night I asked Mom how she wanted me to pray, this is where I was tested in my will submitting in love to hers. You see, if I had imposed my will on her I would have chosen to fight with my entire being to get my mother a miracle and keep her here a while longer with me. I would not even have considered what she may have wanted. Selfishness has no justification, no matter how well seeming it is. I loved her so completely that I was willing to let her make the choice, and she did. I said, "Mom, do you want us to pray for a miracle or are you ready to go home?" She answered, "I want to go home and be with Daddy and Jesus." Mom always referred to my father as Dad or Daddy when she spoke to us kids. It was not a hard choice for me to accept her decision, I want you to know, but walking it out was the hardest thing I have ever done.

That night Mom and I both had the same dream. In the dream we saw Dad standing at the open gates of heaven with a big smile on his face and with his arms open wide, as if welcoming her. I told her about my dream in the morning and she said she had had the exact same dream! She also saw an angel in her room just before she fell asleep that night. These were confirmations of her soon departure from this earth.

Her body was strong and it was the process of it shutting down that we had to walk through. It is, after all, the natural process of things. Just as it takes time for us to be developed in our mother's womb before the process of being birthed, so is the death of this mortal body but in reverse. For the saint there is no sting in death and it is simply going to sleep and waking up on the other side. Eternal life is the promise and so whatever it takes to walk through that portal here on earth, we should do it with confidence and joy.

Mom made her decision and she was never afraid. She was covered in this amazing peace that truly passed all understanding. The favor of God was upon her and she did not suffer. On her way out we sang songs of praise together, we prayed together and we read the word together. She only complained of pain a couple times and we prayed and the pain would go away. Our dear friend Dawn came and stayed with us for almost a week and she was such a great help to us. She had gone through the death process not long before with her own mother. She is a quiet pillar of strength who came and united with us to reinforce our strength.

After Dad had passed away Dawn established a covenant with Mom, much like the one she had made with Dad. She told Mom that she would be faithful and provide for any need she may have, knowing Mom did not have a paying job or an abundance of money to live off of once Dad had passed. Dawn was faithful to the end, one of only a few who also established similar covenants with Mom. Dawn sat with Mom when I needed rest, and she prayed with her and loved on her and us. For her selflessness in those days, I know God is going to bless her in ways that cannot be comprehended. I could never thank her enough or make her to understand the impact it had on me. I will however, always love her for it.

The night after Dawn had gone back to Massachusetts, I was with Mom in her room and she asked me to anoint her head with oil. She also asked me to call Dawn so we could all pray together. So I anointed Mom's head while Dawn prayed on speaker phone. In the midst of this atmosphere, Jesus came in the room. I did not get to see his face but there is no mistaking His presence! I physically felt His hand touch my head and then gently stoke my hair. As I was anointing her, He was blessing me. May you know the love of our Saviour in such a way! He was there all the time in the midst of us and He honored my faithfulness with His presence in the time I needed Him the most. I will never, ever forget that moment.

Jeremiah and Katie did come back from vacation, as soon as they were able to, and spent time with Mom before she went home. The Lord sent a friend who was a hospice nurse to come and talk me through the process and that was a great comfort. Many things happened during that short time. The devil even tried to shake me but my peace could not be shaken because I was in the center of God's will. I was being His hands and feet and operating in His heart and I could stand on that in confidence. Nothing can shake your peace if you know Who the Source of your peace is. I was tested and I passed with flying colors! It wasn't easy but it was beautiful! Like Mary not knowing, I went forward in faith and brought forth God's plan. My sweet, beautiful mother went to be with Daddy and Jesus on November 30, 2018.

The birthday party we were planning turned into a going home celebration that we called The Reunion By The River. We celebrated the reunion of Dad and Mom by the River of Life in heaven. Dad always said that he asked the Lord for his mansion to be river-side property, because he wanted to swim in the river and sit on the bottom and blow bubbles, something he liked to do in the natural. He would say, "You can sit on the bottom of the River of Life as long as you like without having to come up for air. Because in the River of Life you cannot die!" So after Mom joined Dad in heaven we knew they were now together at the river. Many people gathered for this celebration from all over the world to honor and remember the love that was poured out on each of their lives by my parents. There were only tears of joy at this gathering!

Not long after I ushered Mom into heaven, the Lord spoke very clearly to me and said, "Write down the revelations I have given you and the stories of the lives of those who have gone before you." He spoke of the revelation of not imposing my will on others, but little did I know it would open up into something even more. Through the process of writing this book, He has revealed to me that I am in that new dispensation my Dad spoke of. I could have never put the pieces together unless I had obeyed the Lord in writing this book. The legacy of being able to hear and know His voice has taught me more than I could have ever asked or thought of. Not only have I been made aware of this new dispensation but I have been given a revelation of my own of the new that we are now living in.

People would often ask Dad where he got his revelations from because they were so different from a lot of the teaching most were accustomed to hearing. He would say that the revelations flowed from the Spirit of Melchizedek, who had no beginning and no end, like Jesus who is the River of Life. Dad did not base his sermons on someone else's theology but for every new move of God he was brought to, God moved in him and gave him new words to share. The word was always fresh and pure. He said, "The River of Life is flowing through me and it has no beginning and no end. A river purifies itself, no matter what trash gets thrown in it, it never stops flowing and it just keeps purifying itself. To receive what He has to give us, we must become like a river flowing out of Emmanuel." Dad learned of Jesus as the Holy Spirit revealed to him the nature of God. As he came to understand Our God With Us, it in turn not only changed his life but countless other lives for the glory of God. Not because he was a learned man with great head knowledge or a degree from a Bible college. Not because he had a "covering", other than the covering of the Holy Spirit, but because He learned to hear and obey the voice of God.

Writing this book has given me such incredible insight into the lives of those who have gone before. I never knew my Grandma and now that I have told her story, to the best of my ability, I have a more palpable connection with her. Growing up I always heard people say how much of my Grandma they saw in me and I can see now we are definitely a lot alike. I also know why I believe the way I believe, because a piece of her faith is living inside of me. I came to know my Dad in a profound way as well. Knowing him in a way that I could have never known unless I had written his story. I knew the Virgil who was mature in the Lord and so sure of who God was in Him. Through this process of writing this book I met the Virgil who had to deal with himself and die to the carnal so he could become the man I knew. The same goes for my Mom. She and I were always best friends and I was very close to her my whole life, but now I identify with her even more deeply. Through writing this book I came to know another aspect of her heart as I wrote about all the sacrifices she made and the heart aches she walked through and the victories she won. She walked beside him and because of it they were stronger together. I came to have a deeper love and respect for them all and now I can identify with their experiences so much more.

Mine and my families lives are in that River of Life. In one life that River began to flow with a decision to press in for the things of God, my Grandma began the work. The next generation carried on in that River and now it has gone on to the next. Since I began the project of this book I have poured over every bit of literature and audio and video I had of Grandma and Dad preaching. I gleaned details from family genealogy and news paper clippings to help me with the time line. I reached out to people who I knew would have additional insight to share with me. It took a lot of digging and searching to find details that were needed for the telling of this story. Through it all my prayer has been, "Holy Spirit, let me write what You want written." This has most certainly been a collaborative work with Him. Some of you may find that a bold statement but that's ok, I know who I am, and I do not boast in myself but only in my Lord.

Why did all these stories need to be told? Is it merely for history sake? Simply a documentation of life and death? No, these are the testimonies of God's goodness towards us. This is what had to be inscribed to testify the the realities of the Kingdom of God. This is the evidence of a God who is not dead, of a Holy Spirit who comes in power and a Savior who calls us friend. If you are walking after the things of God's world then you will be known for His marvelous works. It's a story that never ends, a story of His glory and His love.

The grave has no victory for those whose story I have told because they fought the good fight, finished their races and kept the faith and their story lives on in me. And you, if you knew them.

I believe this is a timely book and I believe that God has laid out a way for us to look back and see how He has moved in the past so that we may see how He is moving now. What do we mean when we say "how God is moving"? It is a way of saying how He is actively working in each and every individual, who is in Him. We also say "a move of God" to indicate not just what He is doing in each individual, but how He brings those individual's work together to bring about His plan. He comes to do a new thing and to make us new. Oppression from fleshly doctrines have come over and over again to bring the people of God into bondage. God has always sent the Holy Spirit in at just the right time to breathe on His people through revival so that they could be brought out of that bondage. Revival is not a series of meetings in churches for the sake of building more churches or gaining more members. There is a clear difference between the two.

~

"Therefore we ought to give the more earnest heed to the things which we have heard, lest at any time we should let them slip." Hebrews 2:1 (KJV)

~

Why has He had to send revival over and over? It is not the Holy Spirit who wavers but man. It is us in our carnal thinking, in our sleepy forgetfulness. The things we have seen and heard slip away by us becoming complacent or conforming to a system instead of working out our own salvation. If we do not remember who we are then we become blind to the truth. The written word has been a guiding light for us all and it is where the answers for our questions are found. In addition to knowing the Bible we must have the spoken word of God breathed into our lives that we may establish who we are in Him. The Bible is nothing but dead letter if it is not received with Holy Spirit revelation, and the Spirit cannot be fully revealed if the flesh is in the way. Carnal thinking keeps a veil over the eyes of the believer so that he cannot see God clearly. When the word becomes alive to us we become no longer children tossed to and fro by every wind of doctrine and we are no longer under the ministry of death and condemnation but in the ministry of righteousness in Christ Jesus. The Bible is beautiful but God speaking directly to us is even better. Both must come together to bring us into His fullness.

~

"But our sufficiency is from God, who also made us sufficient as ministers of the new covenant, not of the letter but of the Spirit; for the letter kills, but the Spirit gives life. But if the ministry of death, written and engraved on stones, was glorious..., which glory was passing away, how will the ministry of the Spirit not be more glorious? For if the ministry of condemnation had glory, the ministry of righteousness exceeds much more in glory." 2 Corinthians 3:5-9 (NKJV)

~

Words from Him confirmed unto us that God Himself might bear witness. And we know it is from Him when He speaks because His Holy Spirt backs up every word. This is His will, He wants open communication with us. He wants to do away with the ministry of condemnation and make us ministers of the new covenant by the Spirit. What is so overwhelmingly wonderful about His will is that it will always be done in earth as it is in heaven, if we let Him bear witness in us of who He is. We have to identify with Jesus and seek to know Him in His fullness. Not a portion of Him, but all of Him. He exists only within the Father and the Holy Spirit and they within Him. According to Matthew 2:10-11, the church that tries to separate Them is like a whited tomb filled with dead mens bones, beautiful outwardly and unclean within.

In the Prayer of Jesus when he cried out to God to strengthen Him to do His will on earth and to go to the cross He said in John 17:1, "Glorify Me that I might glorify You!" He has given us the power to become the sons and daughters of God because He wants us to be the carriers of His presence. As He reveals His glory to us we should reveal His glory to the earth. If we stay in our carnal ways of thinking, in that worldly way of understanding, then we always be in bondage. So many people believe the love of God and step into that freedom only to step out of the world and into the church world to find more bondage. Bondage in the form of man made shackles of doctrines steeped in tradition. Doctrines that may be similar to the gospel of Jesus, yet contrary nonetheless. He has fulfilled the law, He has paid every price, He has gone to sit at the right hand of God so that we would have a constant advocate with the Father, and He has given us His power.

~

> "Forasmuch then as the children are partakers of flesh and blood, he also himself likewise took part of the same; that through death he might destroy him that had the power of death, that is, the devil; And deliver them who through fear of death were all their lifetime subject to bondage." Hebrews 2:14-15 (KJV)

~

Paul declared this to all his brethren in the midst of the church so that they might know the power they inherited. Jesus has destroyed any power the devil ever had. He has given us power over all flesh and given us this promise, that if we are in Him, the devil's power over us has been destroyed. So if we know the devil has no power and the flesh has no power, then we will live in the knowledge that He has delivered to us all the power we could ever need to take on His mind. The devil is powerless in his ability to win any victory over us unless we stay in our carnal way of thinking and agree with the lies that he tells us. Satan knows he's been defeated. Do you know he's been defeated? If you are in fear, then you are in some form of bondage, and you are giving him back power to keep you in that bondage. Change is not as difficult as it is painful, and who wants to experience pain? But we must! We must die so that He may live and so that we will know we are set free from the power of the enemy because Jesus DESTROYED it! We must let go of the things of the flesh, the things of this world, the ideas of man and seek first the Kingdom of God!

We must become determined to learn of Jesus and to become confident of who we are in Him if we are to comprehend the power He has given us! We don't know if we aren't taught and flesh cannot teach you what is spiritual. If we stay in our carnal understanding we will look to be taught by whatever the church world says is right, instead of what God wants to personally reveal to us through oneness with Him. We seek out who may teach us or where we may be taught because it is a natural way of learning, and there is nothing wrong with that, but the church world has created the idea that the church is the only option for being taught. Even Paul tells us in 2 Timothy 2:2 to "commit to faithful men who are able to teach others." I do not discount that wisdom, but I do see that now is the time that we must put on the mind of Christ and seek to be supernaturally taught. My Dad didn't teach me just what he knew, but lived a reality of faith that could have only been deposited into me by the Spirt. No amount of training by ways of his own understanding could have accomplished this. I have set out to know Him and to be consistent in that. Will I always get everything right or have all the answers? Maybe not, but in my unwavering pursuit of Him, He will be found.

~

"Study to shew thyself approved unto God, a workman that needeth not to be ashamed, rightly dividing the word of truth." 2 Timothy 2:15 (KJV)

~

Study Jesus by letting the Holy Spirit reveal the Truth to you and you will be able to rightly divide the word. My Dad taught me that conquering the carnal mind is the greater miracle that Jesus said we would do. He was born with the mind of The Father and we were born with Adam's mind, that which must be overcome to think like Jesus. I believe God would not have encouraged us to do so if we could not do it! If His mind is in us, then we can rightly divide the word of truth. We can stand before any man and know whether they are in their flesh, or whether they are in the Spirit. This gives us a much needed advantage over the enemy. Over and over again Jesus told us that we have the authority and power. He is not a mean task master who taunts us with the opportunity to become one with Him and then says, "Nope! You can't ever have this!" He is a loving friend who says, "Come, follow me, learn of me, eat the Bread of Life. I share all things with you, if you will but come and taste and see that I am good." All He wants is to be known, for His people to have the eyes of their understanding open that they may know that He is a rewarder of those who diligently seek Him! But He must be sought to be found. Study Him! Be like Him!

Not so you can be a leader of men but so you can have that ministry like Mary the sister of Lazarus.

~

"Now when Jesus was in Bethany, in the house of Simon the leper, There came unto him a woman having an alabaster box of very precious ointment, and poured it on his head, as he sat at meat. But when his disciples saw it, they had indignation, saying, To what purpose is this waste? For this ointment might have been sold for much, and given to the poor. When Jesus understood it, he said unto them, Why trouble ye the woman? for she hath wrought a good work upon me. For ye have the poor always with you; but me ye have not always. For in that she hath poured this ointment on my body, she did it for my burial. Verily I say unto you, Wheresoever this gospel shall be preached in the whole world, there shall also this, that this woman hath done, be told for a memorial of her." Matthew 26:6-13 (KJV)

~

Whenever something pivotal happened throughout the Bible, there was a woman at the heart of it, my Dad taught me that. God does not discount the ministry of a woman who moves in the Holy Spirit. Like my Grandma who had such a dynamic and successful ministry. Throughout the Bible so many stories could not have come about without the women who played a part in them. The conception of Jesus, Mary and Elizabeth having the Holy Spirit confirm through the children in their wombs that Jesus was the Messiah, Jesus' birth, his anointing, his death, his resurrection, etc. Countless miracles have happened throughout history surrounding women of faith. And women of faith still are being used of Him to this day. Because being male or female has nothing to do with a persons ministry, if that person ministers by the Holy Spirit.

Mary poured out that which cost her much and Jesus said that she had an understanding that the disciples didn't yet quite grasp. Why? Because she had a deeper knowledge of the love of God towards her. They had not experienced the love of God like she had in her relationship with Jesus. So she knew that oil was not being wasted, but that it had been given to her for the very purpose of pouring it all out for Jesus. She comprehended how Jesus' love had been poured out on her, and He hadn't even endured the cross yet. That means she believed Him at His word and knew He was the Son of the most High God who is worthy of everything we have. A revelation of how He gave of Himself created in her a desire to give it all away. She had learned from Jesus and Jesus said her testimony would be told to the whole world, throughout the ages, because He knew she believed. She was a woman who brought about the will of God and was not ashamed to give all to Him.

~

"That the God of our Lord Jesus Christ, the Father of glory, may give unto you the spirit of wisdom and revelation in the knowledge of him: The eyes of your understanding being enlightened; that ye may know what is the hope of his calling, and what the riches of the glory of his inheritance in the saints, And what is the exceeding greatness of his power to us-ward who believe, according to the working of his mighty power, Which he wrought in Christ, when he raised him from the dead, and set him at his own right hand in the heavenly places, Far above all principality, and power, and might, and dominion, and every name that is named, not only in this world, but also in that which is to come: And hath put all things under his feet, and gave him to be the head over all things to the church, Which is his body, the fulness of him that filleth all in all." Ephesians 1:16-23 (KJV)

~

That you may know what is the hope of your calling and the riches of the glory of His inheritance. Believer, you are an inheritor of all that Jesus was and is and did and is doing. He wants us to know the greatness of His power in us! He gave us that power in the Holy Ghost and it has been flowing from the throne of God ever since. It is a living, working power within us, if we choose to activate it with the baptism of fire, which comes to burn up all of the old man in us and make us new! Our God is an all consuming fire and He wants every part of us. So that we can no longer be carnally minded creatures but supernaturally minded like Jesus! So many people have not been taught their value and their worth and both are directly linked to understanding our authority in Christ Jesus. So many have been led to believe that salvation is the only thing to be obtained, besides church membership. It may be the natural order within the church world but it is most certainly not the heavenly way of God's world.

I will remind you that Jesus did not come to build a church or a synagogue or a temple, He came to dwell in man. He came to live in us and after we believed on Him He sent the Holy Spirit to dwell in us that we may be vessels of honor unto Him. We are the physical dwelling place for God on earth. How great is our God! That He would humble Himself and come in the form of man with the ultimate goal of dwelling in us! The God-head bodily dwelling inside the vessel They created.

John the Revelator was given a vision of heaven, the place where every believer will one day dwell for eternity. He saw the wall around the city of New Jerusalem and its foundation that is made of precious gem stones. He saw the gates made of pearl and the streets made of gold. In this perfect place that has been prepared for us, John also had it revealed to him that there were a few things that were not in this glorious place because there we have no need of them.

~

"But I saw no temple in it, for the Lord God Almighty and the Lamb are its temple. The city had no need of the sun or of the moon to shine in it, for the glory of God illuminated it. The Lamb is its light." Revelation 21:22-23

~

A temple is a building devoted to worshiping God. Church has, in the common vernacular, become another word for temple. A building where people gather and consider it to be a holy place. But if you believe that Jesus came not to dwell in structures made by mans hand, but in us, then how can a church building, or temple, be the ultimate plan of God? I see a definitive difference between who He is and who the church world has made Him out to be. I see millions of believers who are being restrained by mans traditions and doctrines and laws. I see a system that has been elevated above the ways of God. I see parents sacrificing their children on the alter of religion. I see people being crushed by the enemy through oppression and controlled by man with legalism. This is not the way of heaven, but the byproduct of the flesh attempting to mix itself with that which is Holy.

He is the only Temple that we can run into and dwell if we want to share in His glory and perfection. He takes this mortal body that He created and renovates it into His dwelling place, which is what the temple in the Bible was originally for, to house Him. If we are now that dwelling place, or temple, then there is no need for a church building, if He is to be worshiped in Spirit and in truth. Him dwelling in me and I in Him is the definition of being one. The Father and the Lamb and the Holy Ghost, who are All in All, are all I will ever need and They reside in me. Could it be possible that the understanding of us being His only earthly temple could set us free from believing we need a physical temple or church made with mans hands in order to worship Him? Heaven is God's perfect plan being fulfilled. He made me and now He is alive in me. How much greater is the earthly temple He made in His image?

If He is the only temple in heaven, then why do we think we can live in God's world by having our lives revolve around the church world system here on earth? Do you see the contrast? If we, the Body of Christ, are a living breathing entity, then a building made by our hands, crafted by carnal understanding, is not where God is truly meant to be worshipped. His church is made of lively stones, made free in Him and Him alone. So why do we keep going back to mans ways and knowledge? It is so very limited! We do not need a body of people to make us accountable for anything, when we are walking in the Spirit and operating with the mind of Christ. And if we are in the Spirit we will come together to make a Body that is actively living in the Spirit realm while walking through this world, just like Jesus did. Not hiding our light under a bushel and keeping the world in the darkness as we sit comfortable on our pews in complacency. Churches have become the keepers of the law once again and Jesus died to set us free from that very thing.

The time has come that no man should impose his will on another, that we may all come into the perfect will of the Father. And into the unity faith and of the knowledge of the Son of God, to a perfect man, to the measure of the stature of the fullness of Christ. (Ephesians 4)

# 9

## The New Has Come

I believe God has been raising up His people to see this new way in which He is moving. I believe He is raising us up in this revelation of what He desires within us and how different that looks compared to the current church world-order. That which is so filled with and run by the flesh. He Himself has been teaching those who are hungry and seeking for a different and better way. It is a One-on-one experience of being brought into the fullness of Him. In His perfect plan we have no need of a temple or building because HE IS IT! But where will people assemble? Perhaps the answer is anywhere and everywhere. Maybe it is nowhere specific but where He leads us to, moment by moment.

Nothing that is man made can bring us to Him. No system, no doctrine of man, no religious way of doing things, no program or ritual. The word says He cannot be known by those means, so why do we seek Him by way of our carnal understanding? The church world sings about His power, prays to have more of Him, reads book, after book, after book to see what He has done in other people's lives. They hold seminars and activities and seven step programs. They hold prescheduled meetings and call them revival. They do all they can do to make themselves different from the world by outward appearance, or worse, through self righteousness condemn the world instead of loving it. Then there are those who make themselves so much like the world that there is no discernible difference between the two. We can only be set apart by Him because only He, can radically change us. No denomination on earth has that power. He wants to change us so we no longer dwell in the church world but walk in the world while living and dwelling in the realities of God's world.

Jesus sat with sinners but after they came to Him they could no longer stay sinners. His is pure religion, undefiled and full of the Holy Spirit. The power of God working in Him brought Light into those people who were lost in darkness. Not because He imposed His will on people and made them try to understand His message but because He loved them so well and gave them the freedom to choose. He only gave answers when a question was asked.

One of the most beautiful examples of how Jesus ministered was when He sat at the well and had a simple conversation with a broken and hurt woman. By the end of that conversation she was set free of the hold the devil had on her, and what's more is, that she found her satisfaction in Him as she believed He was the Christ, her Redeemer. I believe ministry is really that simple, when the power of the Holy Ghost is in you. Sit down, have a conversation, reveal the love of God for that person when they hunger and thirst for it and He gives you the opportunity to pour out what He has done for you to that person.

All He wants of us is a relationship, just like what He offered to the woman at the well. That, to me, is a glorious picture of how to minister and the most effective way possible to reach the lost. He discerned what was in her, through the Holy Spirit, so He could set her free. He did not sign her up to become a member, in fact He told her she didn't need to be religious any more. He even told her He came to set her free from the religious system of having to worship God in a certain place. And He knew that revelation of who He was and what He had come to do for her would set her free to worship in Spirit and in Truth.

~

"Jesus answered and said unto her, If thou knewest the gift of God, and who it is that saith to thee, Give me to drink; thou wouldest have asked of him, and he would have given thee living water. The woman saith unto him, Sir, thou hast nothing to draw with, and the well is deep: from whence then hast thou that living water? Jesus answered and said unto her, Whosoever drinketh of this water shall thirst again: But whosoever drinketh of the water that I shall give him shall never thirst; but the water that I shall give him shall be in him a well of water springing up into everlasting life, But the hour cometh, and now is, when the true worshippers shall worship the Father in spirit and in truth: for the Father seeketh such to worship him. God is a Spirit: and they that worship him must worship him in spirit and in truth."
John 4:10-11 & 13 & 23-24 (KJV)

~

He says, come learn, come drink, come eat, come partake, come dwell in Me! A radical change is coming about right now and the church world will not even recognize it because it is like nothing they have ever seen. But to those whose eyes can be opened to see Him, they will be set free to turn and give Him their all, and then they will tell everyone they know about Him, just like the Samaritan woman when she met her Messiah.

My Dad prophesied of this radical change within the church world before the Lord took him home and I believe I have been given the interpretation of that prophecy. This last revival he spoke of, is the Bride being made aware that it is time for their lamps to be filled with oil. Matthew 25 speaks of the five wise virgins who had their lamps filled with oil and were ready when the Master came like a thief in the night to take them to the place He had prepared for them.

~

"At that time the kingdom of heaven will be like ten virgins who took their lamps and went out to meet the bridegroom. Five of them were foolish, and five were wise. The foolish ones took their lamps but did not take along any extra oil. But the wise ones took oil in flasks along with their lamps. When the bridegroom was delayed, they all became drowsy and fell asleep. At midnight the cry rang out: 'Here is the bridegroom! Come out to meet him!' Then all the virgins woke up and trimmed their lamps. The foolish ones said to the wise, 'Give us some of your oil; our lamps are going out.' 'No,' said the wise ones, 'or there may not be enough for both us and you. Instead, go to those who sell oil and buy some for yourselves.' But while they were on their way to buy it, the bridegroom arrived. Those who were ready went in with him to the wedding banquet, and the door was shut. Later the other virgins arrived and said, 'Lord, lord, open the door for us!' But he replied, 'Truly I tell you, I do not know you.' Therefore keep watch, because you do not know the day or the hour." Matthew 25:1-13 (NKJV)

This new way is a call to action, for His coming is soon at hand! Prepare ye the way of the Lord! Thousands of years have passed and it has been but a few days to God. His plan has been carried out through the ages and we can read the signs of the time everywhere. The eternal plan has always been Him coming to take His Bride to be with Him in the place that He has prepared for us. This is that. Hallelujah! I am excited for what He is doing and what He is about to do! This is not a revelation that I have the market cornered on by any means, in fact I believe that an activation has happened to countless men and women of God around the world to be ready for this breath of God that is being breathed upon the whole earth.

I believe it is world wide but it is within the understanding of how it first is activated in the individual, that will bring about the unity of the church. Not a large amount of people reaching just a few but a few reaching a large amount of people by the Holy Spirit igniting the fire. Those few are having the eyes of their understanding opened to see the new way that He is moving in, and they will rise up as beacons of light to those who are seeking. I believe buildings will have very little to do with this last move of God and will only be used should we need to get out of the weather. This move of God will be outside the walls of the churches. If you are looking for revival in the same way it has come in the past, you seek amiss.

The Holy Spirit has fallen on the people of God throughout the history of church and we commonly call it revival. I feel this new way is something even more. John 5 recounts the story of the pool of Bethesda and how an angel would come during a certain season and trouble the water. The angel, brought power to heal the people and it only happened ever so often. Sounds like what we have known as revival, doesn't it?

At the pool there was a man who had been sick for thirty-eight years and he went to the place where he was told he would find healing, a picture of the church. He waited for that Holy Spirit power to heal him and yet he had no one to put him in the water to receive, a picture of the powerless church member. He hungered to be set free and year after year no one would help him and then came Jesus! But He did not come to trouble the water or bring temporary revival. He did not offer something that would happen every once in a while or for a season. The Holy Spirit was in Him and everywhere Jesus went He brought that transformative power of God that would leave a lasting effect.

When the angel troubled the water the effect of the angel's touch only lasted for a very short time. When Jesus came He was the manifestation of the Presence of God, the real deal in the flesh! The invalid man craved revival through the water being refreshed and here comes Jesus bringing something so much better, the very presence of God.

Him indwelling in us is not about the Presence falling to merely revive us but the very presence of God Himself living in us that we may bring His power wherever WE go. That is more than revival but true lasting transformation through the power of God in us. When Jesus brought the presence of God to the pool of Bethesda He didn't come with the intention of picking up this man and putting him in the water. He came to share the presence of God with Him, to transfer His power and set the man free. He brought healing through the authority given to Him by His Father.

Out of all the people on the five porches who were in need of healing Jesus only went to this one man. Why do you think that was? Because God directed Jesus to the one He knew would receive of Himself on that Sabbath day. This healing required Jesus to break the Sabbath tradition in order to fulfill the Sabbath law, in so doing revealing Himself as our Rest. One man's heart was ready for the presence to shake him out of the confines of the law so that he could truly be set free. What was the result?

~

> "When Jesus saw him lying there and realized that he had spent a long time in this condition, He asked him, 'Do you want to get well?', 'Sir,' the invalid replied, 'I have no one to help me into the pool when the water is stirred. While I am on my way, someone else goes in before me.' Then Jesus told him, 'Get up, pick up your mat, and walk.' Immediately the man was made well, and he picked up his mat and began to walk."
> John 5:6-9 (NKJV)

~

This is not a statement of judgment upon any church or anyone. This is simply a revealing of something new and a call to examine what it is and what it can mean for you. I see so clearly now that this is why I have walked through the journey of writing this book. I have been made to see how God has moved in the decades past so that I could see that I am in the center of the new and watching it unfold. All that He is doing is only ever for His glory and our good, so that He may establish His Kingdom in us. So that we may be a part of His eternal kingdom when He comes to take us there. All so that we may comprehend the breadth, length, depth and height of His love for us. So we can comprehend what it means to have the God-head in us and the ability to live in God's world!

You can worship Him in your flesh, within the confines of your carnal thinking and He will allow it. He will love you just the same! But you will never know the power He has given you to take with you on your journey here on earth. He wants you to know Him in His fullness! God is a Spirit and we who worship Him must worship Him in spirit and in truth! I know I am repeating myself on this one point, but it cannot be overstressed enough. Come to Him and learn of Jesus. Let the Holy Spirit reside in you, being made alive in you, that He may have His way in you. Let the love of God be your motivation in all things so that you might do everything out of His heart. God made you for His glory! Jesus did all that He did for you to be His friend! He sent the Comforter for you that all the mysteries of who He is may be revealed to you! Let no man speak against these truths, for in them is liberty found.

~

"God, who made the world and everything in it, since He is Lord of heaven and earth, does not dwell in temples made with hands. Nor is He worshiped with men's hands, as though He needed anything, since He gives to all life, breath, and all things...for in Him we live and move and have our being, as also some of your own poets have said, 'For we are also His offspring.' Therefore, since we are the offspring of God, we ought not to think that the Divine Nature is like gold or silver or stone, something shaped by art and man's devising." Acts 17:24-25 & 28-29 (NKJV)

~

Do you think Paul received this revelation by a man telling him so or perhaps by his own carnal reasoning? No. He received this revelation from the Holy Ghost because the eyes of his understanding had been opened. He preached to men and women who thought God could be found in temples. He told the people they were created by God, in His image, and that He could only be found in believing in Jesus who is the Son of God. If we are made in His image then we cannot have life outside of Him. John 14:6 says He is "The Way, The Truth and The Life." He wants all of His creation to know Him, but not all will believe. We are not called to make them believe, only to speak the truth in love that they may have a choice. Thousands of years of people imposing their will upon others within the church world has brought us to this place. If sin was dealt with on the cross for every single Christian then it is not sin that holds back the church from His fullness, but the carnal mind that perpetuates the alienation of a person from comprehending who Jesus is. In other words, the blind leading the blind.

The Be Like Jesus move has raised up a people that have been chosen to bring forth a radical, life transforming, word of freedom. Paul the apostle did a great work but our work will be even greater. Because I believe through history God has brought His people from deeper understanding to deeper understanding. Building and expounding upon each revelation from generation to generation to bring us to today. This is not just a declaration of another revival but a cry to announce that the time of Jesus as at hand. Jesus in me means the presence of God goes wherever I go. This is more than a revival, more than a spiritual awakening, it is the comprehension of the power of God indwelling in man. Those who are within the sleeping-church are being awakened to see God and that He was never meant to be put in the confines of a building or a system or a carnal way of understanding! Come to Him and know Him as He longs to be known, because He is calling us home! Don't be so busy doing everything the world or the church world says you must do that you miss Him when He comes like a thief in the night.

~

"For yourselves know perfectly that the day of the Lord so cometh as a thief in the night. For when they shall say, Peace and safety; then sudden destruction cometh upon them, as travail upon a woman with child; and they shall not escape. But ye, brethren, are not in darkness, that that day should overtake you as a thief. Ye are all the children of light, and the children of the day: we are not of the night, nor of darkness. Therefore let us not sleep, as do others; but let us watch and be sober. But let us, who are of the day, be sober, putting on the breastplate of faith and love; and for an helmet, the hope of salvation. For God hath not appointed us to wrath, but to obtain salvation by our Lord Jesus Christ, Who died for us, that, whether we wake or sleep, we should live together with him." 1 Thessalonians 5:1-10 (KJV)

~

My Dad taught me that the Holy Spirit is wild, like the wind that blows where it wishes. And that I should not assume to know what He is doing or how He will work through me. But I must simply yield myself to Him so that I can be made ready to be a part of whatever it is He is doing. The Holy Spirit cannot be controlled and most certainly cannot be understood through fleshly or carnal reasoning. That is why we need the gift of faith to really believe we can be made knew creations by being born again into the family of God. A second growing up. This time maturing spiritually instead of physically.

~

"Jesus answered, 'Most assuredly, I say to you, unless one is born of water and the Spirit, he cannot enter the kingdom of God. That which is born of the flesh is flesh, and that which is born of the Spirit is spirit. Do not marvel that I said to you, 'You must be born again.' The wind blows where it wishes, and you hear the sound of it, but cannot tell where it comes from and where it goes. So is everyone who is born of the Spirit." John 3:5-8 (NKJV)

~

Ready yourself by pressing in to obtain everything that is rightfully yours as a born again child of the King. Once the carnal mind is undone and its fleshly ways of thinking are silenced, then you will begin to hear His voice more and more. Hear and obey. Have your lamp filled with that Holy Ghost anointing oil. Be under His wings and in His heart and sure of your oneness with Him so that in your spirit you will know what He is doing in the Spirit. Let your eyes and ears be open so that you can be made ready for what is to come. We do not need to know how or when or where, but we do need to know His voice and hear Him when He says how or when to do it. It is not for us to know the plan in its entirety, for we cannot contain such things, but He wants us to co-labor with Him and be a part of it all. Oneness is two working together as one.

You can mark my life and the lives of those gone before me as an example of who God is because our conversation is in Heaven and we look to the Savior. I do not believe that my revelation is the revelation to trump all revelations but is the sum of all the revelations handed down to me added to the ones He has given to me. I will not take my revelation and build my own kingdom with it, but I present what it is I am sure of so that others may come to know how He is moving now. This is simply what the Lord has shown me and my testimony that I share with you, because I love you. God never wanted to see man's kingdom established, only His own. I openly say that He has come and He is living in me because I am not ashamed of the gospel of Jesus Christ!

~

"Let this mind be in you, which was also in Christ Jesus: Who, being in the form of God, thought it not robbery to be equal with God:" Philippians 2:5-6 (KJV)

~

My Dad was known for the revelation that God gave him about that passage in Philippians 2. If I am one with God through Jesus, if the power of the Holy Spirit is living in me and transforming my mind to be like the mind of Christ, then I know I can believe that it is not robbery to be equal with God. Do you want to know how to walk in power? THAT is how you walk in power. Confidence in the Holy Spirit being in you. It is understanding the reality of the God-headed bodily dwelling within you and making you more than a conqueror. Some people wanted that same understanding my Dad had come to cultivate, and some people loathed him for his boldness in declaring it. Love him or hate him, he had results! Not just because he moved powerfully in the gifts but because his life bore the fruit of the Spirit and the evidence of the presence of the Living God in him.

If everything Jesus did is for each and everyone of us who believes, then why doesn't everyone walk in this way? It's the question that anyone would have when looking into the heart of this truth. Because in my experience growing up within the realm of the pentecostal church world, there has always been this declaration of power but little proof to back it up. I see the power of God and know that it can break every chain, heal every wound, every sickness and every disease. It can set the addict free, renovate the mind, create unity, enable us to love one another. Many churches even teach that we have all this power. They claim it and yet where is the proof of it?

If we really believe the word, as it is written and spoken, God confirms it in us through the fruits and gifts of the Holy Ghost being the evidence of our faith. We should have results in our lives just like Jesus did! Maybe that's where things go askew and confusion causes complacency that makes church people just go along with the way things are, without hungering for change or deeper understanding. The church has become a people who claim to have everything that Jesus has but that do not live it. A defeated people living under condemnation because they don't know why they can't seem to live like Jesus did.

This is where the great men and women of God like Paul the Apostle, Smith Wigglesworth, John G. Lakes, Rebecca Johnson, Kathryn Kuhlman, Reinhard Bonnke, Virgil Johnson, etc., differ from the masses. They were willing to die, whatever the cost, no matter the pain or the hurt, the ridicule or persecution. To die to self and die to the flesh, so they could not be swayed by man's opinion. They were made to understand what it is to lay down their will in exchange for His. I hope you have been able to see in these life stories I have told, this taking up His will in replace of ours means a life time of giving the flesh no occasion to have its own way. It isn't easy but it is good. It is so incredibly radical that most people don't want to go through what it takes to obtain it and thus are simply satisfied with sitting in a crowd and hearing about the works of God that someone else has done. To live a transformed life it takes an excellent spirit like Daniel had who saw miracles in the lion's den! But you have to first be willing to die.

My Dad taught me the importance of dying to the flesh. He spoke of his experience with these words saying, "The first year after my first wife died I didn't want to live. Even during the first months after I married Melonie, I still struggled. Because everything that I had been living for, ministry and miracles, I had done, but I had not comprehended. After fasting on and off for weeks on end for an entire year and praying for the breakthrough, Jesus appeared for the second time to me and I got it. He told me how I was going to do what I was going to do and how I had died to the flesh. In that dying I began to live. I began to live in a world I had never lived in before, a spiritual world. I began to bring my thoughts into captivity through the Holy Spirit in a way I had never before. I was dealing with a lot of questions in my mind during that year, even though I was a successful pastor and preacher. I was greatly respected and thought to be a great up and coming presence in the church world. I want to tell you how to die without having to go through all I went through. I had to learn what it was to die to flesh, so that I could teach you."

This quote was taken from a sermon Dad preached on our last mission to South Africa. During this time he and I were writing his life story. We completed the story up to the time when he was fifteen years old. My Mom even did her best to motivate him to write the story, knowing it would be a help to many people. But the completion never came about. He wasn't able to finish it and now I know why, because it was part of what I have been chosen to do. To not only tell his story but learn from his story in a deeper way. I was there on the front row in the church in South Africa as he said those words about his experience of dying to the flesh. I was there and I watched him weep as he told the story of his first wife's death and how he didn't have the will to live because he was so broken. If no one ever understands what has been written in this book, I have been radically changed by it and that is far greater than I could have ever hoped for! If not even a single person ever reads it, it really doesn't matter to me, because I have a new understanding now.

    I see more clearly now the true impact it has had on my life that my Dad chose to die to the flesh. He died so that I might learn how to live in the Spirit and become like Jesus. He had his flesh crucified so it wouldn't be so hard for me to deal with mine. I was witness to the end result of what life after the death of the flesh looks like. He carried the presence of God wherever he went and he had an active faith that was alive because he had taken on the mind of Christ! He did it. So I know I can do it and I am doing it! He conquered that old Johnson and Sim's nature so I wouldn't have to struggle so much or fight as hard to get rid of that same nature in me. He made it look easy, and it is easy, once the flesh is dead. But if there is flesh fighting tooth and nail for its will to be done, then there will always be struggle and very little victory. This walk is an everything on the line, to the death commitment! Why? So that you may know Him and that others will see Him in you.

    I remember Dad telling about a vision the Lord had given him when he was younger. He saw himself standing before a mirror that was dirty. He took his hand and began to clean the mirror and as he cleaned it he began to see his own reflection. He immediately began to vomit in reaction to what he saw. He knew that when he looked in that mirror, he should have seen Jesus and not himself. If we as the body of Christ want to be victorious, we must die to self and crucify the carnal mind that it may be replaced with the mind of Christ. To the point that we are no longer found. It is a foreign idea to the human way of thinking but to be like Jesus is the ultimate goal. Not to receive power to have miracles and build churches and gain members, but to receive power that will transform us. To be so set apart from the world that they will know Him in His glory through us. We must be willing to die, willing to "waste" it all on him and pour out that which is precious to us for Jesus.

~

> "I could have easily stood in the shadow of my mother's great ministry and basked in the glory of her victories. Instead, I went beyond the inspiration of my mother and touched God for myself. Too many preacher's children live in the shadow of their parent's ministry. Too many church members live in the shadow of their pastors. We must know God for ourselves. HEAVEN IS YOURS, TAKE IT BY FAITH!"
> -Excerpt from Beyond The Faith of Man

~

The church has been notorious for the studying of one man or woman's success in the ministry and trying to duplicate it. "Let us be like Billy Graham or Oral Roberts", they say. Let us build churches and universities and have seminars on how to reproduce what the great men and women of God did because they did it with immense success! We have TV programs and a ridiculous amounts of Bible translations, how to books, and a church on every street corner. There are more and more churches and less and less righteousness in the world. It would stand to reason that if churches were the answer to the salvation of the world then the opposite would be true. I do not say this to be critical but to make a point. It is time that eyes be open to see that there is a separation between the church world and God's world. When you live in God's world you will be one of those wise virgins who's lamp was filled with oil.

~

"Hereby know we that we dwell in him, and he in us, because he hath given us of his Spirit. And we have seen and do testify that the Father sent the Son to be the Saviour of the world. Whosoever shall confess that Jesus is the Son of God, God dwelleth in him, and he in God. And we have known and believed the love that God hath to us. God is love; and he that dwelleth in love dwelleth in God, and God in him. Herein is our love made perfect, that we may have boldness in the day of judgment: because as he is, so are we in this world. There is no fear in love; but perfect love casteth out fear: because fear hath torment. He that feareth is not made perfect in love. We love him, because he first loved us." 1 John 4:13-19 (KJV)

~

Those scriptures hold within them the reality of God. It is an alternate reality that can be lived in only by the transforming of the carnal mind. I have seen people who out of the last move of God came to understand that they had authority because it was written in the word but they never really claimed it. It's like having an inheritance that is just sitting in a bank without ever touching the money. What good is an inheritance if you don't spend it? If you have that authority why aren't you healed? If you have the authority to raise people from the dead, why haven't you? My Grandma did. My Dad did. We need to comprehend the practical application of understanding authority. Let this mind be in you which was also in Christ Jesus! May we all no longer lean on the arm of flesh for our answers as we lay down our lives in exchange for His all-sufficiency. That we might have boldness in the day of judgment! And declare that as He is SO ARE WE!

The church has failed time after time to teach the next step because it has nothing to do with man and everything to do with hearing directly from the Source. Instead of going forward, the church regressed to saying, "We could have what we ask if we wanted to, but instead we will just build a church or a school or hold a seminar." For the saint, believing you have the authority is not faith, it's a fact. Faith is acting on it and going and getting your inheritance because it is the very word of God! It is carnal-mind blowing! Faith is doing it and not just talking about it. It's laying it all on the line, come hell or high water. Even if it means being burned at the stake or crucified upside down or being stoned or being hated and mocked and ridiculed. Or being thrown out of church by those who are not able to see Him as He is.

~

"That which has no life-giving sound is the cry of the soul. How are we, as pastors, going to develop the inner man rather than the flesh unless we have the gift of interpretation? We only hear what the flesh permits us to hear, not the cry of the soul. Yet as men and women of God we should go beyond the flesh and meet the need of that inner man. We have met the needs of the flesh by building beautiful edifices. We need to go beyond the flesh and separate the soul and spirit from the flesh."
-Excerpt from How To Discern Spirits

~

I want you to know that the old way of doing things is done. Even some of the early churches didn't get it quite right in their application because they are dealt with in the book of Revelations. Proving the church world has a mix of the fleshly and the spiritual dwelling in it. A handful fully understood the message in Paul's day but the majority did not. And so the church has had its dark ages and its spiritual awakenings. God has always known it would take time to work the carnal mind out of the descendants of Adam. Like the Israelites who were taken out of Egypt from bondage, it took forty years to let the old die off so the new generation could take the land and live in the promise. If we can come into the full understanding that we are being led into now, we will be that spotless Bride. When His Bride is ready, He will come and take us. All these thousands of years He has had a purpose and a plan to breakthrough the carnal mind and have a people called by His name that will live in Oneness with Him. The church world religiousness is the veil that blocks our vision from seeing God's world in the same way the carnal mind causes us to be blinded to the truth of knowing we can have the mind of Christ.

~

"Then Jesus spoke to the multitudes and to His disciples, saying: "The scribes and the Pharisees sit in Moses' seat. Therefore whatever they tell you to observe, that observe and do, but do not do according to their works; for they say, and do not do. For they bind heavy burdens, hard to bear, and lay them on men's shoulders; but they themselves will not move them with one of their fingers. But all their works they do to be seen by men...They love the best places at feasts, the best seats in the synagogues, greetings in the marketplaces, and to be called by men, 'Rabbi, Rabbi.' But you, do not be called 'Rabbi'; for One is your Teacher, the Christ, and you are all brethren. Do not call anyone on earth your father; for One is your Father, He who is in heaven. And do not be called teachers; for One is your Teacher, the Christ." Matthew 23:1-11 (NKJV)

~

Even Paul has been the source of many doctrinal laws, that perhaps he never meant to become laws, and yet, they have. Taking the letter and mixing in the law creates the ministry of death and condemnation. Paul would be the first to point us to freedom in Christ and the Holy Spirit being the only Teacher we will ever need. Yet fleshly interpretations of things that were written to edify a church thousands of years ago have become laws throughout church history that are practiced within certain churches even to this day. Such as women wearing hats in church, or men not being allowed to grow their hair long. Seemingly small things but laws none the less, binding people with the heavy burden of being condemned into keeping the law. The church world is full to the brim with these "little laws" and a little leaven, leavens the whole lump! Man's tendency to create a systematic approach to understanding Jesus takes something that is sound advice or wisdom and turns it into a law that must be kept to prove ones holiness. Out of our logical minds we seek to find who He is and He cannot be found through carnal minded approaches.

Paul himself said in 1 Corinthians 10:23 that, "All things are lawful for me, but all things are not expedient: all things are lawful for me, but all things edify not." All things are permissible for those who have been set free in Jesus because sin is no longer an issue, for it was dealt with at the cross. If we sin, it's covered by the blood but we no longer sin because according to 1 John 3:9 "whoever has been born of God does not sin, for His seed remains in him; and he cannot sin, because he has been born of God." There are no more laws by which we must be held accountable because we have been redeemed and made overcomers by the blood of the Lamb and the word of our testimony. All things are permissible or lawful, but not all things edify us. Living carnal mindedly is not expedient or beneficial, but we are allowed to do it, if we choose to. It is better to become sanctified through the Holy Ghost purification process than to stay in our flesh. The nature of God can only be known and revealed to us though the taking on of the mind of Christ, it cannot be revealed in being taught in church while being made to live under doctrinal laws.

This new way is the same gospel of Jesus Christ. Same gospel, new dispensation. This move is all about the presence of God. Jesus Himself is about to show up on the scene. But before He shows up to take us home, He is going to show Himself to the world by revealing Himself through us. The Be Like Jesus move is producing a generation who knows that they are the carriers of the presence of God and His presence is His glory. We shall not seek any glory for ourselves but will be found spotless when He comes to call us home. We will see that which Peter preached at the first outpouring of the Holy Spirit on the day of Pentecost and that which Joel prophesied of a pouring out of the Spirit of God upon all flesh.

~

"And it shall come to pass afterward, That I will pour out My Spirit on all flesh; Your sons and your daughters shall prophesy, Your old men shall dream dreams, Your young men shall see visions. And also on My menservants and on My maidservants I will pour out My Spirit in those days. 'And I will show wonders in the heavens and in the earth:
Blood and fire and pillars of smoke. The sun shall be turned into darkness, And the moon into blood, Before the coming of the great and awesome day of the Lord. And it shall come to pass that whoever calls on the name of the Lord shall be saved. For there

shall be deliverance, As the Lord has said, Among the remnant whom the Lord calls."
Joel 2:28-32 (NKJV)

~

Revival is coming just as Peter said it would in Acts 2. After Jesus died and was resurrected He gave to Peter and the others in the upper room that promise of another Comforter that would become the very Presence of the Living God dwelling inside of them. It came when they were all in one accord and in agreement that His word would be fulfilled. I believe as the people of God around the world begin to agree that He is soon returning, we indeed shall see that outpouring. The Kingdom of God has been established in us by the word of God through Jesus and we are citizens of Heaven looking for that city to come. The day is coming when we will meet Him face to face and let us all have the faith to believe that the time is at hand.

From now until eternity we should spend our lives fine tuning the ability to hear His voice, because if we don't hear Him then we don't have confidence in Him. If we don't have confidence in Him, in His love for us and in who we are in Him, we are powerless. Those who have ears, let them hear what the Spirit is saying! The Kingdom of God is at hand, prepare ye the way of the Lord! Jesus never did anything without hearing from the Father first. This is the reality of God, to hear from Him and believe it, live it, have it tested and see results. For He is a rewarder of those who diligently seek Him! If you have faith to believe that the glory of God resides in you, you will have results!

I know that not everyone will be able to make this transition, but I believe He wants that we should all know it is available. May we all press in for more of Him and no longer be complacent with the current church world order. Let us rise up and show the world a people who have been transformed by the power of God unto righteousness by walking in power and victory! Come out and be ye separate from the world and the church world. God's world is where you were created to live, only believe!

~

"Nevertheless even among the rulers many believed in Him, but because of the Pharisees they did not confess Him, lest they should be put out of the synagogue; for they loved the praise of men more than the praise of God. Then Jesus cried out and said, 'He who believes in Me, believes not in Me but in Him who sent Me. And he who sees Me sees Him who sent Me. I have come as a light into the world, that whoever believes in Me should not abide in darkness. And if anyone hears My words and does not believe, I do not judge him; for I did not come to judge the world but to save the world. He who rejects Me, and does not receive My words, has that which judges him, the word that I have spoken will judge him in the last day. For I have not spoken on My own authority; but the Father who sent Me gave Me a command, what I should say and what I should speak. And I know that His command is everlasting life. Therefore, whatever I speak, just as the Father has told Me, so I speak." John 12:42-50 (NKJV)

~

If you speak let it be as Jesus spoke, speak as the oracle of God. Confess that He is the God of the impossible, no matter what the cost, and do not let the opinion of man sway you from speaking in boldness your confession! Speak as He speaks to you and the words the Spirit gives will cause the chains to fall off of every heart that hears and believes. For as they hear and believe, they will see God and no longer abide in darkness. The truth of who Jesus is and how great God loves us all will demolish every stronghold of the devil's lies. Be a vessel, be an instrument of love and tell everyone God does not impose His will on any of us.

~

"As each one has received a gift, minister it to one another, as good stewards of the manifold grace of God. If anyone speaks, let him speak as the oracles of God. If anyone ministers, let him do it as with the ability which God supplies, that in all things God may be glorified through Jesus Christ, to whom belong the glory and the dominion forever and ever. Amen." 1 Peter 4:10-11 (NKJV)

~

I believe with everything that is in me, that right now the Body of Christ is actively being His hands and feet and reaching the lost in a way that has never been done before, and it has only just begun! Those who have been fed by every word that proceeds out of the mouth of God are being transformed by that heavenly mana. It is so subtle, so real and so supernatural that the church world cannot comprehend it. But when it comes in its fullness, all will be sifted like wheat and known for their hearts motivation. The church age is coming to an end as His chosen are coming into their identities as citizens of God's world. His Bride, the true worshipers, are all over the world filling their lamps with oil! I believe it, because I am living it.

The reality of God's world tastes better than anything the world or the church world has ever offered me!

I find it not robbery to be equal with God.

This is the legacy given to me.

Let this mind be in you.

The new has come.

Made in the USA
Columbia, SC
10 June 2022